Jerome

Edmun…
Security Pacific Investment Managers, Inc.

Quantitative Techniques for Financial Analysis

The Research Foundation of
The Institute of Chartered Financial Analysts

Research Foundation Publications

Canadian Stocks, Bonds, Bills, and Inflation: 1950–1987
by James E. Hatch and Robert E. White

Closed-Form Duration Measures and Strategy Applications
by Nelson J. Lacey and Sanjay K. Nawalkha

Corporate Bond Rating Drift: An Examination of Credit Quality Rating Changes Over Time
by Edward I. Altman and Duen Li Kao

Default Risk, Mortality Rates, and the Performance of Corporate Bonds
by Edward I. Altman

Durations of Nondefault-Free Securities
by Gerald O. Bierwag and George G. Kaufman

Earnings Forecasts and Share Price Reversals
by Werner F.M. De Bondt

The Effect of Illiquidity on Bond Price Data: Some Symptoms and Remedies
by Oded Sarig and Arthur Warga

Ethics in the Investment Profession: A Survey
by E. Theodore Veit, CFA, and Michael R. Murphy, CFA

The Founders of Modern Finance: Their Prize-winning Concepts and 1990 Nobel Lectures

Initial Public Offerings: The Role of Venture Capitalists
by Joseph Lim and Anthony Saunders

A New Method for Valuing Treasury Bond Futures Options
by Ehud I. Ronn and Robert R. Bliss, Jr.

A New Perspective on Asset Allocation
by Martin L. Leibowitz

The Poison Pill Anti-takeover Defense: The Price of Strategic Deterrence
by Robert F. Bruner

Program Trading and Systematic Risk
by A.J. Senchack, Jr., and John D. Martin

The Role of Risk Tolerance in the Asset Allocation Process: A New Perspective
by W.V. Harlow III, CFA, and Keith C. Brown, CFA

Selecting Superior Securities
by Marc R. Reinganum

Stock Market Structure, Volatility, and Volume
by Hans R. Stoll and Robert E. Whaley

Stocks, Bonds, Bills, and Inflation: Historical Returns (1926–1987)
by Roger G. Ibbotson and Rex A. Sinquefield
(Published with Business One Irwin)

Note

This book first was published in 1971 as a cooperative venture between the CFA Research Foundation (which subsequently was reconstituted as the Financial Analysts Research Foundation and now is known as the Research Foundation of the Institute of Chartered Financial Analysts) and Richard D. Irwin, Inc. (which today is part of the publishing company Business One Irwin).

It was revised in 1980. This reprint—specially created for use in the 1993 Curriculum of the CFA Candidate Program sponsored by the Association for Investment Management and Research—is a copy of the 1980 revised edition.

For purposes of readability, the tables at the back have been re-typeset, and the front cover and title page have been redesigned; otherwise, the text is unchanged.

Katrina F. Sherrerd, CFA
Vice President, Publications and Research
Association for Investment Management and Research

Mission

The mission of the Research Foundation is to identify, fund, and publish research material that:

- expands the body of relevant and useful knowledge available to practitioners;
- assists practitioners in understanding and applying this knowledge; and
- enhances the investment management community's effectiveness in serving clients.

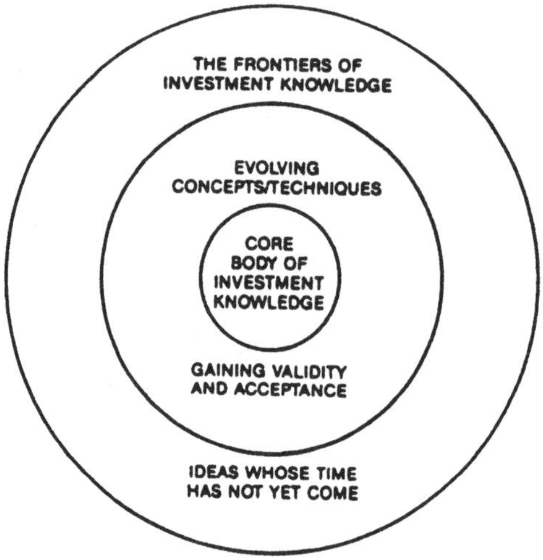

The Research Foundation of
The Institute of Chartered Financial Analysts
P. O. Box 3668
Charlottesville, Virginia 22903
Telephone: 804/977-6600
Fax: 804/977-1103

revised edition

Quantitative techniques for financial analysis

Jerome L. Valentine, C.F.A.
Financial Consultant and Adjunct Professor
of Administrative Science,
Rice University

Edmund A. Mennis, C.F.A.
Chairman of the Board,
Security Pacific Investment Managers, Inc.

To
NICHOLAS MOLODOVSKY
1898–1969

ISBN 0-256-02268-2
Library of Congress Catalog Card No. 79-88782

Printed in the United States of America

4567890ML7654

Preface

When the first edition of this book was published in 1971, quantitative techniques were just beginning to be applied in a major way to financial analysis. The computer was introduced in many investment organizations, although it then was viewed primarily as a massive number cruncher that could digest and array the large body of numerical data the analyst used as a part of the daily work. The interest of the academic community in the securities markets and investment management was increasing, as indicated by the growing number of articles in the professional literature and the content of investment courses in graduate schools. This work from academia, however, had not yet had a significant impact on the investment profession. Nevertheless, The Institute of Chartered Financial Analysts believed that quantitative techniques would be of increasing importance to practicing financial analysts, and these techniques were established as a regular topic in the C.F.A. examination program. In order to provide a useful text for this part of the program, The Financial Analysts Research Foundation commissioned the writing of the first edition of this book. The emphasis in the book was to be on the practical application of quantitative tools to the techniques of professional financial analysis or portfolio management.

Much has happened in the past nine years. The literature has proliferated and many areas of the investment process, especially portfolio theory, have been explored. Partly because of the emphasis in the C.F.A. examination program and the infusion of many quantitatively trained analysts into the profession, the use of quantitative techniques has increased significantly. Computer applications are used not just to crunch numbers, but to analyze, to construct portfolios, and to explore and challenge many investment ideas intuitively held for years. The investment profession has changed dramatically. Consequently, a revision of this text to reflect these changes was needed.

In this revision, the authors have decided to retain some of the elementary information in the previous edition that can be used as a reference or as a refresher for the analyst who may have forgotten some part of a course taken years ago. Therefore, the first four chapters are essentially unchanged. In addition, the last two chapters on computer programming and computer usage again have been included. The remaining chapters of the book have been revised with a view of making it more meaningful as a text for the C.F.A. examinations. Certain subjects that were considered too advanced for broad use or too difficult to treat effectively in the space available have been eliminated—the calculus, analysis of variance, matrix algebra, and certain theoretical parts of multiple regression. Other topics have been expanded, especially the mathematics of compound growth, portfolio models, and applications of multiple regression. We hope that the resulting text will prove of value and interest not just to the new generation of C.F.A. candidates but also to the many practicing analysts who are expanding their use of these many new techniques.

The sources of financial support for this publication may be of interest. In 1968 the Financial Analysts Federation created the Nicholas Molodovsky Award, the highest honor that can be bestowed by the federation. It is presented only to those individuals who have made an outstanding contribution of such significance as to change the direction of the profession and to raise it to higher standards of accomplishment. This award was established to honor Dr. Nicholas Molodovsky, one of the profession's outstanding scholars and the first recipient of the award. Primarily in his capacity as editor of the *Financial Analysts Journal,* but also as a writer and critic, Dr. Molodovsky labored long and hard to bridge the gap between the academic and professional worlds and struggled to make the growing use of quantitative techniques in financial analysis more palatable. The Nicholas Molodovsky Award consists of a financial contribution in the recipient's name to a research project of special personal interest. Thus, the initial financial support for this study was received from the Financial Analysts Federation in recognition of the significant professional contributions of the late Dr. Nicholas Molodovsky to quantitative financial analysis. Additional financial support was provided by the Nicholas Molodovsky Fund, representing the contribution of a large number of financial analysts who wished to be identified with a publication dedicated to a major leader in their industry.

The authors benefited considerably and wish to acknowledge their debt to the Review Committee for this revision established by The Financial Analysts Research Foundation: Robert D. Milne, C.F.A., Partner, Boyd, Watterson & Co., Cleveland, Ohio; Dr. W. Scott Bauman, C.F.A., Colgate Darden Graduate School of Business Administration, University of Virginia, Charlottesville, Virginia; and Dr. Robert F. Vandell, Research Director, The Financial Analysts Research Foundation, Charlottesville, Virginia. The authors also received many comments and suggestions from C.F.A. candidates who have used the text, and their contributions are gratefully acknowledged. The final manuscript was not submitted to the Trustees of The Financial Analysts Research Foundation for approval prior to publication, and the authors assume all responsibility for the content of this work.

The authors also are indebted to the Literary Executor of the late Sir Ronald A. Fisher, F.R.S., and to Oliver & Boyd, Edinburgh, for their permission to reprint Table III from their book *Statistical Methods for Research Workers;* and to the Literary Executor of the late Sir Ronald A. Fisher, F.R.S., to Dr. Frank Yates, F.R.S., and to Oliver & Boyd, Edinburgh, for permission to reprint Tables III and V from their book *Statistical Tables for Biological, Agricultural, and Medical Research.*

December 1979

Jerome L. Valentine
Edmund A. Mennis

Contents

Introduction: What this book is about

As the world has become more complex, the quantitative techniques of statistics and mathematics have been used with increasing success to simplify analysis and to solve problems in many fields. In recent years the proliferation of quantitative techniques in the field of financial analysis has been enormous, but the busy analyst has found it difficult to acquire an understanding of the necessary tools because of the special language in which they have been presented. Assuming only an understanding of elementary algebra, this book will attempt to bridge the gap between the practitioner and the quantitative theorist, with emphasis on understanding the functions of the tools rather than describing elaborate computations and proofs. Thus, the practitioner will know what to use and when, and what it can do for him (her) with the "how" in most instances being accomplished by a statistician or a computer.

The growth of quantitative techniques

The quantitative techniques of statistics and mathematics have been applied with success to a large number of disciplines. These form the backbone of the scientific approach to problem solving, and it has become fairly obvious that the scientific method has provided the more significant successes in man's attempt to probe the objective world. The successes of the quantitative approach occurred first in the natural sciences, but in recent decades the social sciences have moved rapidly toward the use of mathematical analysis as more powerful techniques have been developed, as the computer has made practical the computations which these techniques require, and as the demands for precision and objectivity rose in these newly developed disciplines. Psychometrics now stands beside psychology, just as econometrics has joined economics. Sociology and anthropology have developed quantitative applications, and a number of techniques have been used in political science. Although these developments do not yet rival the constructs of physics or chemistry, we are now beginning to apply the methodology that has explained the behavior of falling apples and atomic energy to the problems we face in the socio-economic world in which we live.

Finance and economics have hardly been immune to this trend. Financial journal articles now bristle with equations, and the output of models of the national economy has an influence upon national policy. The financial analyst, responsible for a critical appraisal and projection of developments in these two fields, is directly challenged by this trend. The quantitative method can provide tools for probing problems that can remain only guesswork on the intuitive level. Without an understanding of how these tools work, the analyst is left to attack a modernized army of problems with only the sniper's rifle of isolated intuitive insight. That a rifle is an excellent weapon cannot be denied, but it cannot be expected to stop a tank. In the growing complexity of the world and the growing sophistication of the investment profession, problems are now so imposing that it is appropriate for the analyst to begin to develop weapons in defense. Quantitative weapons are the most logical choice because of the precision with which they consider the structure of the data and also because their objectivity permits results to be used by different analysts. In addition, quantitative techniques permit existing theory to be subjected to tests of validity, and the results of various quantitative studies can be used as the basis upon which more sophisticated theories can be built. This cumulative property of scientific knowledge can produce a complex theoretical structure that would be only speculation if built by intuition.

Problems in learning quantitative tools

Unfortunately, it is extremely difficult for the practicing financial analyst to acquire the tools of mathematics and statistics. The demands on the average analyst's time are too severe to permit formal academic course work, and in most regions of the country such courses are available only during business hours and are rarely directed toward the specific needs of the financial analyst. Conversations of any duration with quantitative specialists are difficult because of the shortage of trained personnel in this area, the demands upon their time, and the presence of a language barrier. The literature of mathematics and statistics is voluminous and of very high quality but suffers from several drawbacks. It is oriented either toward trained specialists or toward course work where a professor is available to explain techniques. In the former case, decoding is virtually impossible; in the latter case, the material that relates the description of the technique to the concrete problems of the real world is omitted under the assumption that the instructor will provide motivation. The literature that describes techniques in verbal terms invariably deals only with the simplest of tools and does little in expanding understanding of the more complex aspects of the subject.

Actually, solid institutional reasons exist for this problem. Traditionally, mathematical tools have been used by individuals in certain specialized functions—academic mathematicians, physicists, chemists, professional statisticians, and the like. These individuals undertook formal training in quantitative techniques before beginning their careers and then continued their professional development after receiving their degrees. Therefore, the market for literature in the area was fragmented into three basic divisions. Textbooks trained the initiate under the direction of a master craftsman, journals informed the experienced technician of new developments and assumed a high level of expertise, and elementary works provided youth with the basic material necessary before initiation.

This system served its purpose quite well, but when new disciplines began to require information concerning certain aspects of quantitative theory, the institutional framework was slow to adjust. A quite similar problem has developed in the less easily described realm of professional values. The standards of value in quantitative work were developed under the specialized system. As a result, the literature in the field is considered to be worthwhile if: (1) it is as brief as possible; (2) it omits "trivial" intermediate steps in reasoning; (3) it emphasizes proofs instead of intuitive justification; (4) it contains a high degree of theoretical generality and a minimum of practical application; (5) it deletes "unnecessary" verbal rephrasing of mathematical formulations. As a result, work by professional academicians is considered to be significant for almost exactly the same reasons that it is unintelligible to the uninitiated.

A reaction to this traditional approach has developed, and a number of business schools and economics departments have started their own quantitative departments. Although this move is helpful toward broadening the usage of these tools, the same forces that created the older mathematical institutional and value structure appear to be operating now in these new social structures. Once again access to the techniques requires formal preparation and once again the literature appears to be dropping into the three basic market fragments. Only this time the apprentice is initiated into the cult of econometrics or management science instead of math or physics. An intelligent verbal description of the uses of the more advanced techniques for those who may wish to apply the tools without having to present a mathematical proof of their internal structure is once again beginning to acquire an aura of intellectual unacceptability.

In addition to the problems stemming from the specialized nature of the literature and the values motivating the style of presentation, the financial analyst attempting to begin explorations in the field will soon discover that those applications which are presented do not directly relate to the particular problems that are encountered daily. This too is quite natural, for the applications in general texts will relate to disciplines having an established tradition of quantitative methodology simply because most readers will be oriented toward this type of work (examples might be quality control, inventory management, scientific experiments, or physics). The general nature of those illustrations is unfortunate, because the techniques can most easily be understood in terms of a particular, practical example from which the analyst can generalize to other, more complicated applications.

Approach used in this book

When The Institute of Chartered Financial Analysts decided to include quantitative methods in the C. F. A. program, these considerations presented a more than usually difficult problem. The material used for the candidate's preparation needed to assume a level of professional competence equivalent to the MBA, but a quantitative orientation at the beginning of the program could not be required. The use of the techniques should be presented, but without any emphasis upon the actual computations required and without any proofs whatsoever. The material would be more valuable if it were application-oriented and if the applications were directly related to the normal work of the analyst (although possibly simplified for ease in presentation). The shortage of material having these unusual characteristics explains the presence of this book.

An attempt has been made through all of the chapters to conform (as rigidly as the authors' capability permits) to the following basic principles. The verbal text is written on a level that should not insult the intelligence of the practicing analyst, but the mathematical development assumes no training beyond a long-forgotten course in high school algebra. The presentation is essentially verbal, with the mathematical formulation presented only insofar as it is necessary. The emphasis throughout is upon an intuitive understanding of the various techniques as practical tools that can and should be used in everyday situations. Each quantitative tool is considered to be a "black box" requiring a certain type of input, solving a certain type of problem, and producing output which possesses certain clearly defined characteristics. The phrase "black box" used throughout the book is not used in its precise mathematical sense. Instead, it refers to any tool that need not be subjected to intellectual dissection to be useful in practical analysis. A telephone is the most obvious example. This book is not intended to provide the analyst with a knowledge of the computational aspects of the tools described, for this information is available in numerous texts for reference when needed and ordinarily can be handled by a technician. Instead, a conscious attempt has been made to provide the reader with a working knowledge of the basic quantitative concepts, the approach implied in the method and the manner in which the quantitative techniques can be used effectively.

The choice of techniques to be included in the book has been based upon the ease with which the tools can be applied to the investment function but an effort has been made to include the tools that are basic to an entire area of research or that help to illuminate fundamental quantitative concepts.

The first chapter treats notation and attempts to show why the apparently abstruse language of mathematics is actually quite valuable. In addition, this arrangement allows the majority of notational problems to be eliminated before new concepts are introduced.

The chapters on algebra and elementary statistics are included as a refresher for those who have forgotten basic material. An attempt has been made, however, to show the intuitive basis for a number of the simple operations upon numbers.

The mathematics of finance covers compound growth, present value, annuities and the use of present value in valuation models and bond mathematics.

Probability theory is treated from the standpoint of subjective probabilities simply because this approach permits practical applications without complex theoretical developments.

The chapter on hypothesis testing introduces the basic concepts of statistical inference and is the first chapter that provides some of the flavor of the statistical method.

The chapter on regression develops the basic ideas of simple and multiple regression in light of the material contained in hypothesis testing.

Portfolio theory begins with linear programming as the basis upon which a larger literature in the area of maximization techniques has been built. This material is then broadened to include a discussion of the more common portfolio models and a discussion of efficient market theory as well as the capital asset pricing model.

The two chapters treating the computer are included because this tool, while not necessarily quantitative, has been the fundamental reason why the other techniques have become economically practical in investment work. The first chapter on computers discusses the nature of the machine and how programmers provide it with instructions. The second chapter discusses the much more complex problems of project control and systems development.

A number of tables have been included as appendixes to the book. Although the various chapters can be read without reference to these tables, a deeper understanding of a number of the examples in the text can be gained if the tables are referred to by the reader.

A list of additional readings that will permit the analyst to explore models in some detail has been included at the end of a number of the chapters. A brief description of the books is provided in order to permit the reader to select readings most likely to satisfy his personal objectives. The particular works chosen in these lists are, quite naturally, the result of the authors' personal backgrounds and biases. It would be absurd to maintain that the works that have been included are the only valuable material in their particular field, and it is probably impossible to find a set of readings clearly superior to alternatives. Hopefully, the reader will find that the material selected emphasizes the aspects of the techniques that are meaningful to an analyst and provides a substantial broadening of intellectual horizons.

Simplifying the problem of reading quantitative material

A few comments concerning how this material can most effectively be used in self-study may prove beneficial. The most important point in reading any quantitative material is to remember that one of the main advantages of mathematics is that it is concise. As a result, even when the techniques are described verbally in some detail, one page of material has the same information content as a large number of pages covering qualitative subjects. This implies that a reading rate one-fifth to one-tenth of the reader's regular rate is quite normal—the information content is really being digested at normal speed. If the material is read at a normal reading rate, unless the reader is very familiar with both the content and the authors' syntax, comprehension will be extremely low.

Another feature unique to quantitative subjects is the importance of equations and graphs. In verbal subjects, such scribblings serve to amplify and illuminate the text; however, in this type of material, they *constitute* the text, and the verbal description serves to amplify and illuminate. As a result, an abnormally serious consideration of numbers and graphs is needed. The reader should therefore accept without discouragement the likelihood that he will cover only a few pages of text in some normal study periods. Other sections will tend to go much faster simply because the same number of concepts is expressed in a larger number of pages.

A great deal of time can be saved if each chapter is skimmed before it is read carefully. Mathematical developments tend to move methodically from point to point, and comprehension is greatly simplified if a preliminary scan of the chapter has shown the reader roughly where the development is leading. This tendency toward point-by-point development produces an additional reading problem, for it is difficult to proceed if an earlier step in the analysis is not understood. For this reason, it is important to attempt to reread and rethink each point within a chapter before continuing to the next concept. The chapters are largely independent, and a failure to understand the material in one chapter should not greatly affect the others, although the chapters should be read in order if possible. Each chapter is preceded by a brief summary describing the material that follows, so that the reader will have an overview of the tools and their applications before their more detailed presentation. The chapters on notation and algebra are the backbone of all other chapters and should be read until thoroughly mastered. Hypothesis testing contains concepts that are important in almost all of the advanced techniques and that are vital to the understanding of the quantitative methodology.

No claim is made that the content of this book exhausts the set of quantitative techniques that have value in financial analysis or that this is an exhaustive treatment of the subjects covered. The approach taken is that an understanding of the functions of the various tools is more important than an understanding of either the computations or the related proofs. As a result, the function of the technique should be presented first in order to deepen the understanding of more technical material that may be encountered by the analyst at a later time.

The dual purposes of the book are to assist the analyst in his attempt to acquire more powerful methods for research and to assist the profession in its attempt to move toward a more scientific methodology. Academic rigor has been avoided in order to create a simple presentation. Hopefully, as a result of this material the analyst will be motivated to continue reading in the quantitative area and this material will provide him with the intuitive foundation upon which a solid understanding of these techniques can be built. If any such analyst should develop the mathematical sophistication eventually to return to this book and consider it to be a naïve presentation, the highest aims of the authors will have been achieved.

Models: Their nature and value

With this introduction to the book completed, an introduction to the nature of the tools that later will be discussed individually may be helpful. Each quantitative tool can be regarded as a model of reality, and the most fundamental characteristic common to all models is that they inevitably are an abstraction from the real world. As an example, a child's airplane model is an abstraction of a real airplane that portrays the plane's shape and color but does not bother to reproduce the unwanted characteristics—its size, weight, expense, and so forth. On the other hand, an accounting model of the same airplane would abstract a picture of its expense very accurately but would disregard its shape and color as well as its size and weight. As can be seen by these simple examples, models definitely have a common feature. They do not give a *complete* picture of reality; they only give a good picture of certain *important aspects* of reality. The particular aspect that is seen as important has nothing to do with the model; it depends upon whether the user is a schoolboy or an accountant. As a result, there is no such thing as a *good* model, only an appropriate one—a model that adequately abstracts from the real world those aspects needed by the particular user at that time. A model, then, stands in direct relation to a need, and a model satisfying many diverse needs is said (at least by mathematicians) to be *powerful*.

In the above example, the accounting model is powerful because it can be applied to an airplane, or to a car, a diversified business, or anything having financial aspects that need to be pictured. The accounting system represents, or "abstracts" those financial aspects and disregards the rest of the plane, car, etc. If this abstraction did not take place, the investment analyst would have an impossible job in comparing General Foods to General Motors. The accounting model is powerful *because* it is abstract; and mathematics, being the most abstract of all disciplines, could naturally be expected to provide the most powerful models. The usefulness, precision, and generality of the quantitative technique have become so accepted in the exact sciences that at the present time a theory is not regarded as completely formulated unless it is stated mathematically.

Mathematical models are abstract techniques, or procedures, that are known to yield the correct (or approximately correct) answers. A simple example of a mathematical model is the compound interest table used by the analyst to calculate the growth rate of, say, the earnings per share of IBM during the past ten years. Another model is the arithmetic mean or "average" used many times each day by almost all businessmen. The advantage of these and more complicated models is that they solve real problems, that is, they satisfy real needs, which is, of course, the only justification for any model. The "quantitative model" is divided into a large set of smaller tools, so that it is possible to regard basic arithmetic, algebra, the calculus, multivariate statistics, and the like as more specific models used to solve more specific and unique problems. Each of these vague areas, of course, is further divided into a number of smaller tools. Each technique is designed to provide an accurate solution to a very specific type of problem; as a result the most significant problem in the use of the quantitative model as a whole is the selection of the appropriate tool for any given problem.

The major advantage to using these mathematical techniques is that they make it possible to draw upon a "storehouse" of knowledge that required several thousands of years and no small number of geniuses to develop. By using a mathematical model to solve the particular investment problem at hand, the solution technique is provided by, for example, Newton, thus leaving the analyst free to select techniques and to cast problems into a form solvable by some established procedure. In effect, the analyst is using the thoughts of Pythagoras, Newton, and others to solve certain technical problems defined by the senior analyst. Using this approach, the researcher is able greatly to extend his power to analyze his problems, and superior investment results might reasonably be expected.

The use of any technique or model is possible only if a particular problem is molded into a form that the model can accept. Because this molding of the problem into available solution patterns can be done only by a man who understands the real nature of the problem and the characteristics of the available tools, the techniques of mathematics must be understood by the analyst or these models cannot be applied effectively.

Mathematics has its models too. The use of graphs to show the relationships between variables implied by various equations, as well as the analogy of "space" to represent the variables being considered, illustrate the fact that mathematics itself utilizes the abstractions and the molding patterns common to all models.

One very interesting point basic to all that follows is that the English language, like all languages, is in itself a model of reality. It has its own notation, its rules of punctuation and syntax, and a very complex set of symbols (words) that are manipulated within the given set of rules. By using the alphabet, building words and then sentences, paragraphs, and books, English is capable of expressing virtually any set of concepts. As a result, English is one of the most powerful of all of the models. But *the language of mathematics* is a very complex model that closely parallels the verbal language of English in function. Using mathematical notation, "expressions" can be built that are permitted by the mathematical rules and then are manipulated by the established grammar in the system. The notation of math "communicates," and the disadvantage of complexity is more than offset by precision. In addition, the structure of the permissible expressions of mathematics, although more unfamiliar than the grammar of English, permits greater accuracy in portraying the problem and also allows greater generality. One of the main advantages of the use of all mathematical models is their ability to communicate meaning without the possibility of misinterpretation.

Chapter 1

Notation, or the language of symbols and what they mean

In order to use quantitative techniques, some method must be used to represent real world relationships in a simple and precise form. Mathematical symbols, which on the surface appear unintelligible, are merely conventional notations to permit the statement of complex relationships in a clear and readily understandable manner. As the letters of the alphabet became inadequate, mathematicians used letters of the Greek alphabet as a supplement. This chapter provides an explanation of simple and more complicated mathematical expressions, and explains the use of subscripts, exponents, and the important summation symbol, the Greek letter Σ. At the end of the chapter, a table describes the implied or conventional usage of a number of symbols that can help decode many apparently complicated formulas.

ELEMENTARY NOTATION

As discussed in the preface, mathematics can be viewed as a system of models used to represent the real world in purely quantitative terms. Although this representation must necessarily involve some abstraction and therefore some distortion of reality, the precision and manipulative power of the system more than offset its inability to consider problems from a qualitative standpoint. But the precision that has been emphasized stems largely from the notation of mathematics, and this notation is in itself a model expressing mathematical concepts. Over the course of the development of mathematics, a number of conventions have evolved that permit mathematical ideas to be easily conveyed, and the most useful of these have been gradually consolidated into the quantitative notation we now use.

As a matter of fact, the initial use of Arabic numerals is considered by many to be the greatest single advance ever made in the entire history of quantitative methods. The use of this system of numbers in arithmetic was expanded when, in the Middle Ages, algebra was first introduced in Europe. This development in turn established the need for a symbol that could be used to represent some unknown quantity, some number known to have a value but the value of which was as yet concealed from the researcher. This quantity, now referred to as a *variable*, was expressed as the letter x. The manipulation of numbers and variables progressed rapidly, with symbols used to express even the operations being performed upon these values. The *Encyclopaedia Britannica,* in its article on mathematical notations, indicates that the use of two parallel lines (=) to express equality began in the 16th century, with Robert Recorde: ". . . bicause noe .2. thynges, can be moare equalle." The "+" and "−" signs apparently were introduced in the 15th century as a result of a system of recording warehouse weights. Later, "×" for multiplication and "÷" for division were added. Modern algebraic notation tends to rely heavily upon the use of parentheses to indicate both the order in which the operations are to be performed and also to imply multiplication. As a result: $5 \times x$ or $5 \cdot x$ or $(5)(x)$ means "5" times "x", and can be written simply as "$5x$". $(5)(x)(x)$ means "5" times "x" times "x".

In addition, x, y, and z were pressed into service as symbols to permit the analysis of problems involving more than one variable. Eventually, letters were used to stand for unchanging quantities. These "constants" were represented by the earlier letters of the alphabet, such as "a", "b", or "c". Notation at this point permitted people to write such statements as

1. $4 = 2 + 2$
2. $4x = 16$
3. $y = a + b + c$
4. $y = ax$
5. $y = a + bx$

These examples show several types of important mathematical quantities. The most fundamental quantity, of course, is simply a number such as "2" or "4." When mathematical thought moved beyond simple arithmetic by introducing letters such as "x" or "y," it was really introducing a new type of quantity. This quantity, a variable, was a number as real as the numbers 2 or 4, but with the new characteristic of having a value that was unknown. This unknown value could be 2, 4, or any other number, but the variable could be manipulated exactly as if its value were known. This discovery was the foundation for the development of algebra. Viewed another way, a variable was a number that could assume any value, a number whose value could be allowed to vary. The older type of quantity exemplified by 2 and 4 therefore became known as "constants" to distinguish their fixed character from the more flexible variable.

Letters such as a or b were used to denote constants in mathematical expressions in order to show that the quantities represented had constant, unchanging qualities even though the expression did not specify their numerical value. The quantity represented by a was not specified as being either 2 or 4, but represented a value that would be known whenever the expression was evaluated and did not vary in value during the course of the analysis.

In this new notational framework, the value of one variable could be expressed in terms of another variable. For example, y could be said to equal $a+bx$, meaning that the actual numerical value of y was known only indirectly through a knowledge of the numerical value of x. The relationship between unknowns could be specified, defining variables in terms of other variables. Such a definition is called a "function," and in this particular case y is expressed as a function of x. This indirect assignment of value is the cornerstone of mathematics, and all quantitative techniques are merely the reshuffling of these assignments or (stated another way) the manipulation of functions.

Recalling for a moment the "word problems" of high school days, it would be possible to translate the earlier statements 1 through 5 into the following English sentences:

1. Two added to two equals four.
2. Four times an unknown quantity (x) equals sixteen.
3. A quantity (y) exists that is equal to the sum of three other quantities (a, b, and c).
4. A variable (y) is equal to the product of a constant quantity (a) times another variable (x); or two quantities exist that are proportional to each other.
5. A variable (y) exists that is equal to the sum of a constant factor (a) and a proportional quantity (bx).

As can be seen, mathematical notation is substantially simpler than English.

In effect, comparing the relationship between mathematical equations and their corresponding English statements similar to that used above is an attempt to compare the relative merits of two different models of the same item. When the models deal with quantitative relationships and become even moderately complex, the advantage of the symbolic notation of mathematics relative to the verbal model increases very rapidly.

As mathematical applications were expanded beyond the simple basic algebra used in the above statements, additional notational requirements were rapidly encountered. First, problems realistic enough to serve some practical purpose quickly began to involve more symbols than the alphabet could accommodate. As a result the Greek alphabet was added. When even this became inadequate, subscripts were added to the letters to permit a distinction between variables. As expressions became more complicated, parentheses were introduced to indicate the order in which calculations were to be performed, with all operations within parentheses performed before other calculations were begun. Another problem stemmed from the development of completely new models in order to subject additional problems to quantitative manipulation. Examples of this are the calculus, differential equations, probability theory, and more recently the development of statistics. In each of these disciplines, specialized operations and frequently used numbers had to be represented, and new symbols were quickly developed in order to give precision to the advanced approaches. By examining a few of these streamlining techniques at this point, it is possible to introduce symbols that can be used to simplify the later discussion of more complicated mathematical tools. The following sections are not an exhaustive treatment of the notation used throughout this book but can be regarded as an introduction to a few basic symbols frequently encountered in almost all quantitative work.

Special jargon has been developed to allow mathematical quantities to be referenced in English format. Some of the most basic terms are shown in Figure 1-1.

A number of relations other than equality are treated in mathematics and have been given special symbols. The notation for the most common "relational operators" is shown in Table 1-1.

Several other frequently encountered symbols should be described at this point. $|x|$ means "the absolute value of x" or the value of x without regard to the sign., The symbol "±" means "plus or minus"; in everyday language, it could be translated as "give or take" some amount. An example might be 4,376 feet ± 20 feet, meaning "4,376 feet, give or take 20 feet as an allowance for errors in measurement." The symbol ". . ." means "and so forth" or "etc." The dots stand for the missing numbers that are not shown for convenience in notation. An

Figure 1-1

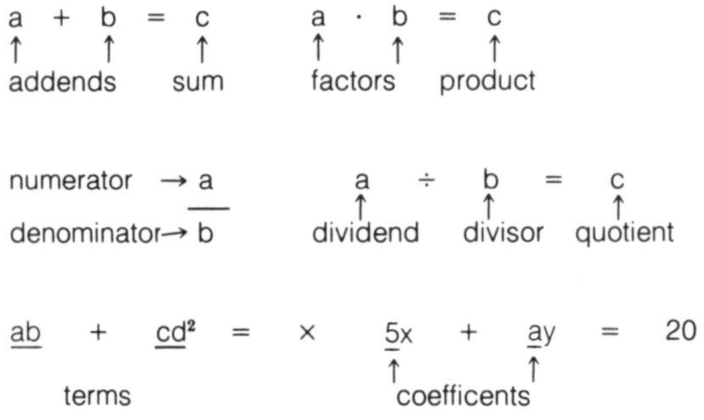

Table 1-1

Symbol	*Significance*
$=$	Equals
$>$	Is greater than
$<$	Is less than
$\leq$	Is less than or equal to
$\geq$	Is greater than or equal to
$\neq$	Is not equal to

example is 1, 2, 3 . . . n, which simply means 1, 2, 3, and so forth until the number n is reached. The symbol "$\therefore$" means "therefore."

EXPONENTS

One of the most useful additions to the notation so far introduced is the use of exponents. Recall that x^2 is another way of writing $(x)(x)$, or x times x. Obviously, x^3 is a simpler way of writing $(x)(x)(x)$. It is relatively simple to expand the use of exponents well beyond this extremely simple application. For example, mathematicians have used x^{-1} as a symbol for $1/x$ for quite some time. Using this approach, it is possible to write

$$\frac{10x + 5}{(5y + 50)} \quad \text{as } (10x + 5)(5y + 50)^{-1}$$

and keep the formula in a more convenient form by writing it on only one line. The approach can be expanded somewhat by writing x^{-2} for $\frac{1}{x^2}$. Using this extension, we can write

$$\frac{10x + 5}{(5y + 50)^2} \quad \text{as } (10x + 5)(5y + 50)^{-2}$$

and keep the relationships in the formula from appearing to be more difficult than is the case.

A number of the formulas in statistics use the radical sign $\sqrt{}$ to express the operation of taking the square root of a number. An exponent can easily be used to accomplish this same purpose by defining $x^{1/2}$ as being simply another way of stating $\sqrt{x}$. By using this approach, $x^{1/3} = \sqrt[3]{x}$, which is the cube root of x. From this it is relatively simple to regard $x^{2/3}$ as simply another way of writing $\sqrt[3]{x^2}$.

SUBSCRIPTS

Unfortunately, not enough letters are available in the alphabet to permit a reasonably complicated mathematical argument to be presented without a great deal of confusion. As a result, subscripts have been used so that the reader may differentiate between variables. For example x_1 is not the same as x_2. Similarly, $y = a + bx$ could easily be expressed as $x_1 = a + bx_2$. Because any number can be used as a subscript, it is simple within this notational system to create as many variables as are needed in the statement of the mathematical problem. Although the flexibility of the system virtually eliminates the problem of precisely representing numerous variables, a major notational advantage of a completely different sort has made subscripts even more valuable. Because both x and y were available for subscripts, it became possible to have x_1, x_2, and x_3 as three separate and distinct variables that nevertheless had something in common—the quality of "x"ness. Each of the x's or the group of all x's could then be related to, say, y_1, y_2, and y_3, which were similar to each other with respect to "y"ness but nevertheless were three separate and distinct variables. The three y's could be regarded as different from each other but *very* different from the three x's.

As an example of this notational scheme, consider x and y as two men each owning a personal portfolio. The portfolio manager for both men typically analyzes portfolios by dividing the stocks in the account into three categories—basic industrial, moderate growth, and high growth. He then takes the total market value of the portfolio in each category as a percentage of the total market value of the entire portfolio in order to derive an account's diversification. By using subscripts, the portfolio manager can call the percentage of x's portfolio invested in basic industrial stocks by the symbol "x_1." Similarly, x_2 equals the exposure of account x in moderate growth stocks, and x_3 indicates participation in the high growth issues. Naturally, $x_1 + x_2 + x_3 = 100\%$ if 100% of the portfolio is invested. Inasmuch as the account executive also does the same thing for y's account, $y_1 + y_2 + y_3 = 100\%$. And certainly it is possible to say $x_1 + x_2 + x_3 = y_1 + y_2 + y_3$ simply because $100\% = 100\%$ even if the two portfolios differ substantially in composition and size.

If all of this seems to be somewhat academic, the problem is probably that this particular example is an extremely simple situation. Real business problems involve many more variables, making the advantages of subscripts more obvious. However, even in this somewhat artificial situation, the expression using subscripts is substantially more meaningful than the equivalent statement without subscripts: $u + v + w = x + y + z$. If the different groups in the two portfolios are to be analyzed, the portfolio manager is able to refer to the same group in both portfolios by simply using the same subscript for both x and y. For example, both x_1 and y_1 are percentage figures relating to "basic industry" stocks because they both have the same subscript. Because the letters are different, the portfolios to which the percentages refer are different. When the portfolio manager concentrates his attention on x_1

versus y_1, he is dealing with the difference between the two portfolios from the standpoint of their concentration in the basic industrial area. If, on the other hand, he considers x_1 versus x_2, he is dealing with the relative emphasis of one portfolio in the basic industries versus the moderate growth industries. Although this form of treatment is somewhat unfamiliar, it is definitely better than talking about "u" versus "x" and "u" versus "y," which would be the case if subscripts were not used.

In both statistics and financial analysis, it is quite common to deal with a number of cases of a similar nature, for example, the price of one stock at the close of 12 different months. Instead of referring to these values as $a, b, c, d, e, f, g, h, i, j, k, l$, it is certainly more meaningful to call them $x_1, x_2, \ldots x_{12}$. It is then very simple to refer to the group of all x's as x_i, meaning "x regardless of the particular subscript." In this particular case, of course, this would mean the stock's price regardless of the particular month being considered (or the monthly closing prices for stock x during the year). By using subscripts in this case, instead of having to define the meaning of a, then the meaning of b, and so on, it is possible to make a general statement by defining the meaning of x_i. As a result of this power to control large quantities of numbers within a simple logical framework, subscripted variables are the stock-in-trade of statisticians. In fact, it would be difficult to conceive of the expression of most statistical concepts without subscripts. For example, $\Sigma(x_i)$ means "add all of the x_i's." It would be much more cumbersome to write the same statement in nonsubscripted form.

Σ (SIGMA)

The Σ (sigma) notation is very useful in many practical applications. It simply indicates that something is to be totaled. $\Sigma(x_i)$ = total of all of the observations of the quantity "x." A number of variations of this basic idea are helpful. For example,

$$\sum_{i=1}^{10} (x_i)$$

is a mathematical expression using the subscript "i" to indicate that all of the x_i are to be totaled, with the "i" going from 1 through 10. The expression is therefore equivalent to:

$$x_1 + x_2 + x_3 + x_4 + x_5 + x_6 + x_7 + x_8 + x_9 + x_{10}.$$

Another way of saying this is: "Sum over i the variable x_i; i = 1, 10." Replacing the "i" with a "j," we can say that if the symbol were

$$\sum_{j=1}^{10} (x_j)$$

the reader would total the "j" observations, knowing that 10 numbers would be added together. If we encountered

$$\sum_{i=1}^{20} (x_i)$$

we would "sum over i," knowing that 20 numbers would be added. It is important to point out that

$$\sum_{i=1}^{10} (x_i)$$

is a number, in exactly the same sense that y or x is a number. It is the total of the x_i's. As a simple example;

$$\sum_{i=1}^{5} (x_i) = x_1 + x_2 + x_3 + x_4 + x_5$$

and if

$$x_1 = 3, x_2 = 4, x_3 = 7, x_4 = 2, x_5 = 6,$$

then

$$\sum_{i=1}^{5} (x_i) = 3 + 4 + 7 + 2 + 6 = 22.$$

Now, because we know from algebra that $(x-y)$ is a number in precisely the same sense that both x and y are numbers, it is perfectly logical that $(x-y)$ can be given a subscript just as easily as x or y.

$$\sum_{i=1}^{5} (x-y)_i$$

is therefore a reasonable use of the notation we have described.

At this point, it is possible to say something like:

$$\frac{\sum_{i=1}^{10} \frac{(x + y)_i}{2}}{10}$$

where:

x = the stock's high price for the year
y = the stock's low price for the year
i = the year

in order to ask for the average of a stock's mean price for the past ten years using *annual* high and low prices. This equation, of course, could be a junior analyst's nightmare, but a senior analyst could take great pride in the precision of the statement of the assignment. His assistant may not *understand* the assignment, but he could never *misinterpret* it. And if the junior analyst is sufficiently familiar with statistics, the correct calculations will always be performed.

Such might not be the case if the assignment were given as: "Get me the average of the stock's average price for the past ten years." In fact, a rigorous senior analyst with a good junior might even write in June, 1978,

$$\frac{\sum_{i=1968}^{1977} \frac{(x + y)_i}{2}}{10}$$

where

x = high price
y = low price
i = year

and be certain that the junior man does not use the mean price *to date* for the year 1978 as one of the ten items being totaled. In fact, if both men were familiar with both subscripts and exponents, the senior could write

$$\frac{\sum_{i=1968}^{1977} (x_i + y_i)(2)^{-1}}{10}$$

where

x = high price
y = low price
i = year

which is, as can be seen from what has been said before, a brief and also a precise statement of the particular number desired. Once a familiarity with the notation has been gained, this expression can be written as rapidly as an English description of comparable accuracy.

MORE SUBSCRIPTS

With a knowledge of the advantages obtained from a subscript, the most natural development, of course, is the use of two or more subscripts. This apparently complex application is actually no more difficult than the tables investment men have always used. For example, Table 1-2 can be set into subscript form very easily if we let i be the number of the row and j be the number of the column. If the analyst is

Table 1-2: Average annual price earnings ratio of industry X (International Oils)

Name	*1978*	*1977*	*1976*	*1975*	*1974*
Exxon	8.4	9.3	8.4	7.1	5.5
Gulf	6.3	7.4	5.9	5.7	3.8
Royal Dutch	6.6	4.8	4.3	3.8	2.4
Standard (California)	6.7	7.0	6.8	6.1	5.0
Texaco	8.5	8.2	8.1	8.1	4.5

discussing Gulf in a meeting of the Investment Committee, he is talking about the second row, and as a result, $i = 2$. If he is dealing with Exxon, the first row is being used, and $i = 1$. Now if he considers Gulf's P/E in 1977, he is dealing with a particular column; in this particular case it is the second column that is important, making $j = 2$. If he considers 1978, $j = 1$.

If the analyst would bother to rewrite the table with all of the subscript values entered, it would look like Table 1-3.

Table 1-3: Industry X

$i = 1$ $j = 1$	$i = 1$ $j = 2$	$i = 1$ $j = 3$	$i = 1$ $j = 4$	$i = 1$ $j = 5$
$i = 2$ $j = 1$	$i = 2$ $j = 2$	$i = 2$ $j = 3$	$i = 2$ $j = 4$	$i = 2$ $j = 5$
$i = 3$ $j = 1$	$i = 3$ $j = 2$	$i = 3$ $j = 3$	$i = 3$ $j = 4$	$i = 3$ $j = 5$
$i = 4$ $j = 1$	$i = 4$ $j = 2$	$i = 4$ $j = 3$	$i = 4$ $j = 4$	$i = 4$ $j = 5$
$i = 5$ $j = 1$	$i = 5$ $j = 2$	$i = 5$ $j = 3$	$i = 5$ $j = 4$	$i = 5$ $j = 5$

Each "element" in the table obviously has a unique set of subscripts, so that the analyst can easily refer to each element by its subscript values, as shown in Table 1-4.

Table 1-4

$X_{1,1}$	$X_{1,2}$	$X_{1,3}$	$X_{1,4}$	$X_{1,5}$
$X_{2,1}$	$X_{2,2}$	$X_{2,3}$	$X_{2,4}$	$X_{2,5}$
$X_{3,1}$	$X_{3,2}$	$X_{3,3}$	$X_{3,4}$	$X_{3,5}$
$X_{4,1}$	$X_{4,2}$	$X_{4,3}$	$X_{4,4}$	$X_{4,5}$
$X_{5,1}$	$X_{5,2}$	$X_{5,3}$	$X_{5,4}$	$X_{5,5}$

First subscript = i = row
Second subscript = j = column

Using this approach, $x_{5,5}$ stands for the price/earnings ratio of Texaco in 1974.

The notation permits us to identify each number, but it does much more than that. It gives each and every number in the entire table the basic name "x," indicating that it is an element in industry X. All of the numbers have something in common: they are from the "X" table, dealing with P/E's in the oil industry. In fact, it is now possible to refer to the entire block, or "matrix" of numbers by simply referring to X as opposed to, say, Y. What could Y stand for? The oil industry's sales figures, or possibly the chemical industry's P/E's.

Two additional advantages to this extremely valuable approach need to be described before passing on to new material. First, we can now talk about *all five* years of Exxon by referring to one symbol; that symbol is $x_{1,j}$ meaning the first row and any column. (The j, instead of a specific number as a column subscript, means "any column.") The tabulation $x_{2,j}$ therefore means the *second* row and any column. In the notation, it is just as simple to discuss the results of all companies in 1976 by saying $x_{i,3}$, meaning any row and the third column, because the "i," instead of a number in the *row* subscript's position, means "any row." The tabulation $x_{i,1}$ = any row in the first column = the P/E of any of the companies in 1978. Now it is possible to write the symbol for the average P/E for Exxon for the five years we are considering:

$x_{1,j}$ = Exxon, any column, as we already know.

Therefore,

$\sum_{j=1}^{5} (x_{1,j})$ = The total of the columns for Exxon, using notation that we have already developed.

Therefore,

$(5^{-1}) \sum_{j=1}^{5} (x_{1,j})$ = The average of the individual annual P/E's of Exxon for the five years.

In the same way, we can find the expression for the average P/E of all companies in industry X in 1978, which we need, let's say, in order to compare the market's valuation of the industry relative to the S&P 500 at the close of 1978:

$x_{i,1}$ = Any company in 1978, because 1978 is the first column.

Therefore,

$\sum_{i=1}^{5} (x_{i,1})$ = The total of the 1978 P/E's of all of the companies.

Therefore,

$$(5^{-1}) \sum_{i=1}^{5} (x_{i,1}) = \text{The average 1978 } P/E \text{ of the companies in industry X.}$$

Placing the two averages in the table (and showing the notation for several other averages as well) we have Table 1-5.

Table 1-5

Name	*1978*	*1977*	*1976*	*1975*	*1974*	*Average for each company*
Exxon	$x_{1,1}$	$x_{1,2}$	$x_{1,3}$	$x_{1,4}$	$x_{1,5}$	$\frac{\Sigma_j(x_{1,j})}{5}$
Gulf	$x_{2,1}$	$x_{2,2}$	$x_{2,3}$	$x_{2,4}$	$x_{2,5}$	$\frac{\Sigma_j(x_{2,j})}{5}$
Royal Dutch	$x_{3,1}$	$x_{3,2}$	$x_{3,3}$	$x_{3,4}$	$x_{3,5}$	$\frac{\Sigma_j(x_{3,j})}{5}$
Standard (California)	$x_{4,1}$	$x_{4,2}$	$x_{4,3}$	$x_{4,4}$	$x_{4,5}$	$\frac{\Sigma_j(x_{4,j})}{5}$
Texaco	$x_{5,1}$	$x_{5,2}$	$x_{5,3}$	$x_{5,4}$	$x_{5,5}$	$\frac{\Sigma_j(x_{5,j})}{5}$
Average for each year	$\frac{\Sigma_i(x_{i,1})}{5}$	$\frac{\Sigma_i(x_{i,2})}{5}$	$\frac{\Sigma_i(x_{i,3})}{5}$	$\frac{\Sigma_i(x_{i,4})}{5}$	$\frac{\Sigma_i(x_{i,5})}{5}$	

Note: The Σ does not need the "1 to 5" symbols because the meaning is obvious from the table. It is useful to specify whether the meaning is "sum over *i*" or "sum over *j*" only because this technique is being presented for the first time. Once the material becomes more familiar, the meaning of the subscript can also be inferred from the table.

This table shows the actual calculations that the analyst already makes when he creates an average "spread sheet." Going one small step further, how would the analyst have his statistical assistant calculate the number in the lower right corner of the table—the average of "the average *P/E*'s in each particular year"?

He would want to average the expression covering each year's average:

$$\frac{\sum_{i=1}^{5} (x_{i,1})}{5} = \text{The first year's average.}$$

Therefore, this is needed for every year:

$$\frac{\sum_{i=1}^{5} (x_{i,j})}{5} = \text{The year's average for } \textit{any} \text{ year; for the } j\text{th year.}$$

This expression must be totaled for all five years (all five values for j):

$$\sum_{j=1}^{5}\left[\frac{\sum_{i=1}^{5}(x_{i,j})}{5}\right].$$

And in order to find the average, we must divide the total by five:

$$\frac{\sum_{j=1}^{5}\left[\frac{\sum_{i=1}^{5}(x_{i,j})}{5}\right]}{5}.$$

Although the final statement of the average appears to be a little forbidding, it is an accurate statement of what is to be done—of what the number is. The expression in this notation could be given to a junior analyst familiar with elementary statistics, and the precise answer desired as well as the procedure for computing that answer would be fully defined.

The symbol Π, called pi, can be used instead of the symbol Σ for some types of applications. The usage is exactly the same, except that instead of *summing* $x_1, x_2, x_3 \ldots x_n$, the *product* is taken. In other words, if the symbol is Σ, the numbers are added together; if the symbol is Π, the numbers are multiplied together.

ALPHABETS

Earlier in this chapter, the use of Greek letters was said to have originated in the shortage of letters in the "normal" alphabet. Since the early stages of notation development, however, a number of conventions have been added to the use of Greek symbols. Although the usage has never been strictly formalized, writers frequently assume that the reader will be able to infer the meaning of symbols from a knowledge of these general rules and the context in which the symbol appears. As a result, a brief description of the implied usage of the alphabets can be of great value in a reader's attempt to "decode" apparently abstruse mathematical formulations, as outlined in Table 1-6.

In statistical usage, notational problems become even more unwieldy. Statistics is a discipline that deals with the description of a *population*. A population is a clearly defined group. Alternative definitions are "class" or "set." Examples are the set of all C.F.A. candidates, the set of all financial analysts, the set of all stocks, and the like. Any population has one or more characteristics that may be treated quantitatively. Unfortunately, the characteristics usually are amenable only to estimation. For example, it is not practical to find the average

Table 1-6: Mathematical usage

Greek alphabet	English alphabet	Description
α alpha β beta γ gamma	a b c	Used as constants in mathematical expressions.
δ delta Δ U.C.* delta	*d* *D*	Used to denote small changes in the value of variables.
ϕ phi Φ U.C. phi ψ psi Ψ U.C. psi	*f* *F* *g* *G*	Used to indicate a particular function. (Functions are discussed in the chapter on algebra, but can be briefly defined as numbers whose values are indirectly defined; numbers that are defined in terms of other variables.)
	i *j*	Index numbers used to show the value of subscripts. The maximum value that may be assumed by the subscript is usually denoted by *m* or *n*.
κ kappa λ lambda μ mu	*k* *l* *m* *n*	Used as constants or parameters. Parameters are artificial or relational quantities used to tie together real variables in mathematical expressions.
ξ xi η ēta ζ zēta	*x* *y* *z*	Used to denote a variable being described in mathematical terms.
Π U.C. pi		Used to indicate that the product of a number of quantities is to be taken.
Σ U.C. sigma		Used to indicate that the sum of a number of quantities is to be taken.

*Note: U.C. stands for upper case.

intelligence of all financial analysts—this value must be estimated. Statistics calls the actual characteristics of the population being studied *parameters*, and these parameters are denoted by Greek letters. The estimate found for the value of the parameter (the estimated intelligence of financial analysts) is denoted by an English letter or by a Greek letter with a caret. An example of such an estimate might be $\hat{\sigma}$ (read "sigma hat"), which means the estimate for the population characteristic σ regardless of what kind of characteristic that might be. More complex distinctions than this are basic to mathematical literature, but this book is designed for an introductory level and will avoid wherever possible the introduction of notational complexity. The statistical notation actually used will be developed as needed in the later chapters.

All of the advantages of any type of mathematical notation, however, can be utilized only when the symbols are used together to form expressions, and these expressions are manipulated in order to provide a meaning more useful to the researcher. The most basic rules for changing mathematical statements are found in elementary algebra.

Chapter 2

A review of elementary algebra

Algebra provides a set of rules for the manipulation of mathematical expressions, and an understanding of these rules is essential to a comprehension of the material in the chapters that follow. The elementary operations of addition, subtraction, division, and multiplication are explained, and then more complex combinations are considered. Fractions and exponent treatment are reviewed, and a description of the "how" may make logarithms more comprehensible. Finally, functions and equations are introduced to prepare for more detailed treatment later.

INTRODUCTION

The system for manipulating numbers and variables known as basic algebra has gained an unwarranted reputation for difficulty. Actually, it is only a system for manipulating quantitative expressions as a means of improving their understandability. A fundamental problem of algebra is the solution of equations, that is, finding the hidden numbers defined by mathematical statements of "screens." The set of rules involved in the process of algebraic simplification is actually much less complex than, say, the rules for playing contract bridge. If algebra also has gained a reputation for being dull, there are understandable reasons for this attitude. Learning algebra is equivalent to learning the rules of bridge, and the enjoyment of the game is not in memorizing the rules. Nevertheless, without rules there could be no game.

This section will serve as a refresher to readers who are already familiar with the elementary aspect of algebra but who have not used it since school days. An intuitive "feel" for the operations is emphasized. Fortunately, the subject is actually very limited, and it is only necessary to cover:

1. The elementary operations
2. Fractions
3. Exponents

4. Logarithms
5. Equations and functions

THE ELEMENTARY OPERATIONS

The simplest mathematical results are achieved through the use of addition, subtraction, multiplication, and division. Although every analyst is familiar with these operations, a few words may place them into the context of the other sections.

Addition is the simplest operation of mathematics, but it nevertheless took the human race millennia to develop it as a useful tool. The technique could have developed from a situation like this: A shepherd would pick up a stone when each sheep would leave the pen in the morning. In the evening, when each sheep was returned to the pen, he would throw one pebble away. If, after the sheep were in the pen, he had a pebble remaining, one sheep would be lost. If, instead of one pebble remaining at the end of the day, he found that he had the following collection of pebbles:

he would realize that he had a serious problem!

If two herds were placed together, the pebbles could be "pooled" in one pouch, and the system could continue with the result of this "addition."

The next step was probably the use of symbols less cumbersome than stones, and then came the attempt to "predict" the outcome of the changes in the stones. For example, if three stones were added to four stones, the result was always the same, seven stones. As a result, the following table of "predicted" results could be built. Modern man, of course, is quite familiar with the sum of any two numbers, and it is difficult to realize that the entries in Table 2-1 had to be developed

Table 2-1: Additions

	0	1	2	3	4	5	6	7	8	9
0	0	1	2	3	4	5	6	7	8	9
1		2	3	4	5	6	7	8	9	10
2			4	5	6	7	8	9	10	11
3				6	7	8	9	10	11	12
4					8	9	10	11	12	13
5						10	11	12	13	14
6							12	13	14	15
7								14	15	16
8									16	17
9										18

gradually by practical experience of what happened when two groups were placed together.

By using this table, or by memorizing it, anyone could predict the number of pebbles that would result from adding two pouches together. Why is the entry in the fourth row and the fifth column equal to seven? Simply because it *works*—it agrees with what would happen in the real world. From this, it can be seen that addition is a model and is valid only because it agrees with the reality it represents.

If the shepherd sold eight sheep, he would throw away eight stones in order to keep his "books" in balance. Eventually, this technique gave way to subtraction. Using the subtraction table, the results of the manipulation of the stones can be "simulated," and because the stones simulated the sheep, the table is a model of the sheep. In Table 2-2, the entry in the table is equal to the value at the left of each row subtracted from the value at the top of the column.

Table 2-2: Subtractions

	1	2	3	4	5	6	7	8	9
0	1	2	3	4	5	6	7	8	9
1	0	1	2	3	4	5	6	7	8
2		0	1	2	3	4	5	6	7
3			0	1	2	3	4	5	6
4				0	1	2	3	4	5
5					0	1	2	3	4
6						0	1	2	3
7							0	1	2
8								0	1
9									0

In the addition table, the unentered elements were blank because they were not needed. 3 + 2 is not in the table because it equals 2 + 3, and this value *is* entered, etc.; but in the subtraction table the unentered elements do not stem from 3 − 2 equalling 2 − 3; they stem from the fact that the entry cannot be expressed in terms of pebbles because it is a negative number. In prehistory, the shepherd would have a severe problem if a stray sheep were accidentally mixed into his herd. When the sheep entered the pen, he would run out of pebbles and still have one sheep left. Intuitively, he would know that this was the opposite of what he was trying to avoid, and, because he would have been unhappy if he had been "long" pebbles, he would be happy being "short." This is the fundamental idea of the negative, the idea of "opposite." But it was not until the Middle Ages that rudimentary definitions for the use of negative numbers were developed. Table 2-3 therefore goes beyond the mathematical capabilities of the ancient Greeks.

Table 2-3: Subtractions giving negative results

	1	2	3	4	5	6	7	8	9
0	1	2	3	4	5	6	7	8	9
1	0	1	2	3	4	5	6	7	8
2	−1	0	1	2	3	4	5	6	7
3	−2	−1	0	1	2	3	4	5	6
4	−3	−2	−1	0	1	2	3	4	5
5	−4	−3	−2	−1	0	1	2	3	4
6	−5	−4	−3	−2	−1	0	1	2	3
7	−6	−5	−4	−3	−2	−1	0	1	2
8	−7	−6	−5	−4	−3	−2	−1	0	1
9	−8	−7	−6	−5	−4	−3	−2	−1	0

Division, as used by financial analysts, is a process by which numbers can be made more comparable through the use of a common "base." The net income available to common of two companies cannot be usefully compared from the standpoint of a stockholder unless it is changed to net income per common share. Division, then, is the technique by which a researcher can remove an unwanted weighting—a bias that "loads" the data in a disadvantageous way. The dollars of dividends declared for one fiscal year of a company is "biased" from the standpoint of an individual shareholder because it is implicitly "weighted" by the number of shares outstanding. In order to discover the "meaning" of total dividends, the stockholder needs to divide by shares outstanding. In other words, because the implicit weighting by shares outstanding is unwanted in this case, it should be removed or the study will have to allow for the bias at every step. The weighting can, of course, be removed by division. Division, then, is a model that eliminates unwanted weights from base data.

The usefulness of division in analysis stems from the fact that the fundamental function of the investment analyst is to relate many diverse facts and trends. This diversity in large part stems from undesirable weights that must be removed before comparisons are possible. The entire system of ratio analysis is based upon improving the comparability of company data. *Company-relative* data, comparing companies to their industry, the market, or the economy, are based on division. Indexes are a series of numbers set to a common base in order to follow the same principle of improved comparability. A few financial items, their unwanted "bias," and the ratio resulting from adjustment are listed in Table 2-4 as examples.

Multiplication, of course, introduces weights to numbers that should be made either more or less important in a study. For example, suppose an account is 50% IBM, 25% AT&T, and 25% GM. The portfolio

Table 2-4

Item	*Weight (unwanted bias)*	*Result (desired item)*
$ net to common	Number of shares outstanding	Earnings per share
Long term debt	Size of company's capital	L.T. debt as fraction of total capitalization
Pretax income	Sales volume	Pretax margin
Income tax	Pretax income	Effective tax rate
$ investment in IBM	$ size of portfolio	Fraction of investment in IBM

manager wishes to compute the average P/E for stocks in the account. Assume the following P/E's:

$$\begin{aligned} \text{IBM} &= 40 \\ \text{AT\&T} &= 15 \\ \text{GM} &= 15 \end{aligned}$$

In order to represent the average, the manager should *weight* each stock by the size of the holding in the portfolio, that is, he must *introduce* a needed weight not present in the data, as follows:

$$\text{Average } P/E \text{ ratio} = 0.50(40) + 0.25(15) + 0.25(15) = 27.5.$$

FUNDAMENTAL MANIPULATIONS

Working with combined operations is very simple but requires the introduction of a few additional rules. The first set of such rules deals with signs: To add numbers with like signs, add their values without regard for sign and attach their common sign.

$$(+2) + (+2) = +4; \qquad (-2) + (-2) = -4.$$

As an example of the intuitive justification that lies behind the treatment of the signs, assume that a company has two divisions and that each division earns $2,000. The company obviously earns $4,000. If each has a $2,000 deficit, the company has a $4,000 deficit.

To add numbers with unlike signs, subtract the smaller absolute value from the larger and attach the sign of the number having the greater absolute value.

$$(+2) + (-4) = -2; \qquad (+4) + (-2) = +2.$$

The practical meaning of this rule can be clearly seen for a hypothetical company that has only one of its two divisions operating at a deficit. The results of the two divisions will tend to offset each other in this case, but the company (which is the sum of the two divisions) will have a profit or loss depending upon whether the profitable or the deficit division shows the operating results having the largest absolute value. If one division earns +\$2,000 and the other earns −\$4,000, the result of adding the divisions into the company is −\$2,000, a \$2,000 deficit.

To subtract two numbers, change the sign of the number being subtracted and then use the rules for addition.

$$(+4) - (+2) \text{ therefore becomes } (+4) + (-2) = +2;$$
$$(+4) - (-2) \text{ therefore becomes } (+4) + (+2) = +6.$$

Since addition indicated the "pooling" of divisions, subtraction can be regarded as the "removal" of a division. For example, assume that the hypothetical company decides to sell one of its divisions. The earnings of that division will be subtracted from the total. Assume:

Company earnings	+\$2,000	
Division A	+\$4,000	(operating at a profit)
Division B	−\$2,000	(operating at a deficit).

Now if Division B is sold, the new total earnings of the company will be equal to the \$2,000 company earnings minus Division A's earnings of −\$2,000, producing the earnings of the "new" company of \$4,000. This, naturally, equals the profits of Division A because this is the only division left in the company. Therefore, minus a minus equals a plus because selling a deficit division raises profits.

Multiplication and division follow these rules:

1. Multiplication or division of two numbers with like signs produces a positive result;
2. Multiplication or division of two numbers with unlike signs produces a negative result.

In terms of the hypothetical company:

1. If the company in the example decides to expand Division A to four times its present size, its divisional earnings will be (\$4,000) (4) = \$16,000.
2. If it expands Division B to four times its present size, the impact on the company's profits will be (−\$2,000)(4) = −\$8,000.
3. If it sells two operations identical to the profitable Division A, we have (−2)(\$4,000) = −\$8,000 benefit to the company (showing that "minusing out" a plus to the company is obviously a disadvantage).
4. If it sells two operations identical to the unprofitable Division B,

we have $(-2)(-\$2{,}000) = \$4{,}000$ benefit to the company (showing that "minusing out" a negative to the company is beneficial).

The order in which operations are to be performed is indicated by parentheses or brackets. All operations inside parentheses are to be performed first. For example:

$$\begin{aligned} (4 + 7)(8) &= \\ (11)(8) &= 88. \end{aligned}$$

or:

$$\begin{aligned} (4 + 7)(8) + 7 &= \\ (11)(8) + 7 &= \\ 88 + 7 &= 95. \end{aligned}$$

If there are parentheses enclosed within parentheses, such as $((3 + 4)(2 + 2) + 2)$, the calculations in the innermost parentheses must be performed first:

$$((3 + 4)(2 + 2) + 2) = ((7)(4) + 2) = 30.$$

In the absence of parentheses, the following priority for operations will be used:

First:	Exponentiation
Second:	Multiplication
Third:	Division
Fourth:	Addition and subtraction.

Illustrations:

$$\begin{aligned}
(2)(8) + 7 &= 16 + 7 &&= 23 \\
8 + 7 - (6)(2) &= 15 - 12 &&= 3 \\
8 \div 2 - 4 &= 4 - 4 &&= 0 \\
8 \div (2 - 4) &= 8 \div -2 &&= -4 \\
4^2 \div 2 - 4 &= (16 \div 2) - 4 &&= 4 \\
4^2 \div (2 - 4) &= 16 \div -2 &&= -8
\end{aligned}$$

$$\begin{aligned}
(2^3)(2) \div (4)(1) &= (8)(2) \div (4)(1) &&= 16 \div 4 = 4 \\
(2^4 \div 4)^2 \div 2 &= (16 \div 4)^2 \div 2 &&= 4^2 \div 2 = 8 \\
(3^2 + 4^2)(2) - 20 &= (9 + 16)(2) - 20 &&= 50 - 20 = 30 \\
75 - (3 + 2)^2(2) &= 75 - (5^2)(2) &&= 75 - 50 = 25
\end{aligned}$$

An important warning is necessary at this point: Never divide by zero or by a symbol that has a zero value.

FRACTIONS

Only a very small number of operations dealing with fractions need be remembered: addition, subtraction, multiplication, division, and simplification.

If two fractions have the same denominator, their sum is a new fraction with the same denominator; its numerator is found by simply adding the old numerators. The same principle holds true for subtraction:

$$\frac{a}{c} + \frac{b}{c} = \frac{a + b}{c}; \qquad \frac{a}{c} - \frac{b}{c} = \frac{a - b}{c}.$$

If, however, the two fractions do not have identical denominators, they cannot be directly added. It is necessary to first perform an "adjustment," converting the fractions into equivalent fractions that *do* have the same, or common, denominator. This is done by multiplying the fraction by $^2/_2$, $^3/_3$, or $^4/_4$, etc. This, of course, is the same as multiplying by one; the operation leaves the value of the fraction unchanged.
Add:

$$\frac{1}{2} \text{ and } \frac{1}{3}.$$

$$\frac{1}{2} \cdot \frac{3}{3} = \frac{3}{6}; \qquad \frac{1}{3} \cdot \frac{2}{2} = \frac{2}{6}.$$

Therefore:

$$\frac{1}{2} = \frac{3}{6}; \qquad \frac{1}{3} = \frac{2}{6},$$

and:

$$\frac{1}{2} + \frac{1}{3} = \frac{3}{6} + \frac{2}{6} = \frac{5}{6}.$$

This technique of finding a common denominator can be used in the subtraction of fractions as well. For example,

$$\frac{1}{2} - \frac{1}{3} = \frac{3}{6} - \frac{2}{6} = \frac{3 - 2}{6} = \frac{1}{6}.$$

Multiplication and division of fractions are less complicated. To multiply, simply multiply the numerators and then multiply the denominators:

$$\frac{a}{b} \cdot \frac{c}{d} = \frac{ac}{bd} \quad \text{or} \quad \frac{1}{2} \cdot \frac{2}{3} = \frac{1 \cdot 2}{2 \cdot 3} = \frac{2}{6}.$$

In order to divide, invert the divisor (simply turn the fraction upside down, making the numerator the denominator and vice versa) and then multiply the resulting fractions:

$$\frac{a}{b} \div \frac{c}{d} = \frac{a}{b} \cdot \frac{d}{c} = \frac{ad}{bc} \quad \text{or} \quad \frac{1}{3} \div \frac{1}{2} = \frac{1}{3} \cdot \frac{2}{1} = \frac{2}{3}.$$

the ↑ divisor   the ↑ divisor inverted

In order to simplify fractions, virtually all of the previous techniques may be used, but two tools are very important. The first is cancellation. If the same factor appears in the numerator and the denominator, it can be removed from both places:

$$\frac{\cancel{2}(a+b)}{\cancel{2}(c+d)} = \frac{a+b}{c+d}.$$

This can only be done to factors, not to terms. The reason that cancellation is legal is self-evident in the following illustration:

$$\begin{aligned}\frac{2(a+b)}{2(c+d)} &= \frac{2}{2} \cdot \frac{(a+b)}{(c+d)} \\ &= \frac{1}{1} \cdot \frac{a+b}{c+d} \\ &= \frac{a+b}{c+d}.\end{aligned}$$

Cancellation can be used when two fractions are being multiplied just as easily as when considering only one fraction:

$$\frac{c(4+d)}{2(a+b)} \cdot \frac{2(a+b)}{c^2+d^2} = \frac{c(4+d)}{\cancel{2(a+b)}} \cdot \frac{\cancel{2(a+b)}}{c^2+d^2} = \frac{c(4+d)}{c^2+d^2}.$$

This is legal because

$$\begin{aligned}\frac{c(4+d)}{2(a+b)} \cdot \frac{2(a+b)}{c^2+d^2} &= \frac{c(4+d) \cdot 2(a+b)}{2(a+b) \cdot c^2+d^2} \\ &= \frac{2(a+b) \cdot c(4+d)}{2(a+b) \cdot c^2+d^2} \\ &= \frac{1}{1} \cdot \frac{c(4+d)}{c^2+d^2}\end{aligned}$$

The second important device in simplification deals with complex fractions—fractions that have fractional numerators or denominators. When a complex fraction is encountered, it is often useful to eliminate the internal fraction by simply removing its denominator and multiplying it by the nonfractional number:

Example with fractional denominator

$$\frac{2}{1/3} = \frac{2 \cdot 3}{1} = 6$$

Example with fractional numerator

$$\frac{1/3}{2} = \frac{1}{2 \cdot 3} = \frac{1}{6}.$$

This device is a short method for performing the following manipulation:

Fractional denominator

$$\frac{2}{1/3} \cdot \frac{3}{3} = \frac{6}{3/3} = \frac{6}{1} = 6$$

Fractional numerator

$$\frac{1/3}{2} \cdot \frac{3}{3} = \frac{3/3}{6} = \frac{1}{6}.$$

EXPONENTS

In the section on notation, the advantages of exponents were indicated. In this section, the rules governing the manipulation of these exponents need to be covered.

First, $a^m \cdot a^n = a^{m+n}$. This can be seen from the simple illustration:

$$2^3 \cdot 2^4 = 2^7$$

or:

$(2 \cdot 2 \cdot 2)(2 \cdot 2 \cdot 2 \cdot 2) = 2^7$ since there are seven 2's multiplied.

Next, if we raise a number with an exponent to a power:

$$(a^m)^n = a^{mn}.$$

For example,

$$(2^3)^2 = 2^6$$

or:

$$(2 \cdot 2 \cdot 2)(2 \cdot 2 \cdot 2) = 2^6.$$

Next, if a product is raised to a power:

$$(ab)^n = a^n b^n.$$

For example,

$$(2 \cdot 3)^2 = 2^2 \cdot 3^2 = 36$$

or:

$$(2 \cdot 3)(2 \cdot 3) = 2 \cdot 2 \cdot 3 \cdot 3 = 2^2 \cdot 3^2 = 36.$$

Next, if a fraction is raised to a power:

$$\left(\frac{a}{b}\right)^n = \frac{a^n}{b^n}.$$

For example,

$$\left(\frac{2}{3}\right)^2 = \frac{2^2}{3^2}.$$

or:

$$\frac{2}{3} \cdot \frac{2}{3} = \frac{2 \cdot 2}{3 \cdot 3} = \frac{2^2}{3^2}.$$

Next, if a fraction has the same numerator and denominator except for the fact that they are raised to different powers:

$$\frac{a^m}{a^n} = a^{m-n}.$$

For example,

$$\frac{2^3}{2^2} = 2^{3-2} = 2^1$$

or:

$$\frac{2 \cdot \cancel{2} \cdot \cancel{2}}{\cancel{2} \cdot \cancel{2}} = 2^1.$$

Fortunately, these same laws apply to fractional exponents as well as to integer exponents. It has already been shown that square roots, cube roots, and so on, can be expressed as fractional exponents, and the rules for exponents apply to taking roots as well.

LOGARITHMS

Introduction

Logarithms have developed a formidable reputation over the years, largely because it is difficult to grasp intuitively the meaning of calculations regarding their use. Nevertheless, logs, as they are commonly called, are extremely useful in both basic calculations and in advanced mathematical theory. They present the following advantages: (1) they provide the basis for all of the compound interest, annuity, and present value calculations used daily by all analysts; (2) they are used in the theory that makes virtually all of the advanced statistical models available to the business community; and (3) they are easy to use now that most pocket calculators supply the log by simply pushing a button.

In order to gain a feel for the nature of a logarithm, consider the following analogy: A man must prevent a ten-pound weight (which he is holding with a rope) from falling. In order to do this, he must exert ten "pounds" of effort. Now, in order to assist him, he hooks a "black box" to the rope that will increase his "power" tenfold. By exerting one pound of effort, he can hold the ten-pound weight as in Figure 2–1.

It is possible to extend this analogy still further by considering the case of a 100-pound weight. The black box already used by the man had

Figure 2-1

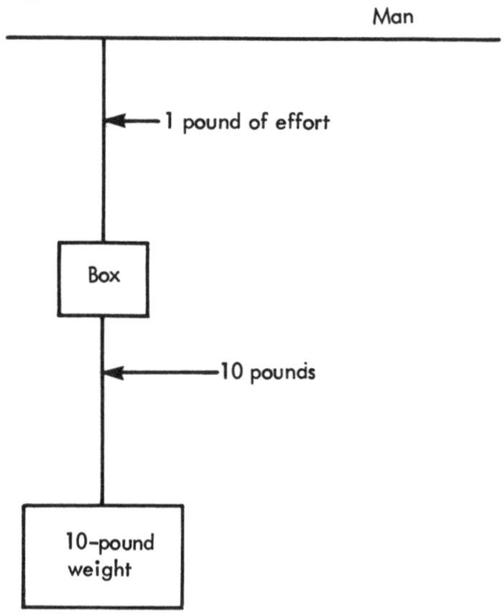

an "input" of one pound of force and an output of 10 pounds, and so the man can simply purchase another box identical to the first and hook it to his rope. This second box will receive the power output by the first one. It will therefore have an input of ten and an output of 100, a tenfold increase. As a result, the man will still need to exert only one pound of effort to hold a 100-pound weight. This can be diagrammed as in Figure 2–2.

This system is getting somewhat cumbersome; in order to keep things simple, the man trades in his two boxes and buys a single deluxe unit with a dial on it. If set at "one," it puts out the power of one box; a "two" setting gives "two boxpower," and so forth. Now his system looks like Figure 2–3.

At this point, if someone puts a 1,000-pound weight on the rope, the man can simply throw the switch to "three" and still maintain control. As a matter of fact, if he encounters a weight of, say, 500 pounds, he is still all right because he can set his dial at some number between two and three that will handle this particular weight. Actually, this "deluxe model" has a "governor" on it that automatically sets the dial at the proper number (fractional or not) that will balance the weight regardless of how heavy it might be. For any weight, an index setting exists that matches it, and for any index setting, a weight exists that it will balance.

The obvious question now is what all of this has to do with logarithms. The answer is that the weight that can take on any value

Figure 2-2

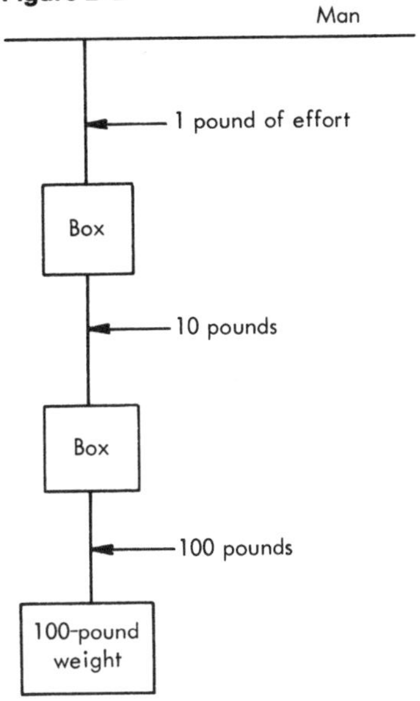

actually stands for any positive number in the number system, and the index setting necessary to balance the weight (number) is the logarithm of that weight (number). There is nothing more mysterious about logs than the use of this index setting on the box instead of the use of the number itself.

This system may not be complex, but it would certainly be superfluous if it didn't assist the analyst in solving practical problems. Two simple properties of logs will point out their usefulness: (1) adding logs is the same as multiplying the numbers; (2) subtracting logs is the same as dividing the numbers. Therefore, the index numbers do not have the same behavior in mathematical operations as do the numbers they

Figure 2-3

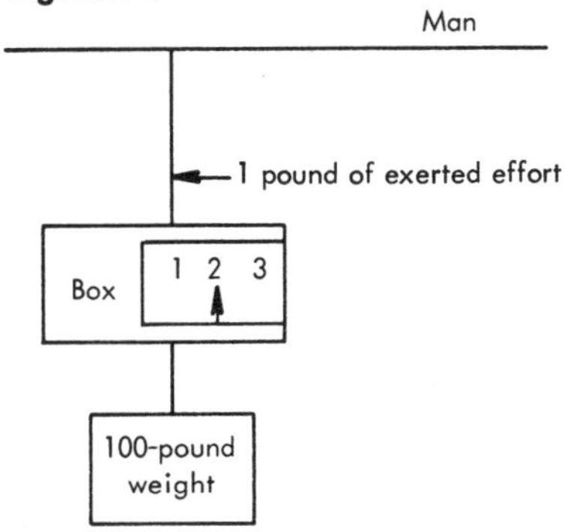

represent. On the positive side, an analyst can work either with a number or its index setting (log), whichever will make the calculations easier. On the negative side, this fact seems to throw logs back into the realm of the mysterious.

Actually, the difference in the behavior of logs and numbers could have been anticipated from the analogy. If someone had inserted a 1,000-pound weight in place of the 100 pounder, the man would have thrown the switch from "2" to "3" and kept everything in balance. Multiplying the weight by 10 is certainly not the same as adding 1 to the index setting. Nevertheless, the setting *did* remain in balance, and if we simply knew how the index numbers behaved relative to the numbers, we could use them without having to refer back to ropes and boxes (although we could always do so with valid results if we wished). Mathematicians have worked out the behavior patterns of the index settings, and it is possible to use their findings instead of working them out for ourselves. Incidentally, if the fact that adding logs is equivalent to multiplying numbers is still confusing, notice that the man's *adding* one to the index setting offset someone *multiplying* the 100-pound weight by 10.

In mathematical notation, the index setting is represented as $\log_a N$ = the logarithm of the number N to the base a. N stands for the weight, and the base a is simply the "power" of the box with its basic setting of one. In our analogy, this number was 10 (a tenfold increase in output over input), and the use of the base 10 is the system of common logarithms. Assuming common logs, the index setting is written as $\log N$. The fundamental fact about logarithms is that if

$$\log N = X$$

(where X stands for some "index" setting), then

$$N = 10^X$$

(which means that the "index" setting is the exponent of 10 that will "bring the number 10 into balance" with the weight N).

This simple mathematical identity makes the analogy of the weight work. The index setting "adjusts" the number 10 to bring it into balance with N, and it adjusts it by acting as an exponent. Only four fundamental properties of logarithms need to be pointed out at this point:

1. $\log (AB) = \log A + \log B$.
   This simply says that adding two index numbers will produce another index number—and the new index is the setting that will balance a weight equal to the product of the two weights associated with the first two indices. In other words, adding indices equals multiplying numbers.

2. $\log \frac{A}{B} = \log A - \log B$

   To divide numbers, subtract indices.

3. $\log A^k = (k) \log A$

   Raising a number to a given power is the same thing as multiplying its index setting by the given number.

4. $\log \sqrt[k]{A} = \frac{(\log A)}{k}$

   Taking the kth root of a number is the same thing as dividing its index number by k.

Two important practical points need to be mentioned. First, if an analyst wishes to add or subtract numbers, logarithms cannot be effectively used. This is no great loss, for resorting to logs would be a waste of time on these simple operations, anyway. Second, if an analyst wishes to use logarithms instead of the numbers, he must convert from "weights" to "index numbers" using tables, perform the simplified calculations, and then *convert back* from indices to numbers. If the log isn't converted back into the number that it represents, the user may make the mistake of thinking that the power setting *is* the number that it represents. This is the same as maintaining that log N is N. The process of getting back to the number from a log is called taking the antilogarithm (usually called antilog). Mathematically, antilog (log N) = N, which means that if the log of a number is found and then the anitlog of the log is found, the result will be the original number.

Determining logarithms

In order to find the log (logarithm) of a number, a table of logarithms is used. Any log is divided into two parts: characteristic and mantissa. The characteristic of the log is the whole number portion of the log. In 1.17609, for example, the characteristic is the number 1. The mantissa is the fractional portion of a log. In 1.17609, the mantissa is .17609. If an analyst wishes to convert a number to a log, he first must determine what the characteristic of the log will be. This process is quite simple, for the characteristic is one less than the number of digits in the number (whole number portion only) for which the log is desired. Examples: log 10 = 1; log 100 = 2; log 10,000 = 4. If the number is less than one, it is written 0.xxxx and the rule still holds (using the entire number), but in this case the characteristic is negative. Examples: log 0.1 = −1; log 0.0001 = −4; log 0.000001 = −6.

The analyst next needs to locate the mantissa, or fractional part of the log. The mantissa is found in a logarithm table using the number for which the log is needed without regard for the decimal point. The characteristic and the mantissa are then added to find the log. If the characteristic is negative, it is more useful to keep the mantissa and the characteristic separated. This is especially important when using a logarithm table in connection with a mantissa.

In order to find the mantissa of 12.5, the analyst would disregard the decimal and go down the rows to 12, then across the columns to 5.

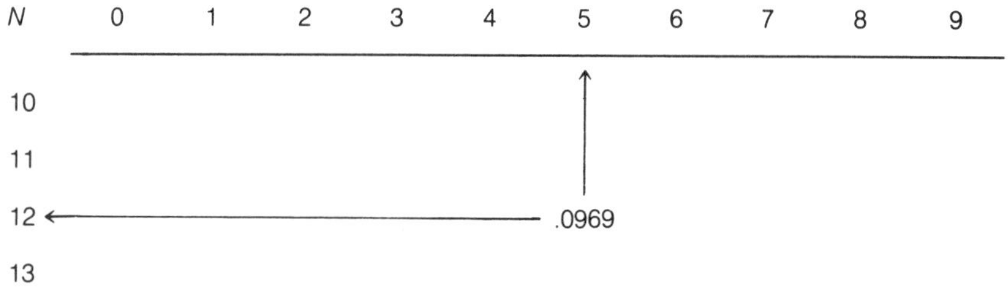

The mantissa of the log of 12.5 therefore equals .0969. Because the location of the decimal point in the number does not affect the mantissa, this is also the mantissa of the log of 125 and 1250. Adding the characteristic to the mantissa for various numbers, we find that

$$
\begin{aligned}
\log 1.25 &= 0.0969 \\
\log 12.5 &= 1.0969 \\
\log 125 &= 2.0969 \\
\log 1250 &= 3.0969 \\
\log 12500 &= 4.0969.
\end{aligned}
$$

To find the antilog of a number, an analyst can use the log's mantissa to find the number in the table and then place the decimal point in the location indicated by the characteristic. For example, if the analyst had performed several calculations using logs and had ended with 4.0969, he would desire the antilog of 4.0969, the number that this log represents. In order to find this number, he would locate the mantissa in the log table.

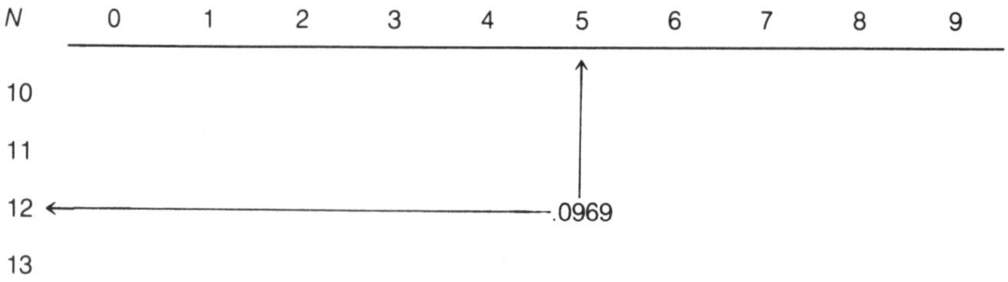

As can be seen, .0969 is the mantissa of 125. But this does not indicate anything about the location of the decimal point in the number. Its value could be 1.25, 12.5, 125, etc. Referring to the characteristic of the log (4, in this case) the analyst moves the decimal four digits to the right of its "base" position at 1.2500 and has the answer of 12500. If the characteristic had been negative, he would have moved the decimal to the left instead of the right (the number would have been made smaller rather than larger).

If the number whose log is desired is less than one, the characteristic will be negative, as has already been mentioned. When using the log table to find the mantissa of such a number, nothing unusual is encountered. For example, the mantissa of 0.125 is .0969. Because the characteristic is negative, however, adding it to this mantissa will produce a negative number having a fractional part different from .0969. When the antilog is taken, the mantissa (.0969) necessary to find the antilog would not be immediately obvious from an inspection of such a logarithm. For this reason, it is standard practice to state the mantissa and characteristic separately when the characteristic is negative. For example, log (.125) = .0969 − 1.0. By following this rule, the fractional portion of the log will always be the mantissa shown in the log tables.

Natural logarithms

In closing this section, we return once again to the original analogy. If a base other than 10 were used, the analogy still holds. Changing bases is the same as trading the box that multiplied the man's power by 10 for a box that would increase his power by, say, about 2.71828 as an example. The settings on the index pointer would need to be adjusted, but this is a simple matter. They need only be multiplied by some number that will keep everything in balance (.43429 in this case). This is true for any shift in base, but our particular example shows the system of *natural* logarithms (or logs to the base *e*, which is approximately equal to 2.71828), and their simple connection to *common* logs (or logarithms to the base 10.) Because logarithms to any base have the same general nature, the analogy always holds. Changing the base is equivalent to changing the power capacity of the box and hence the index setting needed, but the structure of the problem remains essentially unchanged. As a result of this fact, any base may be chosen that is convenient to the user. Common logarithms (base 10) are commonly used for basic calculations, while natural logarithms (base *e* approximately equal to 2.71828) are most natural in advanced mathematical theory.

Behavior of logarithms

In the system of common logarithms, note once again that the characteristic of the logarithm is the "whole number" part of the log (the "1" of "1.17609"). This characteristic is the whole number on the index setting in the analogy, and while a setting of "1" balanced 10 pounds, the characteristic of 10 is two digits minus one, or "1." A setting of "2" balances 100 pounds, which has three minus one or two digits, and so on. For this reason, the "rule of thumb" using the number of digits to determine the characteristic of common logs produces the correct result. Moving one step further, a weight of less than 10 pounds would give the box some trouble, because even with the basic setting of "1" it would still have an output of 10 pounds, which would be too much power. The solution is to use a fractional setting, so that only a fraction of the total power output of one box will be used to hold the weight. As a result, the numbers from 1 to 10 have a log with the form 0.xxx. If the weight is less than one, the black box must actually subtract a portion of the one unit of power that was supplied by the man. This action can be done only if the log is negative, which is the reason why all numbers less than one have a negative characteristic. The negative characteristic will get larger and larger as the numbers get closer and closer to zero. Finally, because a negative weight is absurd, a negative number cannot have a logarithm.

FUNCTIONS AND EQUATIONS

Single equations

The other aspects of algebra usually are viewed as being supplementary tools that facilitate the solution of equations by simplifying the basic equation. Dealing with equations is essentially a matter of performing these preliminary simplifications and then manipulating the data by the use of a basic rule: *Whatever is done to one side of the equation must also be done to the other side for the statement to remain true.*

This rule is grounded in simple logic, for equals plus equals are equal, equals times equals are equal, and so on.

Illustrations:

Given that

$$5x + 12 = 20$$

and subtracting 12 from each side, it must be true that

$$5x = 8.$$

Given that

$$5x = 8$$

and dividing each side by 5, it must be true that

$$\frac{5x}{5} = \frac{8}{5}$$

and upon simplifying, it must be true that

$$x = \frac{8}{5}.$$

Notice that throughout all of the operations used to simplify the equation, x had a value of 8/5, and substituting this value into any of the equations would produce a true equality. The value of x was always 8/5, but its value was not known until the equation was simplified. "Solving" for x is merely this process of simplifying until the unknown value of x becomes obvious.

If an equation is to be solved for, say, x, then the solution requires that x be placed alone on one side of the equation. The other side is then usually stated in the simplest possible way as a matter of convenience. As the first step in accomplishing this, all terms involving x are moved to one side of the equation and all terms not involving x are moved to the other side. This step is done by subtracting terms from both sides as shown in the examples above. A shortcut accomplishing the same thing is called "transposing," whereby the term is simply rewritten on the other side with the sign changed:

$$\begin{aligned} 5x + 12 &= 20 \\ 5x &= 20 - 12 \\ 5x &= 8 \\ x &= \frac{8}{5} \end{aligned}$$

Transposing always will move an unwanted term from one side of the equation to the other. Once all of the terms involving x are on one side and all of the other terms are on the other, the equation still may need to be simplified by adding terms or removing a coefficient from x. For example:

$$\begin{aligned} 3x + 4x &= 5 + 9 \\ 7x &= 14 \\ x &= 2. \end{aligned}$$

Systems of equations

Using the techniques already described will permit the analyst to isolate x when x is the only unknown value to be discovered, that is, if x is the only variable in the equation. But if both x and y are to be discovered, it will be impossible to find the value of x unless the value of y is already known. On the other hand, the value of y cannot be found unless the value of x is already known. The problem is that although one equation provides enough information to permit the value of one variable to be found, it is inadequate when two variables are present. If two unknowns are to be discovered, two equations are needed; if three unknowns are present, three equations are needed, and so forth. The set of equations is called a "system" that must be solved "simultaneously." A system of equations requires two or more different equations, and the equations are not different if they "reduce" to the same equation. For example, $x + y = 1$ is the "same" equation as $2x + 2y = 2$, in that it provides no additional information about the relationship of x to y.

This section considers only linear equations, i.e., equations in which each variable is not raised to a power and enters the equation as a simple addition. Quite naturally, the problem is called the simultaneous solution of a system of linear equations. Only the two-variable case is considered in this chapter.

The following equations show an explicit example of a system of two linear equations with two unknowns as well as the algebraic structure of all such equations:

$$5x + 10y = 50 \text{ has the general form } a_1x + b_1y = c_1;$$
$$2x + y = 25 \text{ has the general form } a_2x + b_2y = c_2.$$

In order to solve any such system, the following formulas can be used by the analyst, although the derivation is not presented here:

$$x = \frac{b_2c_1 - b_1c_2}{a_1b_2 - a_2b_1}; \qquad y = \frac{a_1c_2 - a_2c_1}{a_1b_2 - a_2b_1}.$$

In this particular case, the solution is as follows:

$$x = \frac{1 \cdot 50 - 10 \cdot 25}{5 \cdot 1 - 2 \cdot 10} \qquad y = \frac{5 \cdot 25 - 2 \cdot 50}{5 \cdot 1 - 2 \cdot 10}$$
$$x = \frac{-200}{-15} \qquad y = \frac{25}{-15}$$
$$x = \frac{40}{3}; \qquad y = \frac{-5}{3}.$$

This technique does nothing for the development of an intuitive "feel" of what is happening. An analogy and the use of graphs may make the significance of the simultaneous solution of equations somewhat clearer.

An application of a system of equations

When the computer was first applied to the problems of investment analysis, a technique known as "screening" or "filtering" became very popular. Using this approach, the computer user could specify, for example, all stocks having a P/E below 10, a yield above 4%, and a positive earnings growth rate. The computer would supply the names of all companies that satisfied the user's requirements. This approach of "pulling" certain companies from a larger set of companies according to some user-specified criterion is a precise parallel to what mathematics and statistics do for the quantitative analyst. One of the best examples of mathematics as a "retrieval system" for numbers is the use of equations.

Suppose that an analyst knows that a company has fixed costs of $10 million and that additional costs of $0.8 million are incurred as each additional million units of its product are manufactured. He could then say that the cost of production of the company is expressed by

$$C = 10 + 0.8P$$

where

C = total cost, expressed in millions of dollars;
P = the number of units produced, expressed in millions.

If the company has no production, its cost will equal 10 + (0.8)(0), or 10. This is the level of fixed costs. In addition, for each additional million units produced, an additional $0.8 million will be added to the $10 million cost level. The equation, then, is a model that eliminates many unwanted pairs of values for C and P. For example, ($P = 10$, $C = 25$) is not a reasonable pair of values for the analyst to select if he believes his equation. It is easy to see that the model has "filtered" out many unacceptable pairs of numbers, that is, many unacceptable combinations of production and cost. Inasmuch as the analyst has not indicated the actual level of production, he still has an infinite number of pairs left; but then again, he has removed an infinite number of possibilities as well. At any rate, he has screened out enough numbers to allow himself to find the "normal" cost level for the company as soon as he knows the company's production level.

Now assume that the company under consideration has $8 million of investment income before taxes and that it is assured of the sale of all production at $1.10 per unit. The total dollar inflow to the company from both sources follows the rule:

$$\text{Inflow} = 8 + 1.10P.$$

It is now possible for the analyst to use the information in those two rules to develop additional knowledge by using the technique of solving a system of two simultaneous equations. At some level of production, the dollar inflow will exactly equal the cost, permitting the company to break even. This break-even point will occur, obviously, at the point where Inflow equals Cost. This means that C can be substituted into the second equation, producing the following system:

$$C = 10 + 0.8P$$
$$C = \ \ 8 + 1.10P$$

when the company breaks even. The implied level of production can be found using these equations. Each of these two equations constitutes a "screen" that the company must pass. Each equation screens out a number of inadmissible combinations of production and cost. The company must pass not only the first screen, but the second as well. How many values for Cost pass the requirement $C = 10 + 0.8P$ *and still pass* the requirement $C = 8 + 1.1P$? Only one number for Cost (and for Production) survives the "double screening." As it happens, the surviving value for Cost (and for Production) can be retrieved by applying a model. This model, of course, is the simultaneous solution of a set of linear equations. Using the formulas already developed, we can apply this model to solve the problem. The general form of the equation is

$$a_1x + b_1y = c_1$$
$$a_2x + b_2y = c_2.$$

Our particular equations are:

As already stated	*In "normal" form*
$C = 10 + 0.8P$	$0.8P - C = -10$
$C = \ \ 8 + 1.1P$	$1.1P - C = -\ 8$

The general form of solution is:

$$x = \frac{b_2c_1 - b_1c_2}{a_1b_2 - a_2b_1}$$

$$y = \frac{a_1c_2 - a_2c_1}{a_1b_2 - a_2b_1}$$

In this case, the form is:

$$P = \frac{(-1)(-10)-(-1)(-8)}{(0.8)(-1) - (1.1)(-1)}$$

$$C = \frac{(0.8)(-8) - (1.1)(-10)}{(0.8)(-1) - (1.1)(-1)}$$

At this point, the problem is reduced to simple numerical calculation. We know that:

$$P = \frac{(-1)(-10) - (-1)(-8)}{(0.8)(-1) - (1.1)(-1)}; \qquad C = \frac{(0.8)(-8) - (1.1)(-10)}{(0.8)(-1) - (1.1)(-1)}.$$

It follows by arithmetic that

$$P = \frac{+10 - 8}{-0.8 + 1.1} \qquad C = \frac{-6.4 + 11}{-0.8 + 1.1}$$
$$= \frac{2}{0.3} \qquad = \frac{4.6}{0.3}$$
$$= 6.66; \qquad = 15.33.$$

We can see from this that the sales plus investment income at the break-even point for the company as indicated by the criteria set up by the analyst is $15.33 million and the break-even production level is 6.66 million units.

It is possible to graph the arguments in the preceding analysis by applying a model frequently used by mathematicians as a "display device" for their logical manipulations. Setting up two perpendicular coordinates, we will give the horizontal axis the name "*P*" and the vertical axis "*I*" for dollar inflow, as in Figure 2-4.

Figure 2-4

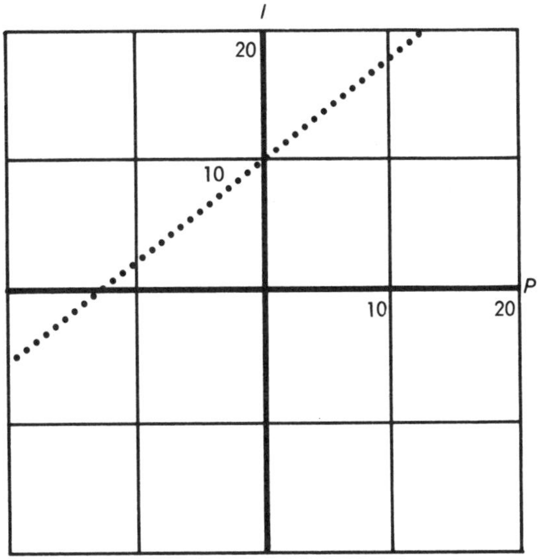

Several possible pairs of values for *P* and *I* have been plotted for reference. If we choose a specific value for *P*, chances are that it would not yet have been plotted, but we could enter it by going "over" to the value on the *P* axis and then "up" to the proper value on the *I* axis. Because *P* can be given any value, let's examine Figure 2-5 where 500,000 values have been plotted. These plots look like a straight line because the points are so "dense" on the page. Actually, if *all* of the pairs of values were plotted, the graph *would* be a straight line, and

Figure 2–5

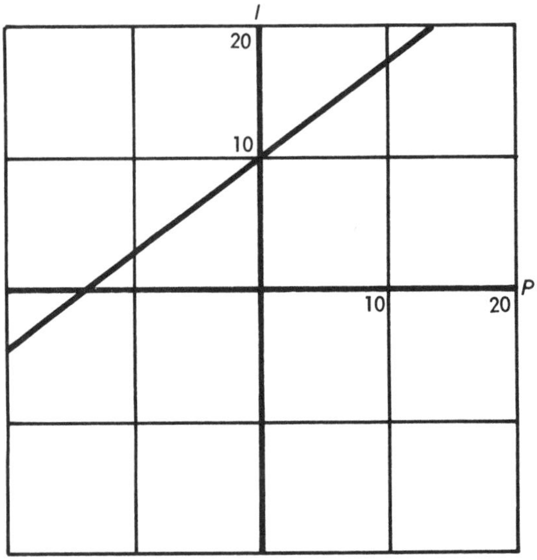

there would be an infinite number of points because there are an infinite number of possible pairs of P and I.

If we plotted the second equation on the same graph, we would have Figure 2–6. Each line is the set of values "permitted" by that equation, that is, each line portrays only those pairs of values that "passed" one

Figure 2–6

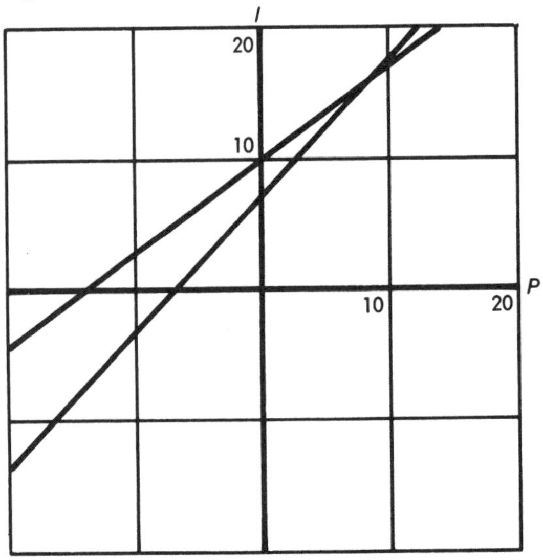

"screen" or equation. Only one point is "permitted" by both equations, as can be seen by the fact that only one point is on both lines, that is, if we screen either line by using the other equation, only one point will pass this second screen. Therefore, on the graph *one point is on both lines,* indicating that one pair of values is *in both sets of acceptable solutions.* Obviously, this "common point" is the point of intersection of the two lines, and this point is the only (P, I) pair permitted by both equations. Naturally, the value of I at that point of "intersection" is 15.33.

In economic theory, the use of simultaneous equations to find the values of economic variables constitutes a major branch of econometrics. From the standpoint of the analyst, this particular type of application is the most important example of the theory of simultaneous equations.

Probably the simplest possible way of looking at the economy is to break the National Income (Y) into two components, Consumption and Investment. This means that

$$Y = C + I.$$

Because this rule is true by definition, it would be impossible to have Consumption at 10, Investment at 1, and the National Income at 15. This means that the equation, like all equations, has screened out a large number of combinations of values. If economists maintain in addition that in this economy consumers save 5% of their income and this rule is never violated, this means that

$$C = 0.95Y.$$

This equation screens out still more combinations of values. For example, it would now be impossible to have Consumption at 10 and National Income at 15.

Obviously, if enough equations can be found that accurately describe the nature of the economy, at some point all of the combinations of values will have been screened out except one value per variable. If all of the equations used are correct, the values for the variables would necessarily be correct. In order to complete this screening, it would be necessary to have one equation for every variable in the model. This is reasonable, because it took two equations to solve for two unknowns, and three unknowns would naturally produce more combinations of values requiring a third equation to screen, four unknowns would require a fourth "screening" equation, and so on.

The quality of any economic model, however, is dependent upon the accuracy of the rules (equations) used, not on the number of equations that are involved. An increase in the number of equations would have a direct benefit only because the number of economic variables being predicted by the model would increase. The reason realistic models are always fairly large is the unfortunate fact that accurate "rules" cannot be found using the more highly aggregated economic variables, so that the equations must relate various lower level components in the economy. This necessarily produces a system having a large number of variables, and it is the large number of variables that forces the use of a large number of equations.

Functions

Actually, what the analyst was saying by an equation and what the graph was saying by a line was simply that two variables have a relationship—that one is a function of the other. In the particular case of the example used in the preceding section, the mathematical statement, or equation, asserted that dollar inflow was a function of P (of production).

Because a function asserts that a definite relationship exists between two different items being analyzed, the function indicates that it is possible to *find* one variable, given the value of the other. In the example of the preceding section, if the dollar inflow of the company is a function of production, it is possible for the financial analyst to find I, given P. More generally, if any y is a function of any x, it is possible to find the value of y, given x. Once x is known, for all practical purposes, y is known also. As a result, if y is a function of x, it is reasonable to say: "You tell me x and I'll tell you y." In effect, what the function does is to tie x and y together in an established mathematical relationship. Because this relationship may in many cases be known by the analyst, once x is known y is simple to find. In our example, once P was known, I was easy to locate because the function (the equation) was clearly defined. Even if the exact function is *not* known, quite often the analyst can find that function by the use of statistical techniques.

From this, it is easy to see that any equation involving two or more variables expresses a function just as does an English sentence that relates two items. If, however, a mathematician wishes to express that "y is a function of x" without specifying *how* they are related, he can write

$$y = f(x) \text{ (pronounced "}f\text{ of }x\text{")}$$

where "f" stands for "function" and not "f" multiplied by "x."

This notation is useful, especially when the precise form of the relationship is unknown. Another use of $f(x)$ is as an abbreviation of the *actual* relationship. In the example used earlier, $I = 10 + 0.8P$ could have been written more simply as $I = f(P)$ if the *form* of the relationship was not a matter of interest. This same type of notation can easily be extended to include many variables instead of the two examined in this simple example. If, for example, the research department maintains that P/E is a function of the growth in earnings (G), the quality of the company (Q), and the stability of earnings (S), we have:

$$P/E = f(G, Q, S).$$

The functional notation can be expanded by the use of subscripts. Therefore, f_1 can refer to one function and f_2 to another. For example, if P/E is a function of growth, $P/E = f_1(G)$, and if growth is a function of rate of return (R), $G = f_2(R)$. In the example

$$P/E = f(G, Q, S),$$

it may be possible to establish that G, Q, and S are not related to each other in any way, in which case the relation could be rewritten as:

$$P/E = f_1(G) + f_2(Q) + f_3(S).$$

From this discussion, it can be seen that functions (definite quantitative relationships) are the main "screening" mechanisms in the mathematical approach. Through a function, it is possible to "transform" a given value for G into a value for P/E. In effect, knowledge of G becomes a "roadmap" by which we can locate the corresponding P/E. The advantage of using this approach in investment work is obvious because the large number of relationships that exist between different items being analyzed can easily be regarded as functions. Thus the analyst can arrive at a conclusion concerning one or two items and then "automatically" deduce his implied conclusions concerning a large number of additional variables. An example of this approach would be to arrive at a conclusion concerning the percentage change in Gross National Product and then deduce the level of Gross Corporate Product in the nonfinancial sector.

Functions, when known by the analyst, are expressed as equations, and as a result equations can be regarded as the basic sentences of the quantitative language. From this, it is possible to argue by analogy that, because success in the English-speaking countries is a function of an individual's use of "English" sentences, success in quantitative problems tends to be a function of the use of "mathematical sentences"—of equations. The basic manipulation of equations and their component parts is, of course, the material that has been covered in this chapter on algebra.

Chapter 3

The mathematics of compound growth explained

Compound growth or compound interest, when a quantity increases at a constant rate rather than a constant amount, is one of the most frequently used techniques in financial analysis. The four major types of compound growth problems are analyzed: (1) the future value of a quantity subject to compound growth; (2) the present value of a future quantity subject to compound growth; (3) the future value of an annuity, that is, a fixed sum paid or received at regular time intervals; and (4) the present value of an annuity. The use of tables in determining these types of values is described and formulas are given for use when tables are not available. In addition, present value is related to security valuation.

INTRODUCTION

One of the most important portions of algebra for the financial analyst is, quite naturally, the mathematics of finance, which is based upon the principle of compound interest. If a man borrows money, he must eventually repay both principal and interest. If he repays the entire obligation at the maturity of the loan, then during the term of the loan he had some interest accrued against him. If he is charged *interest on the interest* due, then the debt is said to be subject to compound interest.

Another example of a compounding process is the growth in the net income of a company. If a company begins with earnings per share of $1 and this figure increases by 10% in the first year, the result is $1.10. But the $0.10 of additional earnings gained during the year is used to provide additional earning power. If the company's per-share earnings grow by 10% in the second year, the earnings per share will be $1.21. This amount represents an additional $0.10 on the original $1 plus

$0.01 gained as a result of the $0.10 earned in the first year. The act of including increases in computing new values for EPS (earnings per share) forces the process to be treated as an example of compound growth.

Compound growth is actually a very simple process in which each new value is a stated constant percentage increase over the preceding value. An example might be EPS growth at 10% per year, producing the series: $1.00, $1.10, $1.21, $1.33, ... Another example might be the 8% per day growth of the number of germs in a culture, producing the series: 1.00, 1.08, 1.17, 1.26, ... Another example is the increase of $1.00 deposited in a 5% per year savings account, producing: $1.00, $1.05, $1.10, $1.16, $1.22, ... Obviously, if more than $1.00 is invested, the series is simply multiplied by the initial amount invested to find the value of total wealth after any given number of periods.

Compound growth can be viewed as the second simplest kind of growth. The simplest way for numbers to increase is to add a constant value to the preceding value, producing, say: 1.00, 1.10, 1.20, 1.30, ... This growth is called linear, and the series is called an arithmetic progression. An example of linear growth might be the behavior in the P/E (the ratio of price to earnings per share) of a stock when the growth rate in EPS increases by 1%. Assume, for example, that an analyst believes that the P/E of a stock can be found by the equation $P/E = 10 + 0.8G$. As additional units of G are added, the P/E will increase from 10 by the constant amount 0.8, producing: 10, 10.8, 11.6, 12.4, ... Compound growth is only slightly more complex, stating that the increase is a constant *percentage* of the preceding value instead of a constant *absolute* amount. Because almost all quantities concerning the financial analyst increase or decrease on the basis of a percentage deviation from their preceding status, compound growth is a matter of importance to the financial community.

Two fundamental distinctions must be thoroughly understood in the theory of compound interest. These are:

1. Future value versus present value
2. Lump sum versus annuity.

Future value is the value at some point in the future of a quantity subject to compound growth. An example would be the value ten years from now of $1,000 invested at 5% compound interest. *Present value*, on the other hand, is the current or beginning value of a quantity subject to compound growth. An example of present value is the value that must be invested now at 5% compound interest in order to have $1,000 accumulated in ten years. The relationship between future and present value can be shown graphically by the use of a time line.

If the present value is known:

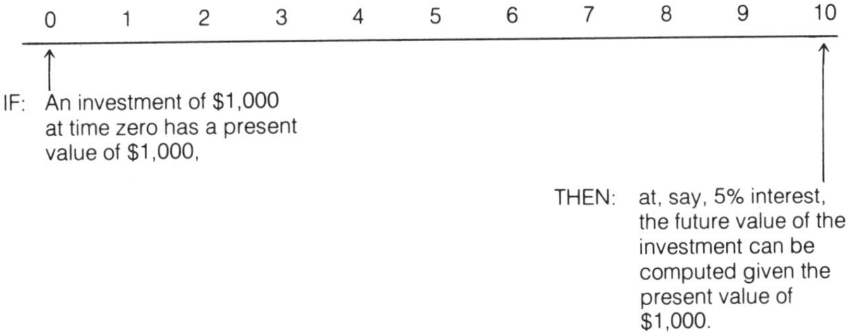

Alternatively, if the future value is known:

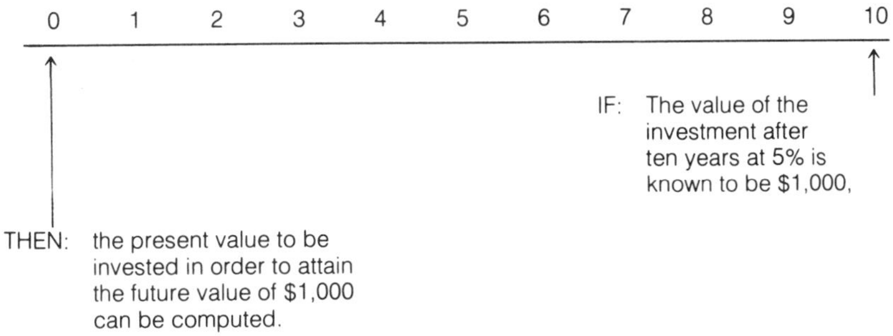

From the time lines, it can be seen that future values can be converted into present values and vice versa. Notice that money can have different values at different times because it is subject to the law of compound growth.

Lump sum quantities are easily explained because they are the quantities with which the analyst is most familiar. The examples in the preceding paragraph were lump sums—the future value of a lump sum of $1,000 or the present value of a lump sum of $1,000 received ten years from now. A lump sum is merely a single payment that is either given or received on a specified date. Annuities are only slightly more complicated, being a fixed amount such as $1,000 that is paid or received once each time period for a stated number of time periods. An example of an annuity received might be an arrangement to receive $1,000 annually for 20 years. An example of an annuity paid might be the investment of $1,000 annually for ten years. In terms of time lines, the annuity can be shown as:

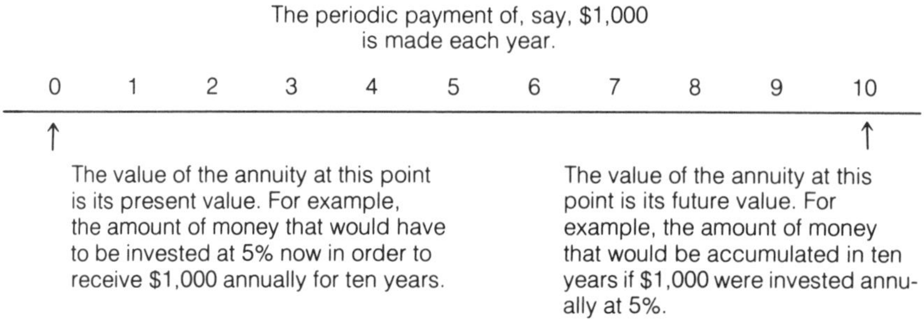

From the time line of the annuity, it can be seen that this type of investment has both a present value and a future value. In this sense, annuities are similar to lump sum payments. In order to solve problems involving the compounding process, then, it is necessary to know whether the problem involves a lump sum or an annuity and then to decide whether it is necessary to begin with a known present value and calculate an unknown future value or to begin with a known future value and calculate an unknown present value. Once the type of problem has been recognized, it is possible to use financial tables simply to look up the solution. Four basic tables are commonly available for this purpose (see Appendix B).

1. *Amount of $1 at Compound Interest.* Table B–1 is used in lump sum problems with a known present worth to compute an unknown future worth.
2. *Present Value of $1 at Compound Interest.* Table B–2 is used in lump sum problems with a known future worth to compute an unknown present worth.
3. *Amount of Annuity of $1 Per Period.* Table B–3 is used in annuity problems when the annual payment is known and the future worth is needed.
4. *Present Value of Annuity of $1 Per Period.* Table B–4 is used in annuity problems when the annual payment is known and the present worth is needed.

ILLUSTRATIVE PROBLEMS

The use of these tables can be explained most easily in the context of practical examples, and a few applications are presented for this purpose. The problems selected do not in any way exhaust the possibilities of this approach in investment analysis.

Example 1

You are preparing a report that will include the *P/E* of a stock based upon earnings five years from now. The company is now earning $2.50 and you are estimating growth at 8% per year. The current price is 32. What is the desired *P/E*?

The problem involves finding the future value of a lump sum of $2.50. Table B–1 is therefore used. This table entry shows $1.4693 after five years at 8% as the value of $1. The value of $2.50 will therefore be 2.5 times $1.4693, or $3.67 rounded to the nearest penny. The desired *P/E* is therefore 32 ÷ 3.67, or 8.72.

Example 2

Assume that in your career planning you would like to have $1 million when you retire in 40 years. How much is $1 million in 40 years worth today, discounted at 8%? In other words, how much would you need to invest now at a return of 8% net of taxes to have $1 million upon retirement?

The problem is to find the present value of a lump sum, so that Table B–2 is appropriate. The table entry for 40 years at 8% is 0.046. The amount of money needed today is therefore 0.046 times $1 million, or $46,000.

Example 3

If you do not presently have $46,000, can you acquire it within ten years by investing $4,000 a year at 8%?

This is an annuity problem, because the $4,000 is invested each year, and the future value of an annuity is desired. Table B–3 is appropriate, and that table's entry for ten years and 8% is 14.4866. The amount available in ten years is therefore $4,000 × 14.4866, or $57,946.

Example 4

If you have an opportunity to invest $5,000 per year for 15 years at an 8% return, how much would you need to invest today to achieve the same results at the end of 15 years?

This is an annuity problem, and the present value is needed, making Table B–4 appropriate. The table entry for 15 years and 8% is 8.5595. The amount needed today to achieve equivalent results is therefore $5,000 × 8.5595, or $42,798.

Example 5

A company had earnings per share ten years ago of $2 and the current EPS is $3.26. If only one growth rate can be used to characterize the increase, what would that growth rate be? This problem is not an annuity, and the problem is to find the return that would convert the present worth of $2 into the future worth of $3.26. This conversion is performed by using Table B–1. By dividing $3.26 by $2, we get $1.63 as the future value per $1.00 of earnings. Looking at Table B–1 under ten years for some rate of return that would produce 1.63, we find an entry of 1.629 under 5%. The EPS can therefore be characterized as having grown at approximately a 5% rate over the past ten years.

Example 6

As a portfolio manager, you are discussing retirement plans with a 55-year-old man. He does not wish to touch his current capital upon retirement, and he wishes to receive $10,000 annually from the additional capital he is willing to place in your care at the beginning of his retirement. He will retire at 65 and you both are willing to assume that he will die at 75. In addition, you agree that a 10% return is possible. How much should he present to you on his 65th birthday?

This problem can be attacked by using the approach outlined above. Is it a lump sum or an annuity problem? Because he wishes $10,000 *annually,* it is an annuity, and it is to run for ten years. Is it necessary to convert the annuity into a present worth or into a future worth? Because he will be presenting the lump sum at the *beginning* of the term of the annuity, the present worth at age 65 is needed. Note that present worth is expressed in terms of the life span of the annuity, not in terms of the particular year that the portfolio manager considers the problem. Because the problem is to convert an annuity to a present worth, Table B–4 is used. The entry in this table for ten periods at 10% interest is 6.145 (or $6.145), the lump sum needed in order to receive $1 per year. Because he needs $10,000, we multiply 6.145 by $10,000, obtaining $61,450, which must be invested at age 65 to receive $10,000 annually for ten years. If he were expected to live 15 years, the table entry would be 7.606, implying that $76,000 would be needed to produce the annuity from age 65 to age 80. If he were expected to live precisely ten years, but a return of only 5% was available, the table for ten periods at 5% shows 7.722, implying that $77,220 would be needed in this case. This amount compares to $61,450 for the same annuity at 10%, a substantial increase in the investment needed. If a 20% return were possible, only $41,930 would be needed.

Example 7

Assuming the original problem stated in Example 6, assume further that the man states that he now has $500,000 capital that he wants safely invested and that he intends to leave to his children. Because he is willing to assume very little risk, a 5% interest rate is assumed. He further states that he is able to save $5,000 per year (at the level of risk associated with a 10% return) toward the annuity he wishes to begin receiving when he retires. He then asks several questions, assuming that the 10% return and 5% low-risk return can be attained. Will he have accumulated enough personal funds to have financed his retirement without drawing upon the money he has set aside for his children? What will be the value of the fund for his children when he retires? When he dies? If he has more than ample funds for retirement and invests these funds at 10% for his children, how much additional money will they have when he dies? We now have a set of problems in compounding theory, and they can be solved by simply breaking them into a series of individual problems.

First, it is already known from Example 6 that $61,450 will be needed at age 65 to finance the annuity. The problem, then, is discovering the value of the $5,000 saved each year for ten years at 10%, which is an annuity problem because more money will be paid each year. The future worth is needed because the problem is to find the value at the *end* of the term of the annuity (this annuity builds funds from age 55 to 65). From the description of the tables, this conversion of annuity to future worth requires the use of Table B–3. The entry in this table for ten periods at 10% interest is 15.937, which is the future value of a $1 annuity. Because $5,000 will be paid annually, we multiply: 15.937 × $5,000 = $79,685, which is the value of the money accumulated by the annual $5,000 payments as of age 65. Because only $61,450 will be needed for retirement, $18,235 will be available to be invested at 10% for the children. The children will receive this money after it has been invested for 10 years (from age 65 to age 75).

What will be the total value of the money at that time? We begin as usual by asking whether the problem is an annuity or a lump sum. It is a lump sum because all of the money to be invested is available at one time. Is the present worth or the future worth needed? The number desired is the value of the fund at the end of the ten-year period that it will be invested. It is therefore a future worth. Referring to the description of the tables, converting lump sum present worth into future worth is solved by using Table B–1. The entry in this table for ten years at 10% is 2.594, which is the value of $1 after ten years at 10%. Because we are investing $18,235, we multiply 2.594 by $18,235 to get $47,301.59 as the value to be received by the children when the investor reaches age 75.

This solves all of the problems except the value of \$500,000 at 5% when the man reaches age 65 and age 75, which is a lump sum, future value problem using Table B–1. The entry at 5% for 10 years is 1.629 and for 20 years is 2.653. The \$500,000 will therefore be worth 1.629 × \$500,000, or \$814,500 at age 65 and 2.653 × \$500,000, or \$1,326,500 at age 75. The total value of the funds available for the children at age 75 is therefore \$47,301 + \$1,326,500, or \$1,373,801.

Example 8

An investor wishes to have \$500,000 in 14 years and expects to be able to achieve an 8% return during this period. How much money does he need to have now in order to achieve his goal? This is a lump sum problem because it asks for the single payment necessary now in order to have \$500,000 in 14 years (assuming that it is invested at 8%). The present worth is the desired value. Referring to the description of the tables, converting lump sum future worth into present worth is the function of Table B–2. The table entry for 14 periods at 8% is 0.340. This is the amount that must be invested now in order to have \$1 in 14 years at 8%. Because we must have \$500,000, we must multiply 0.340 by \$500,000, finding \$170,000 as the necessary amount.

Example 9

The investor in Example 8 is in the unfortunate position of having only \$100,000 available for investment. How far short of his goal will he fall at 8%? What rate of return must he have to achieve his goal? The value of \$100,000 in 14 years at 8% can be found using Table B–1 to convert present worth to future worth. The table entry is 2.937, which when multiplied by \$100,000 equals \$293,700, or \$206,300 below the goal. The solution to the second question is found by dividing \$500,000 by \$100,000, getting 5.0. The rate of return that in 14 years will provide a future value of \$5 for every \$1 in the present is the minimum return that will achieve the goal. Looking in Table B–1 (which converts present worth into future worth) under 14 periods, we find that the table does not contain columns for interest rates high enough to meet the requirement. Undaunted, the resourceful analyst notes that the entries in the table are merely values of the expression $(1 + r)^n$. Taking out his pocket calculator, he solves the equation $(1 + r)^{14} = 5$, finding that r, the required interest rate, is 12.18%.

Example 10

As a portfolio manager, you receive a set of estimates from the research department concerning the future price action of two different stocks that will pay no dividends in the foreseeable future. The first stock is expected to sell at 65 in three years, with a current price of 50. The second stock is currently selling at 30 and, although results from year to year are unpredictable, it can be estimated to be selling at 45 in four years. Assuming that you have no additional information, that you can buy only one of the stocks, and that the estimated rise in the S&P 500 in the intermediate future is 8% per year, which stock do you purchase? One possible solution to this problem is based upon using the 8% per year return on an "average" investment in a "cost of capital" sense. Because this return could be earned on the capital by simply investing in the averages, it seems clear that an investment in either stock recommended by the research department has an expected opportunity cost of 8%. Using Table B–2 (which converts future values into present value) we can find the present value of the capital appreciation per dollar of investment that would be produced by each stock and then select the issue having the largest present value. If the estimates are correct (and we have no other information upon which to base a decision, making the assumption of accuracy necessary), this approach will maximize the capital appreciation of the account relative to the appreciation of the S&P 500. Incidentally, if either stock has a present value less than the assumed $1 initial investment, its purchase would provide less appreciation than the purchase of the "averages." This statement is the same as saying that the stock will provide less benefit than its opportunity cost, which in turn is equivalent to maintaining that the stock should not be purchased.

Actually performing the indicated calculations, we find that:

		Price in		*Indexed appreciation*	
Stock	*Current price*	*3 years*	*4 years*	*3 years*	*4 years*
A	50	65	—	1.30	—
B	30	—	45	—	1.50

These values can be reduced to present values by using Table B–2 at the 8% level with each time period corresponding to the year in which the gain is estimated to be received:

Stock	*Time period*	*Appreciation*	*"Discount" factor*	*Present value*
A	0 yr.–3d yr.	1.30	0.794	1.0322
B	0 yr.–4th yr.	1.50	0.735	1.1025

This table indicates that although both investments would provide a more attractive return than the market average, stock B is expected to be substantially more beneficial to the portfolio than stock A. Note, however, that if the return on stock B were not obtained until the fifth year, the discount factor would be 0.681 and the present value would be 1.0215, which would be less attractive than stock A's 1.0322.

This approach in the selection of securities is more flexible than simply dividing the expected appreciation by the number of years required to achieve the benefit. This flexibility stems from the ability to deal with multiple time periods when using the present value method. For example, if the market were expected to rise 20% in the fourth year, the present value of an investment in stock A would be unaffected but the present value of an investment in stock B would decline very dramatically.

When the portfolio manager has expectations concerning varying returns over varying time periods, for both the averages and the set of stocks being analyzed, the present value technique will still permit him to select the set of stocks most consistent with his set of expectations. Using the average annual rate of return for the different stocks, on the other hand, can never provide the proper weighting of the value of each issue over each time period relative to the behavior of the market during that period. Present value technique reduces the large number of expectations over a complex set of time intervals to a single number indicating the value of each security as an investment vehicle.

FINANCIAL FORMULAS

The financial tables are calculated from four basic formulas that can be used directly when tables are not available. The formula for the compound amount of one that converts present worth into future worth is

$$S = (1 + i)^n \qquad \text{or} \qquad S = \text{antilog}\,[n \log (1 + i)]$$

where

i = The interest rate per period
n = The number of time periods.

This equation can easily be solved by the use of a hand calculator that has a logarithm key. The procedure is simple.

1. Enter $1 + i$ (if 10% is the interest rate, enter 1.10).
2. Find the log of $(1 + i)$ (usually a matter of pushing the "log" button).
3. Multiply this number by n (the number of time periods) to obtain $n \log (1 + i)$.
4. Find the antilog of this number (by pressing "inverse log" if in common logs or "e^x" if in natural logs).
5. The calculator now shows the compound value of $1 in n years. Simply multiply this number by the number of dollars involved.

The formula that provides the discount factor used to find present worth, given future worth, is

$$\text{Discount factor} = (1 + i)^{-n} \qquad \text{or} \qquad \text{antilog}\,[\frac{1}{n} \log (1 + i)].$$

This formula can also be solved using a calculator with log capability. The procedure is basically the same as in the first formula, although it is necessary to divide by n instead of multiplying.

1. Enter $1 + i$ (if 10% is the interest rate, enter 1.10).
2. Find the log of $(1 + i)$.
3. Divide this number by n (the number of time periods) to obtain $\left(\frac{1}{n}\right)\log(1 + i)$.
4. Find the antilog of this number (by pressing "inverse log" if in common logs or "e^x" if in natural logs).
5. The calculator now shows the present value of $1 to be received after n years. Simply multiply this number by the number of dollars involved.

The formula for the future value of an annuity is:

$$\frac{(1 + i)^n - 1}{i} \qquad \text{or} \qquad \frac{[\text{antilog}\,[n \log(1 + i)]] - 1}{i}$$

This procedure on a calculator is only slightly more complex than the two preceding formulas.

1. Enter $1 + i$ (if 10% is the interest rate, enter 1.10).
2. Find the log of $(1 + i)$.
3. Multiply this number by n to obtain $n \log (1 + i)$.
4. Find the antilog of this number, that is, $(1 + i)^n$.
5. Subtract one from this number.
6. Divide the calculator entry by the interest rate. For example, if interest rate is 10%, divide by 0.10.

7. The calculator entry now shows the future value of a $1 annuity. Simply multiply by the number of dollars invested per time period for the total value.

The formula for the present value of an annuity is:

$$\frac{1 - (1 + i)^{-n}}{i} \quad \text{or} \quad \frac{1 - \text{antilog}\left[\frac{1}{n}\log(1 + i)\right]}{i}$$

Using a calculator, the procedure for this formula is as follows:

1. Enter $1 + i$ (if 10% is the interest rate, enter 1.10).
2. Find the log of $(1 + i)$.
3. Divide this number by n.
4. Find the antilog of this number.
5. Subtract this number from 1.0.
6. Divide the calculator entry by the interest rate. For example, if interest rate is 10%, divide by 0.10.
7. The calculator now displays the future value of a $1 annuity. Simply multiply by the number of dollars invested per time period for the total value.

COMPUTING AN UNKNOWN ANNUITY

The techniques presented up to this point will permit the analyst to move easily from present worth to future worth and back again. In addition, we have considered moving from an annuity having a known annual payment to either the present worth or the future worth of the annuity. We have not yet discussed computing an unknown annual payment when the present or future worth is known. The following examples show how to solve this problem and why computing annual payments is important.

Example 11

Assume that you are a portfolio manager and a client wishes to have $100,000 available when he retires in eight years. You agree that a 7% return on investment is possible and use the future worth to present worth conversion table at eight years and 7% to find a discount factor of 0.582. Multiplying this factor by $100,000 you get $58,200, the amount that should be invested now in order to have the desired amount upon retirement. The client, however, indicates that he prefers to make annual payments into the portfolio in order to obtain the $100,000 instead of providing the $58,200 lump sum. He asks for the size of payment needed. Because this problem deals with the conversion of future worth into the size of the annual payment, it is the reverse of Table B–3 (which converts the payment into the future worth). Looking in this table under eight years and 7%, you find 10.260. Because the problem is "reversed," you divide 10.260 into 1.0 in order to find the annual payment, getting $0.0975 as the annual payment needed to have $1 after eight years. Because $100,000 is needed, you multiply 0.0975 by $100,000 to find the payment needed, which produces a solution of $9,750.

Example 12

As a portfolio manager, you are approached by a client for advice concerning an investment opportunity he has encountered. He has a chance to invest $10,000 in a local business that will provide a constant annual return for 12 years, at the end of which the assets will be worthless. What is the minimum annual payment that will make the investment worthwhile if the client has the alternative of obtaining a 9% return by investing in bonds? In this problem, the 9% opportunity cost can be taken in the cost-of-capital sense, and the investment can be regarded as attractive if the present worth of the stream of income generated has a positive value using a 9% discount rate. In other words, the capital the investor would have after 12 years of bond investment would be greater than the capital produced by this investment *unless* the investment produced a return greater than or equal to 9% per year. Any annual payment from the investment that would be less than 9% would dissipate the capital that could have been produced by the purchase of bonds. The present worth is known to be $10,000, and the unknown quantity is the amount of the annual payment that would provide a 9% return. To move from the present worth to the annual payment, we "reverse" the process of moving from payment to present worth, which is covered in Table B–4. This table has no column for a 9% interest rate, but the procedure described in the preceding section can be used to calculate the needed value, which is 7.161. In order to "reverse" this entry, you divide this value into 1.00, getting 0.1396 as the amount for the annual payment that would give a present value of $1. Multiplying 0.1396 by $10,000, you get $1,396 as the minimum annual return that would make the investment profitable (i.e., make it provide a 9% annual return).

PRESENT VALUE AND SECURITIES VALUATION

The mathematics of compound growth is useful not only in solving a large number of the practical problems encountered almost daily by the investment professional, but also in developing theoretical support for the market value of both stocks and bonds. A security, stripped to its barest essentials, can be regarded as simply a series of dividend or interest payments to be received over a period of time. The current price that should be paid for this sequence of payments must be its present value. The mathematical structure used to compute present values is therefore the logical machinery to use in securities valuation.

As a simple example, consider a bond that will pay \$1 per year forever. If the current interest rate in the economy is 5%, the use of the present value mathematical machinery would show that its present value is $1 \div i$, which would give a price of \$1 ÷ 0.05, or \$20. The same formula would apply to a stock having a zero growth rate.

If the bond did not pay its coupon in perpetuity, but rather paid only, say, 40 coupons, then the formula does not apply, but the problem is a fairly simple application of the present value of an annuity and can be solved using the Table B-4 entry for 40 periods and 5%. This entry is 17.1591 and the value of the bond is this number times the payment coupon (\$1 in this example) plus the present value of the principal returned after 40 years. The calculation of bond yields to maturity is done in exactly this way, except that most bonds pay their coupons semi-annually, so that the number of time periods is twice the number of years and the interest rate per period is adjusted accordingly.

The valuation of stocks does not have to be modified to allow for a limited number of payments, because the normal assumption for equities is that they will survive forever. But while the coupon payment of a bond cannot normally change, the dividend payment of a share of stock can change. The basic formula ($D \div i$) needs to be adjusted to reflect this characteristic, and the simplest adjustment is to assume that dividends per share will grow at a constant rate. This assumption can be converted into valuation formulas in a number of ways, only a few of which will be discussed here.

Using the same machinery that established the price as $D \div i$ (or its equivalent, price ÷ dividend = $1 \div i$) to attack the problem of constant growth rate produces the formula

$$\text{price} \div \text{dividend} = \frac{1}{i - g},$$

where i is the "interest rate" or discount rate and g is the growth rate. This formula shows that the growth rate can simply be subtracted from the interest rate demanded before dividing the difference into 1.0. The problem with this approach is that when the growth rate of a company is almost as high as the discount rate, the indicated price approaches infinity. While very high prices are justified for rapid growth that one is certain will occur, the usefulness of the model in these situations is not great in practical applications, where growth is uncertain and some higher discount rate is appropriate though difficult to determine.

An alternative to this formulation is suggested by Ezra Solomon, who divides the market price of a stock into two components. The first component is the present value of the annual earnings (E) received as a result of the operation of *existing* assets. This present value is calculated using as a discount rate (previously referred to as i) the demanded rate of return of investors, called y. This present value is equal to $E \div y$.

The second component of market price is the incremental value awarded in response to the stock's prospects for growth. Each year the company reinvests a proportion, call it b, of its earnings per share, E. This reinvestment, amounting to bE dollars, earns in each following year an amount equal to bEr, where r is the rate of return achieved on the assets. The present value of these returns is bEr/y, which means that each year the company receives a value increment from its reinvestment program equal to bEr/y. The present value of this annual value received from reinvesting can be calculated, the present value of the amount reinvested subtracted from this, and after some manipulations the price is given as

$$P = \frac{E}{y} + \left(\frac{bE}{y}\right)\left(\frac{r - y}{y}\right),$$

which expresses price in terms of the demanded rate of return of investors and the company's rate of return on invested assets. If the price is taken as a given, the demanded return of investors can be calculated as

$$y = \frac{E}{P} + \frac{bE(m - 1)}{P},$$

where m equals the company's rate of return (r) divided by the rate of return (y) available to investors. Both of the above formulas assume that a constant *dollar* amount is being reinvested. If a constant *percentage* of earnings is being invested, Modigliani and Miller have shown that the earnings to price ratio will equal the sum of the yield and the growth rate in earnings. Using these formulas, the investment professional can gain a fairly good insight into either a pricing situation for a stock or the rate of return that investors seem to be demanding for an issue. The results of the formulas must be used with discretion, however, because they assume a constant rate of return on investment by any individual company being considered.

A number of modifications to this basic approach are possible, and many of these variations are an improvement in the models' realism, because they usually allow for some type of variation in the growth rate over time. One of the most interesting of these modifications was advanced by Nicholas Molodovsky, who developed a set of tables showing the justified *P/E* ratio for each discount rate and three inputs estimated by the analysts. The first of these is the growth rate that can be maintained over the intermediate term, the second input is the number of years that the growth rate can be maintained, and the third input is the number of years of declining growth rates that will be required to reduce the company to a zero growth position. This approach provides the professional with a great deal of flexibility in describing the form of the anticipated earnings stream yet retains the discipline that is inherent in the present value formulation of the valuation process. Details of this method are described in Part III of *Investment Values in a Dynamic World: The Collected Papers of Nicholas Molodovsky,* edited by Robert D. Milne and published by the Financial Analysts Research Foundation in 1974.

SUMMARY

Four very simple tables can provide the financial analyst with the solutions to a very substantial set of problems. They can be used to calculate the values for any process that operates according to the compounding principle, and the model of compound growth is useful in an extremely high percentage of the items considered by the investment community. Probably the most important applications stem from the fact that money (and also the products that can be purchased with money) has a time value. A dollar today is worth more than a dollar to be received ten years from now, even if the purchasing power of money is held constant. The analyst deals with many variables, and these variables have values at different points in time. By using the techniques shown in this chapter, he will be able to reduce the diversity of his data by expressing many of the quantities at their present worth. In this way, he will be able to consider a high percentage of his problems without regard to the variations caused by the time dimension and the time value of money.

The specific techniques discussed enable the analyst to convert present worth to future value, convert future worth to present value, convert annual payments to the future total value of an annuity, or convert annual payment to the present worth of an annuity. In addition, if both values are known (both present and future worth or both annual payment and future worth, for example), then the implied table entry can be computed and compared to the actual table values to find the implied interest rate. Example 5 showed how this can have practical application. Finally, problems requiring the conversion of either the future or present worth of an annuity into the required annual payment were found to be solved by simply dividing the appropriate table entry into 1.

Chapter 4

Elementary Statistics

In statistical analysis, it is often necessary to select one number, or an "average" to represent a large collection of numbers. The "average" most often used is the arithmetic mean, but at times other "averages" are more appropriate. The harmonic mean and the geometric mean are explained, as are the median and the mode. In addition, an average is more meaningful if the dispersion of the data around the average is known. The range, the variance, and the standard deviation are illustrated, together with the coefficient of variation, which is used to compare dispersion among several series of data.

INTRODUCTION

Elementary statistics is the study of how data can be effectively summarized. It attempts to describe the important aspects of large sets of data without inundating the reader in a mass of numerical details. By using the simple models of descriptive statistics, the analyst can illuminate important characteristics of the information being studied because the general tendencies of the data are presented clearly and without the distraction of the individual peculiarity of each observed datum. The dangers in the use of the tool of descriptive statistics can be deduced from the purpose of this approach. First, it is possible to fail to locate a significant feature of the data. Second, it is possible to misuse the tools and indicate a characteristic not actually present. The two most important features of a data set are some central value about which it clusters and its tendency to deviate from that central value. These two features are the topics of the two following sections of this chapter.

MEASURES OF CENTRAL TENDENCY

Arithmetic mean

Whenever an analyst wishes to characterize a large group of numbers by a single number, he quite naturally gives serious consideration to using an *average*. The arithmetic mean, commonly called the "average," is probably one of the two most frequently used mathematical models in the investment community (the compound annual growth rate being the other). This section is not an attempt to establish the uses of the average but instead is designed to show the limitations of the model and to show several other "averages" that in certain cases are more appropriate than the arithmetic mean.

The basic, underlying concept implied in the use of an average is that all of the data being used are observations from one population that has a common property. It would, for example, be absurd to average the *P/E* of Exxon, the earnings per share of U.S. Steel, and the current ratio of Xerox. This point is obvious, but it indicates two very important points in the use of the mean. First, the arithmetic of the average is simply

$$\frac{\Sigma x_i}{N}$$

(read: the total of all x's, divided by the number of x's). It will work on any group of numbers indiscriminately, producing absurd results if not used with some care. Second, the characteristic of the population being measured can easily be misrepresented unless some care is taken. The average is a number "pulled" out of the set of data by the model; the number is supposed to *represent* or "stand for" the particular characteristic of the data set that is needed. If the model is not appropriate for the data at hand, or if the data do not refer to the particular item for which a measurement is desired, the results can be fallacious.

One of the most misleading uses of an average is to characterize a highly diverse group with an "average" that is not representative of any member at all. This situation is illustrated by Table 4–1, which shows the five-year price appreciation of an equal investment in five different companies. Although a number of misleading conclusions can be drawn from this "average," the arithmetic procedure used is correct. The model is wrong, in the only sense that a model can be wrong: it is not helpful in analyzing the data.

Table 4–1: "Speculative" industry

Company		*Appreciation ($)*
A		− 40
B		− 60
C		− 80
D		− 20
E		+550
	Average	$70

Another example occurs in the averaging of *P/E* ratios. If the earnings of one company are almost zero, its *P/E* will be enormous and any average that includes this company will be unrealistic. Therefore, great care is necessary when averaging ratios of any sort.

Harmonic mean

In some cases, the *harmonic mean* should be used instead of the more generally known arithmetic mean. This average is employed in certain cases where rates or where prices are being characterized by an average. Mathematically, this average is

$$H = \frac{N}{\sum \left(\frac{1}{x_i}\right)}.$$

It is used when the x_i are such things as miles per hour, dollar earnings per dollar market value, and so forth. Whenever the analyst averages numbers expressed as an "x per something," the harmonic mean should be considered. This mean is more appropriate than the average if the variations in the data are in the "per something" instead of in "x" (as is normally the case). For example, when averaging fixed charge coverage, we typically find that both series are changing, i.e., both the earnings available to cover fixed charges and the charges themselves. Consider the following financial data for General Electric Company:

Year	*Available earnings (millions)*	*Fixed charges (millions)*	*Fixed charge coverage (earnings ÷ charges)*
1964	$ 613	$ 36	17.1
1965	722	42	17.0
1966	708	55	12.9
1967	737	81	9.1
1968	739	91	8.2
1969	603	99	6.1
1970	673	124	5.4
1971	905	120	7.6
1972	1,020	313	7.8
1973	1,157	156	7.4
Averages	$ 788	$ 93	9.9

If we divide the average earnings of GE of $788 million by the average for fixed charges of $93 million, the common sense answer is that earnings averaged 8.5 times fixed charges during this decade. Yet the arithmetic mean of the column for fixed charge coverage ratios indicates an average of 9.9 times, which clearly overstates the actual coverage of fixed charges during the period.

However, by taking the harmonic mean, we come up with the right answer. By pushing the reciprocal button on a pocket calculator we change the fixed charge ratios into reciprocals and obtain this average as follows:

	Fixed charge coverage		*Reciprocal*	
	17.1		0.058	
	17.0		0.059	
	12.9		0.077	
	9.1		0.110	
	8.2		0.122	
	6.1		0.164	
	5.4		0.185	
	7.6		0.131	
	7.8		0.128	
	7.4		0.135	
Average	9.9	Average	0.117	= 8.5 times

The same problem arises in any situation where a change occurs in the series being averaged, the "per something." If fixed charges had been the same each year, use of the harmonic mean would have been unnecessary because the "per something" of fixed charges would have been constant. However, such a development is unlikely to occur in real life. Thus, when making averages of current ratios, price/earnings ratios, fixed charge coverage ratios, and so forth, use the harmonic mean. (The only important exception would be dividend yields, because the yield itself is a reciprocal and inverting a yield would result in a price/dividend ratio and an incorrect average.) In the days before pocket calculators with reciprocal buttons it was inconvenient to calculate harmonic means, and most analysts were content with the less accurate results in using arithmetic means for ratios. Today there is no need to accept less accuracy.

Geometric mean

The geometric mean is frequently used in averaging quantities such as the base data for indices, the observations of a time series that has a compound growth rate, ratios, and ratios of change over time. It is mathematically defined as

$$G = \sqrt[n]{x_1 x_2 x_3 \ldots x_n} \qquad \text{or} \qquad G = \sqrt[n]{\Pi(x_i)}$$

Recall that Π indicates that the product of all x's is to be found, producing a single number.
The simplest way to calculate the geometric mean is to find the logs of x_i, then add these logs, divide by N, and finally take the antilog of the result. Mathematically,

$$\log G = \frac{\Sigma(\log x_i)}{N};$$

then,

$$G = \text{antilog}\ (\log G).$$

A major computational limitation of the technique is that G cannot be found if any x_i is zero or negative.

The main use of the geometric mean in financial analysis is in averaging changes over time. For example, if the rate of return on a portfolio that has received no dividends is needed, calculating the ratio of the current year's value to the preceding year produces the following:

Year	*Market value*		*Market value relative to previous year*
1973	$100.00		—
1974	110.00		1.10
1975	88.00		0.80
1976	101.20		1.15
1977	121.44		1.20
		Total	4.25
		Arithmetic mean	1.06

To compute the geometric mean, add the logs of the x_i:

$$\begin{aligned} \log 1.10 &= 0.04139 \\ \log 0.80 &= -0.09691 \\ \log 1.15 &= 0.06070 \\ \log 1.20 &= 0.07918 \\ \text{Total} &\quad\ \ 0.08436 \end{aligned}$$

We then find the average of the logs:

$$0.08436 \div 4 = 0.02109;$$

and then to find the geometric mean, we take the antilog of the average:

$$\text{Antilog } 0.02109 = 1.05 = \text{Geometric mean.}$$

As a result of these calculations, the arithmetic mean of 1.06 and the geometric mean of 1.05 were found as alternative numbers that might possibly be used to characterize the same set of data. In order to determine which method is more valuable, it is logical to start with the beginning portfolio value and apply the "average" change each year in order to see how accurately the final value of the portfolio is approximated by the use of the averages. For the arithmetic mean:

Beginning portfolio value increased at arithmetic average rate

\$100	× 1.06 =	106.0	in	1974
106	× 1.06 =	112.4	in	1975
112.4	× 1.06 =	119.1	in	1976
119.1	× 1.06 =	126.2	in	1977

Because the arithmetic mean yields a 1977 value of 126.2 instead of the actual 121.44, it has an optimistic bias. For the geometric mean:

Beginning portfolio value increased at geometric average rate

100	× 1.05 =	105	in	1974
105	× 1.05 =	110.2	in	1975
110.2	× 1.05 =	115.7	in	1976
115.7	× 1.05 =	121.5	in	1977

The calculated 1977 value of 121.5 is accurate within rounding error.

Other measures of central tendency

If an analyst divided his stocks into ten equal groups based on their *P/E* ratio, he might display the results in a presentation as shown in Figure 4–1. This graphic presentation is called a histogram and clearly shows the frequency with which events occur and the distribution of these frequencies within a population. The only point to be made by the histogram at this stage, however, is that it is not "balanced"; it has a concentration on the left-hand side, in the area of the low *P/E* ratios. The average used to represent the population, then, must represent a "skewed" population, that is, one with a bias toward one side or another rather than a symmetrical or bell-shaped distribution.

This creates a rather severe problem, because the relatively few observations in the high-priced range are given, obviously, a high *P/E* and hence a heavier weight when the arithmetic mean is computed. The arithmetic mean, in other words, automatically weights the frequencies by their numerical values, which produces distorted results if the distribution is radically skewed. If the weights (the *P/E* ratios) are ignored, it is possible to emphasize the companies themselves by asking which company has exactly half of the companies below it in "expensiveness" and the other half above it. In this way, the "middle"

Figure 4-1

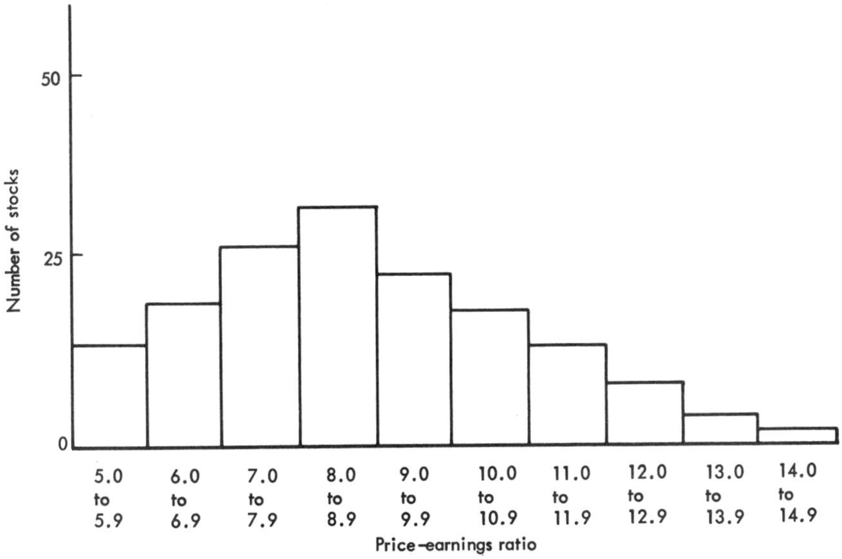

company would be found, and in a very real sense this company is representative of the group as a whole. This type of average is called the *median*. It would be the analyst's "best bet" if he wished to guess what *P/E* a particular company possessed, worrying about the *number of companies* that would fall between his estimate and the actual value.

The arithmetic mean, on the other hand, would be the "best bet" when guessing the *P/E* of a company while worrying about the number of *P/E*'s that would fall between the estimate and the actual value. In other words, the median represents the *companies* while the mean represents the *P/E*'s. The mean is more sensitive to extreme values. Therefore, while the two will be equal in balanced distributions, the mean will tend to be "pulled" off center in skewed populations. Because the median is simply the "middle" number, no mathematical technique is available to calculate it. The median can be found only by examining the set of numbers and selecting the middle value. For example, in the following set,

$$5 \quad 8 \quad 10 \quad 14 \quad 23,$$

the number 10 can be seen to be the median. For larger sets, however, locating the median can be a tedious task. Because of this (and also because it has no mathematical formula that might make it useful in more advanced mathematical use) the median is seldom used in statistical analysis.

The *mode* is defined as the most frequent value in the population. It represents the single *P/E* that the largest number of stocks in our example possess. In balanced distributions, it equals the mean and median, but in skewed distributions it is less sensitive to extreme values than either of the other two measures. If each value in the following set of numbers represents the number of years that a stock has been held in a portfolio,

1 2 [3] 2 [3] 4 [3] 5 4 [3] 2 1

the mode is 3 years, as can be found by counting the frequency with which each value occurs. This procedure is the only means by which the mode can be discovered, and as a result the mode is seldom used.

MEASURES OF DISPERSION

Unfortunately, the use of one of the various types of averages cannot completely describe the basic data. One very important characteristic that the average completely neglects is the "closeness" of the various observations to the average. The need to supplement the average with another measure that characterizes this "spread" has been recognized by analysts for many years, so that, for example, the mean price of a stock frequently is supplemented by the range for the year.

Range

The range as a measure of the amount of dispersion present in a data set has the advantage of conceptual simplicity and ease in calculation. Its disadvantage is that one extreme value will greatly affect the range but is not really typical for the population as a whole. For example, if a stock at the close of each month sells for:

32 34 30 35 33 37 34 38 49 37 35 37

the range can easily be found by inspection to be 30–49. The number 49 was a most unusual value, so that the range presents a picture of greater market volatility than is justified by the data. One possible solution would be simply to throw out extreme observations before finding the range, but because of the difficulty in defining "extreme" with precision, this technique is very subjective.

Variance and standard deviation

If the analyst decided to reject the use of the range and instead used deviation from the mean as a measure of "spread," he would be using the lines in the diagram shown in Figure 4–2.

Figure 4–2

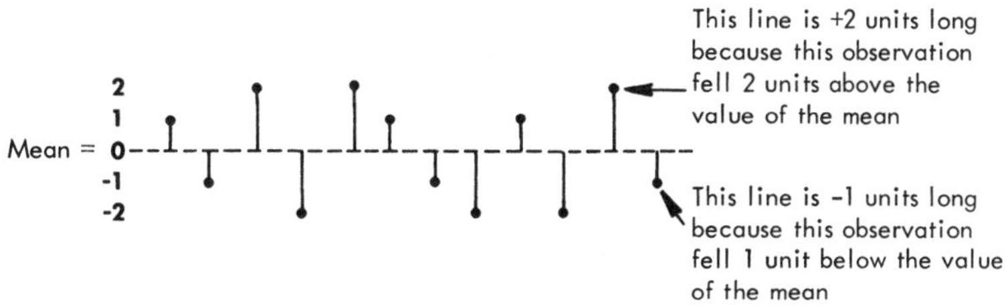

If the total of the length of these vertical lines is large, the population has a large dispersion; if small, a small dispersion. But on closer examination, we find that the lines for observations *below* the average are negative. By the definition of the mean (it must fall in the middle of the observations), the total of the negative lines *must* equal the total of the positive, yielding an answer of zero in every case. In the graph, we find that

$$+1-1+2-2+2+1-1-2+1-2+2-1=0.$$

In order to measure these lines without regard to the sign of the numbers that they touch, it is necessary to do away with the negative signs. A simple way to do this is to square all of the lines, that is, to square every deviation from the mean. This works because $(+2)^2 = +4$ and $(-2)^2 = +4$, showing that equal length lines have equal positive length without regard to the original sign. By summing the squared deviations and then dividing by the number of observations, it is possible to find the "mean squared deviation," which is called the *variance* in statistical theory. If the variance is then "unsquared," the root mean square is found. This is called the standard deviation. The following formulas are helpful:

Variance	*Standard Deviation*
$\sigma^2 = \dfrac{\Sigma(x - \bar{x})_i^2}{N}$	$\sigma = \sqrt{\dfrac{\Sigma(x - \bar{x})_i^2}{N}}$

where:

σ = the greek letter "sigma," traditionally used in statistics to indicate standard deviation.
x_i = the observation value.
$\bar{x}$ = the mean of the observations.
N = the number of observations.

Assume, for example, that the quarterly *P/E* ratio of a stock being analyzed has the set of values:

10 12 14 10 9 11 12 13.

These numbers have a mean of 11.375. The mean value is useful in providing a single number that can be used to characterize the entire set of eight numbers, but it does not give any indication of the "diversity" of the set. The eight values might as easily have been

0 0 0 0 22.750 22.750 22.750 22.750

or

11.25 11.25 11.25 11.25 11.5 11.5 11.5 11.5.

The mean of any of these sets is still 11.375, but the accuracy with which the mean characterizes the data is quite different in each case. The variance indicates the adequacy of the mean as representing the numbers and at the same time is in itself a valuable measure of the variability of the data, which in this case shows the volatility of the market's valuation of the company's earning power. The standard deviation is simply the square root of the variance. Each measure has selected uses in more advanced statistical techniques.

In the first set of numbers shown above, the variance is computed by: (1) subtracting the mean from each number, (2) squaring the result, (3) adding all of these squared values together, (4) dividing this sum by 8. Step one produces the following set of numbers:

−1.375 0.625 2.625 −1.375 −2.375 −0.375 0.625 1.625.

Step two squares these numbers, producing:

1.89 0.39 6.89 1.89 5.64 0.14 0.39 2.64.

Step three simply adds these numbers together, getting 17.625. Step four divides by 8, getting 2.203 as the value for the variance. The standard deviation is the square root of 2.203, or 1.484.

The advantage to the use of the variance or the standard deviation is that it takes every value in the population into account when measuring the dispersion in the group being studied. In a normally distributed set of numbers, approximately 68% of the numbers will fall within one standard deviation of the average. For example, if the average is 48 and the standard deviation is 2, an analyst would expect about 68% of the numbers to be between 46 and 50. He would expect about 95% to lie within 2 σ of the mean (44 to 52), and about 99% to lie within 3 σ (42 to 54). If the data are not normally distributed, this statement will not be true. The standard deviation is always measured in the same units as the average. An average *P/E* of 20 would have a σ of, say, 3 (from 17 to 23); an average sales of $40 million might have a σ of, say, $8 million (from $32 million to $48 million); and so forth. Observations falling more than 3 σ from the mean when the data are assumed normal are very unusual and in many studies are removed from the analysis in the belief that they are not representative of the data as a whole. Removed observations are called "outliers."

Coefficient of variation

The advantage of having the measure of dispersion expressed in the same units as the mean disappears, however, when an analyst wishes to compare the volatility of two different sets of data. For example, it may be necessary to compare the variation from average profit margin in the grocery chain industry to the retail trade industry. If the net margin in grocery chains is 1.5% with σ = 0.45%, and retail trade has a mean margin of 5.0% with a σ of = 0.75%, it is difficult to see which industry has more "scatter." Certainly, the 0.75% of retail trade is greater, but its mean is also higher and so a larger σ is to be expected. The solution is to calculate the standard deviation as a percentage of the mean. This produces the *coefficient of variation*, a "percentage dispersion" figure. In the example, the coefficient of variation (symbolized by V) for grocery chains equals 0.45% ÷ 1.5% = 30%. For retail trade, V = 0.75% ÷ 5.0% = 15%. From the data, it is now clear that grocery chains have about twice the dispersion found in the retail trade industry. It is the data that provide the basis for the conclusion, but the information within the data was made visible to the analyst through the coefficient of variation. For reference, the formula is:

$$V = \frac{\sigma}{\bar{x}} \times 100.$$

Mean absolute deviation

An alternative to the standard deviation as a measure of dispersion is the mean absolute deviation. To obtain this quantity, the absolute values of all deviations from the average are totaled and the resulting sum is then divided by the number of observations. The formula for this procedure is:

$$\text{Mean absolute deviation} = \frac{\Sigma\,|x_i - \bar{x}|}{N}.$$

In the chart of deviations presented in the section on variance, the deviations were:

$$+1 - 1 + 2 - 2 + 2 + 1 - 1 - 2 + 1 - 2 + 2 - 1 = 0.$$

The absolute values can be found and totaled, producing:

$$+1 + 1 + 2 + 2 + 2 + 1 + 1 + 2 + 1 + 2 + 2 + 1 = 18.$$

Because there are 12 observations, the mean absolute deviation equals 18 ÷ 12 = 1.5.

The advantage of the mean absolute deviation is that it is less sensitive to extreme deviations than the variance and it is used extensively in financial descriptive statistics. The disadvantage is that it is not used extensively in more advanced mathematical techniques, while the variance is found in many applications.

QUARTILES, QUINTILES, AND DECILES

Although strictly not measures of dispersion, quartiles, quintiles, and deciles occur in financial analysis fairly frequently and do relate to problems in evaluating the way that data "spreads" away from the mean. In applying these measures, the range of the data (or the range adjusted by removing outliers) is divided into four equal intervals for quartiles, five for quintiles, or ten for deciles. Any individual observation can then be reported as being in the, say, third quartile if four equal intervals were chosen. If ten intervals were used instead, then the observation might fall into, say, the seventh decile.

This approach relates the evaluation of particular observations relative to the overall dispersion of the data. It does not directly measure the dispersion of the data itself. For example, the fact that a particular manager falls in the third decile of the performance of all managers does not indicate the degree of dispersion in the population of all managers' performance. Nevertheless, the information is important in many cases.

SUMMARY

The elementary, or descriptive, statistics discussed in this chapter serve the investment professional well by summarizing essential characteristics of the great masses of data encountered daily. It is important, however, to point out that the field of statistics goes well beyond the simple description of the characteristics of data. Later chapters on hypothesis testing and regression will show some of the power of the statistical method in an analytic instead of a merely descriptive context.

Chapter 5

Probability theory, or how to treat uncertain events

The field of investments constantly deals with uncertainty. Probability theory can be used effectively to make the treatment of uncertainty more realistic and less dependent upon intuition or hunch. Understanding the probability of a single event is relatively simple, but problems become more complex (and the rewards of understanding the theory become greater) when events are combined into joint probabilities, union of probabilities, and conditional probabilities. The concept of maximizing expected values is discussed because it is so useful in considering the benefits and costs of alternative investments and investment strategies. Moreover, consideration is given to measuring the loss in return as a result of the presence of uncertainty, thereby indicating the amount that can be paid for information that will improve choices.

BASIC CONCEPTS

Anyone who has ever played a game of chance has an intuitive feel for the meaning of probability. Because life itself is one of the most uncertain of projects, the gambling forced on man by virtue of his merely being alive makes probabilities one of the most fascinating of subjects. The mathematical theory of probability deals with the "chance" of something occurring that is not certain to occur, but it treats the subject with a precision and objectivity not found in the subjective, experiential approach. Because probabilities provide information concerning uncertain events, they are ideally suited for management and investment functions, which could be *defined* as *decision making in the face of uncertainty.*

Probabilities are expressed on an arbitrary scale, or index. If an event must necessarily occur, it is absolutely probable and has a probability of 100%—expressed as 1.00. If it cannot possibly occur, it has a probability of 0. Naturally, most real-world problems fall somewhere between these extreme values. A probability of .5 means that it is equally likely that an event will occur or not occur. A figure of .25 means one chance in four, .10 means one chance in ten, etc.

The simplest examples stem from the simple games of chance. If a coin is flipped, the probability of heads is .50; if a die is rolled, the probability of a "three" is one in six, or .167. Any analyst can determine these results intuitively. Intuition, however, breaks down in more complicated problems, requiring the use of math. Mathematically, the solution was found by dividing the number of ways the event being analyzed could occur by the number of all possible events (all events being equally likely). In flipping the coin, the probability of heads was therefore

$$\frac{H}{N},$$

where

$$H = 1, \quad N = 2.$$

The problem can be expanded a bit by asking about the behavior of N. If the coin were tossed three times, N would equal $2 \cdot 2 \cdot 2$, or 8. The probability of throwing three successive heads is therefore one in eight, or 0.125. The formula holds for more complicated problems, like the probability of ten successive heads ($N = 2^{10}$), where the answer is one chance in 1,024 or a probability of 0.00098.

CALCULATING PROBABILITIES

These results are not sufficient to make probabilities useful, but the theory can easily be extended by *combining* probabilities. If an analyst estimates that XYZ Corp. has a probability (p_1) equal to 0.10 of dropping 15% in price and Widgets Inc. has a probability (p_2) equal to .20 of dropping 15%, what is the probability of *both* of these events occurring? If the price movements of the two stocks are completely unrelated, the answer is:

$$(p_1)(p_2) = (0.10)(0.20) = 0.02.$$

The probability of *at least one* of the events occurring is slightly more complicated. At first glance, this probability would appear to be the sum of p_1 and p_2, which would produce a probability of 0.30. This result, however, has the probability of both events occurring simultaneously added into the total twice. Figure 5–1 shows how this happens.

When p_1 is added to p_2, the area "p_1 and p_2" is included both in the probability of p_1 *and* in the probability of p_2. The addition therefore adds the "p_1 and p_2" area into the result twice. The solution to this

Figure 5-1

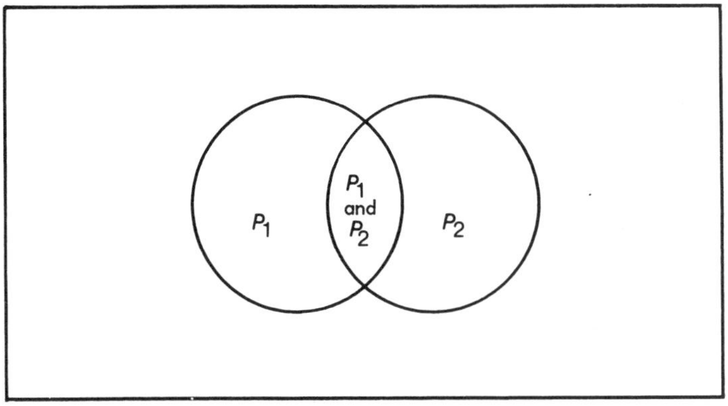

problem is to subtract one of the "p_1 and p_2" values out of the original addition, producing the answer

$$p_1 + p_2 - p_1p_2 = 0.10 + 0.20 - 0.02 = 0.28.$$

If the price movements of the two stocks are related (that is, if a decline in one stock would lead the analyst to expect a decline in the other), then it would be necessary to know the probability of a decline in the second stock, given that a decline in the first stock occurred, before any calculations could be performed.

The notation for the probability concepts developed so far is shown in Table 5-1.

The use of tree diagrams to show the structure of problems in conditional probability has become quite common. For example, assume that a potential investor is giving consideration to the purchase of the common stock of a company. He is, however, faced with possibilities of a good, neutral, or bad market during the coming year. In addition, his

Table 5-1

Mathematical symbol	*Mathematical term*	*English equivalent*
P(A)	Marginal probability	The probability of the occurrence of *A*.
P(A and *B)*	Joint probability	The probability of both *A* and *B* occurring.
P(A or *B)*	Addition of probabilities	The probability of either *A* or *B* occurring.
P(A |B) or *P(A* given *B)*	Conditional probability	The probability of *A* given that *B* has occurred.

particular stock may perform well, neutrally, or poorly relative to the market in any of the three markets. If the hypothetical investor is familiar with probability theory, he would attempt to determine the probabilities of each of the three market conditions and also the probabilities for the particular stock's relative performance in each of the market conditions. Assume that he subjectively provides these probabilities, which are then used to construct the tree diagram, Figure 5–2.

Figure 5–2: Example of a simple decision tree

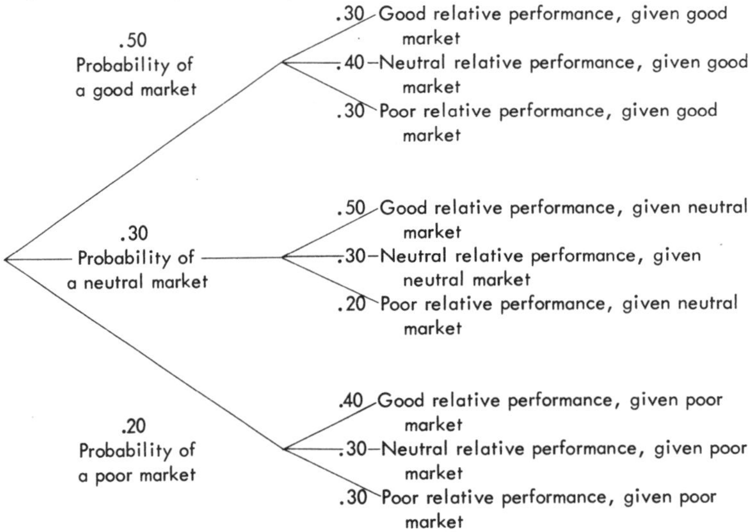

This information is interesting in itself, but it can be manipulated to provide even more interesting results. For example, what is the probability of both a good market and a poor relative performance in the stock? What is the probability of the stock's performing relatively well even though a poor market occurs? In order to answer these questions, Table 5–2 can be constructed.

The column for marginal probability deals with the unconditional probability shown in the tree diagram at the leftmost set of branches, the branches that do not depend upon any prior event. In this particular example, this is the unconditional probability of a given market condition. The conditional probability column gives the probability of each of the branches on the tree diagram that depends upon a prior event. In this particular case these probabilities are related to the performance of the stock relative to the market *given* some specific market condition. The joint probabilities column is the solution column in this particular table and refers to the probability that *both* a given market condition and a given performance for the common stock are in fact realized after

Table 5-2

Marginal probability of market behavior		×	*Conditional probability of stock performance*		=	*Joint probability*
Good	0.50		Good	0.30		0.15
			Neutral	0.40		0.20
			Poor	0.30		0.15
				1.00		
Neutral	0.30		Good	0.50		0.15
			Neutral	0.30		0.09
			Poor	0.20		0.06
				1.00		
Poor	0.20		Good	0.40		0.08
			Neutral	0.30		0.06
			Poor	0.30		0.06
	1.00			1.00		1.00

one year. Joint probabilities are obtained by multiplying the market probability by the stock probability. From this table, it is possible, for example, to discover that the probability of both a good market and a bad relative performance of the common stock occurring is 0.15. In addition, the probability of both a poor market and a good relative performance in the stock is 0.08. By adding together all of the joint probabilities dealing with good relative perfomance, the investor can determine the total probability of his investment proving to be more successful than the alternative investment of a very broadly diversified portfolio that would behave exactly like the market. In this case, his calculation would be

$$0.15 + 0.15 + 0.08 = 0.38.$$

The total probability for a neutral performance would be

$$0.20 + 0.09 + 0.06 = 0.35.$$

The probability of poor results can be calculated as

$$0.15 + 0.06 + 0.06 = 0.27.$$

Naturally, the total for the three possible results of good, neutral, or bad is 1.00:

$$0.35 + 0.27 + 0.38 = 1.00.$$

This total equals 1.00 because there is a 100% probability that the stock will perform *either* well, neutrally, or poorly. By using this form of analysis, the investor has discovered that he can expect his common stock to do somewhat better than average. If his assessments of the probabilities are correct, he would perform fairly well in the long run if enough common stocks having this probability pattern were purchased, because the probability of outperforming the market (0.38) exceeds the probability of performing less well than the market (0.27).

EXPECTED VALUE

One of the most useful results of the theory of probability is the concept of expected value. In a game of chance, there is some price at which a rational gambler would be indifferent to the game because he would expect neither to lose nor to win. If a man offers to flip a coin with you paying $1 if it is heads and gaining $1 otherwise, you would expect to break even—the expected value of the game would be zero. On the other hand, if you received an offer to flip a coin and receive $2 if tails are thrown but nothing for heads, what would you be willing to pay? The game must be worth something, because you have an opportunity to receive money but cannot possibly lose anything other than the amount paid for the privilege of playing the game. The problem is to determine the precise amount that the game is worth. Over the long run, tails will occur about half the time, and so you will receive $2 about half the time. The rest of the time, you receive nothing. It seems reasonable to assume that $2 half the time is the same as $1 all the time, which is the expected value of the game. Over the long run, the game would be profitable for you if you paid anything less than this $1 expected result. Actually, of course, you can pay $1.05 for the privilege of enjoying the game, but over the long run this decision would result in the loss of money.

If this discussion appears to have more value in after-five problems than in business situations, the approach can easily be extended to virtually every situation involving uncertainty. For example, the expected value of a particular stock at the end of the year could be calculated by the use of probabilities. Assume that the analyst estimates the prices and probabilities shown in Table 5-3.

Table 5-3:
Expected value of a typical stock

Probability	*Price*
0.10	70
0.20	75
0.30	80
0.20	85
0.20	90
1.00	

The expected value of the stock would be the "average" of its estimated values at the end of the year. However, because the probabilities vary, a "weighted total" of the various possible prices is needed in order to find the "average":

$$(0.1)(70) + (0.2)(75) + (0.3)(80) + (0.2)(85) + (0.2)(90) = 7 + 15 + 24 + 17 + 18 = 81.$$

The expected value of any investment project to be undertaken, experiment to be performed, or the like, can be calculated in a similar fashion. In investments, the advantage of expected values is that they facilitate a comparison between potential investments, thus providing a way by which probabilistically weighted relative values can be used in decision making, because the maximization of expected value can be regarded as a rational business strategy.

The approach could be broadened somewhat by saying that the maximization of utility can be regarded as a rational business strategy. This modification allows the decision maker to allow for risk. For example, if you received the coin-flipping offer described at the beginning of this chapter, but the wager was for $100,000 if tails occurred, would you be willing to pay, say, $40,000 for the opportunity to play? The expected value of the game is $50,000, but most individuals would prefer to avoid the wager because of the risk involved. Utilities are numerically measured dollar values reduced by the individual's personal feelings concerning his distaste for risk. Techniques for the measurement of utility and also for its maximization exist; however, because of the complexities involved, only maximization of dollar values will be considered in this chapter.

The use of expected values can be expanded by building tables that show the probability of given events and what would happen to various investments if the events actually occurred. As an example, assume that the economist for the investment department has projected three different business assumptions for the next year. Because no additional information is available concerning possible alternatives for the economy, the investment department head chooses to assume that these three events completely exhaust the possibilities for the environment in which the various companies his department analyzes will operate in the near future. Quite naturally, he believes that the price appreciation of most of the various companies covered by the department will depend upon which particular economy actually happens to occur. In addition, he knows that his staff would be much more capable of correctly predicting price appreciation if they were certain of the economic conditions in which the companies were operating.

The preceding analysis implies that the department head can obtain reasonably accurate estimates of price appreciation given the economy (the conditional price appreciation) and also that these estimated returns will vary substantially from one potential "economy" to some alternative potential "economy." As a result of these considerations, he decides to ask each analyst to submit the expected value of each company's price appreciation for each possible economy. After the estimates are returned, the following table (Table 5–4) is presented to him.

Table 5–4: Estimated conditional capital appreciation

	Company				
	A	*B*	*C*	*D*	*E*
Economy I	11%	14%	8%	16%	6%
Economy II	10	12	7	12	6
Economy III	9	6	7	4	5

Because the staff is in this particular case familiar with the theory of probability, each of these numbers is the probabilistically weighted "spread" of possible returns in the company *given* one particular level of economic activity, that is, the 11% entry for Company A in Economy I was derived in the same way that the $81 expected value was derived in Table 5–3. For example, an analyst may believe that stock A in Economy I has a 0.25 probability of rising 14%, a 0.50 probability of 12%, and a 0.25 probability of 6%:

$$(0.25)(14\%) + (0.50)(12\%) + (0.25)(6\%) = 11\%.$$

Given the data in Table 5–3, the department manager then decides to "merge" the three economies together to form a single expected value for each of the stocks being considered. In order to do this, he assigns a probability to each of the economies and then weights the returns for each of the stocks by these probabilities, as in Table 5–5.

Table 5–5: Calculation of expected values from conditional values

	Prob-ability	Company				
		A	*B*	*C*	*D*	*E*
Economy I	0.3	11%	14%	8%	16%	6%
Economy II	0.5	10	12	7	12	6
Economy III	0.2	9	6	7	4	5
Expected value		10.1%	11.4%	7.3%	11.6%	5.8%

At this point, a single expected value has been obtained for each of the stocks. The 10.1% expected return in Company A is obtained by weighting the three possible returns for the company by the three probabilities for the economies. The particular calculations in this case would be:

$$(0.3)(11) + (0.5)(10) + (0.2)(9) = 10.1\%$$

Using Table 5–5, commonly called a payoff table, the manager would direct the purchase of Company D, and he might possibly use Company B as an alternative purchase if circumstances required it. This action is called for because Company D has the highest expected value at 11.6% while Company B is a close second at 11.4%. It is important to point out several facts about this table. First, the probability weights given to the economies obviously had an influence on the expected value of the securities. Second, the sum of the probabilities assigned to the economies was 1.00 because it was absolutely certain that one of the three economies would occur (given the assumption of the department head). Third, each of the rates of return estimated by the analysts was derived by the use of a probability weighting of the various possible performances of each of the issues, given the particular economy in the estimate.

Suppose that the department head decided that the economy next year was somewhat less promising than his initial probability weightings indicated. He could still use the three potential economies developed by the department's economist, but he would want to change the probabilities assigned to these three conditions. As a result, he may profitably set up another payoff table, such as Table 5–6, of the same stocks using different probabilities.

Table 5–6: Revision of expected values

		Company				
	Probability	*A*	*B*	*C*	*D*	*E*
Economy I	0.1	11%	14%	8%	16%	6%
Economy II	0.6	10	12	7	12	6
Economy III	0.3	9	6	7	4	5
Expected value		9.8%	10.4%	7.1%	10.0%	5.7%

Now Company B is the most attractive, because of its more defensive price characteristics. This result follows solely from the change in weightings, for the conditional returns of the various stocks (the returns *given* a specific economy), have not changed. What has happened is that the less promising economy has received a larger weight, and as a result the returns of the stocks in an adverse environment have become more important in determining the final expected value of the stock. Because Company B is more attractive than Company D in an adverse environment and this type of economy has become more important in determining the stock's expected return, Company B quite naturally has become more attractive. If the economic climate continued to worsen and the department head decided to assign the probabilities 0.0, 0.6, and 0.4, Table 5–7 indicates the relative attractiveness of the companies.

Table 5–7: Revision of expected values

		Company				
	Probability	*A*	*B*	*C*	*D*	*E*
Economy I	0.0	11%	14%	8%	16%	6%
Economy II	0.6	10	12	7	12	6
Economy III	0.4	9	6	7	4	5
Expected value		9.6%	9.6%	7.0%	8.8%	5.6%

Companies A and B now tie with an expected return of 9.6% per year. Company D has now dropped to an estimated 8.8%. As can be seen, the application of expected value and payoff tables can portray the impact of changing expectations on the relative attractiveness of alternative investments.

STRATEGIES

The use of expected monetary value as a criterion for business decision is only one of a number of possible strategies. A potential investor may, for example, decide to use an alternative strategy causing him to invest in that stock providing the largest possible gain under some possible condition. For example, in Table 5–5 the payoff table shows that stock D given Economy I has an expected profit of 16%. Because this possible profit is the largest that can be obtained from any investment being considered, this strategy (called "maximax") would direct the purchase of stock D. The problem with this approach is that it does not consider the probability of the various economic developments. It focusses on the largest *possibility* without regard to its *probability*. If the probabilities of various economic developments changed, as shown in Table 5–6, the maximaxer or "crapshooter" would still purchase stock D because of its possible 16% return even though Economy I (and hence the 16% return) is highly improbable.

If the alternative approach of using the expected monetary value of an investment in each of the stocks is applied, this cavalier approach to investment is avoided because the behavior of the stocks under all expected conditions is given the proper consideration (the proper weight). On the other hand, the maximax strategy, if carried to its extreme, will cause the investor to opt for the largest possible value under conditions where the probability of that value occurring is so minute as to be virtually zero, as found in Table 5–7. In this case, the "crapshooter" would still purchase stock D even though the 16% figure is for all practical purposes irrelevant to any investment decision. In fact, he would still purchase stock D (given some minute probability of Economy I) even if the expected returns under Economies II and III for this stock were zero instead of the actual 12% and 4%.

A more reasonable approach toward investment is the "minimax" style. This investor minimizes his maximum loss (or in a bull market maximizes his minimum gain), which means that the minimaxer will choose that particular stock that will perform best given the worst possible development that could occur. Examining Table 5–5, the worst returns that could be produced by each of the stocks are 9%, 6%, 7%, 4%, and 5%, respectively. The minimaxer would choose stock A in order to insure a 9% return regardless of what economy was encountered. This strategy has some intuitive appeal, for it is the most conservative stance that can be taken.

In order to understand the problem in the minimax strategy, it is necessary to examine the minimaxer's choice when the probabilities are changed, as in Table 5–6. In this payoff table, the minimaxer will still choose the stock having the maximum performance under the most adverse conditions and will continue to purchase stock A. This choice will always be the case regardless of the probabilities, because (*given* the economies) the conditional value for the stock does not change when the probabilities of the various economies change. Therefore, the minimaxer completely disregards the probabilities for the various economies. As a result, he would make his selection on the basis of the performance of companies in the most adverse economy regardless of the probability of that economy actually occurring. This procedure appears to be carrying safety to an extreme, because it disregards a great deal of the information available for making business decisions. It disregards the probabilities of the various economies despite the fact that information concerning their relative importance is available.

EXPECTED OPPORTUNITY LOSS

Another strategy that will always produce the same results as the expected monetary value, but is more subtle and provides more value in the more complicated problems of decision theory, is the minimization of the expected opportunity loss. In order to understand this concept, examine Table 5-8, which is the same as Table 5-6 with one minor modification. The value of the stock producing the best conditional return in each economy is boxed. This stock would be purchased if the economy presented in the row were known with absolute certainty to be the actual operating environment for the companies during the coming year. In this particular case, the "best" purchase in each of the three economies in Table 5-8 is different.

Table 5-8: Revision of expected values

		Company				
	Probability	*A*	*B*	*C*	*D*	*E*
Economy I	0.1	11%	14%	8%	[16%]	6%
Economy II	0.6	10	[12]	7	[12]	6
Economy III	0.3	[9]	6	7	4	5
Expected value		9.8%	10.4%	7.1%	10.0%	5.7%

These are the stocks that would be purchased if uncertainty were not present, that is, if one or the other of the economies were known with certainty. Naturally, the presence of uncertainty in the first place required the use of probabilities and the calculation of expected value. Using the Table 5-8, however, we can move one step further in the analysis of the influence of uncertainty by showing the *loss in return* the investor would suffer by choosing the incorrect company *given the occurrence* of the economy. For example, if Economy I does in fact occur and Company A were chosen for investment, the investor will receive only 11% instead of the 16% return that could have been obtained by selecting the best stock given Economy I. Therefore, the choice of Company A would have resulted in a 5% opportunity loss, that is, a 5% lower rate of return than would have been possible if the economy had been known with certainty. If Company B had been chosen and Economy I actually occurred, a 14% rate of return would have been achieved instead of the optimum 16% for Company D. Therefore, a 2% opportunity loss would have been suffered because it was not known with certainty that Economy I would occur. Examining Economy II, the purchase of Company A would produce a 10% return, 2% below the 12% optimum return achieved by Companies B and D. Naturally, if Company B had actually been chosen, opportunity loss would be zero. In Economy III, the purchase of Company D would have produced a 4% return, 5% less than the optimum 9% return achieved by Company A. The fact that the occurrence of Economy III was not known with certainty produced an opportunity loss of 5% given the purchase of Company D. The opportunity losses from each of the investments in these five companies can be placed in a table such as Table 5–9.

Table 5–9: Conditional opportunity loss

	Company				
	A	*B*	*C*	*D*	*E*
Economy I	5%	2%	8%	0%	10%
Economy II	2	0	5	0	6
Economy III	0	3	2	5	4

As can be seen, this table indicates the *conditional* opportunity losses, for the entries are the losses that will be incurred *given* the actual occurrence of one or the other of the various economies. Further analysis is unfortunately impossible unless these conditional opportunity losses are "merged" into a single opportunity loss figure for each of the companies. After all, the objective is to select that company that has a minimum opportunity loss, which would be impossible unless each company were represented by only one number.

Up to this point, the analysis has not considered the problem of uncertainty at all. Each entry in the table is the correct entry for the company given that the economy actually occurs. But each of the economies will occur only with some given degree of probability. As a result, the *actual* opportunity loss resulting from an investment in any of these stocks cannot be discovered. Only the *expected* opportunity loss (EOL) can be computed. In order to calculate EOL, each of the conditional opportunity losses is weighted by its probability and the results are then totaled. This calculation then gives the investment analyst the "best bet" concerning the opportunity loss involved in the purchase of any of the companies. These calculations (using the probabilities that were used in Table 5–5) are shown in Table 5–10.

Table 5–10: Expected opportunity loss

		Company				
	Probability	*A*	*B*	*C*	*D*	*E*
Economy I	0.3	5%	2%	8%	0%	10%
Economy II	0.5	2	0	5	0	6
Economy III	0.2	0	3	2	5	4
EOL		2.5%	1.2%	5.3%	1.0%	6.8%

The company having the lowest expected opportunity loss is Company D, showing that the use of EOL produces the same decision as the use of expected monetary value in Table 5–5.

Table 5–11 calculates EOL using the probabilities in Table 5–6.

Table 5–11: Revised expected opportunity loss

		Company				
	Probability	*A*	*B*	*C*	*D*	*E*
Economy I	0.1	5%	2%	8%	0%	10%
Economy II	0.6	2	0	5	0	6
Economy III	0.3	0	3	2	5	4
EOL		1.7%	1.1%	4.4%	1.5%	5.8%

The minimum EOL is now that of Company B, corresponding to the selection of Company B that was made by the use of expected monetary value with the same probabilities.

As can be seen from the last two tables, the expected opportunity loss (EOL) is not the *actual* opportunity loss that will be incurred from the investment but rather the analyst's *expectation* of the amount of opportunity loss he will suffer. The EOL, then, is the "best bet," in an uncertain world, of the amount of opportunity loss that will be suffered. But because opportunity loss is by definition the amount by which the actual selection will be inferior to the *optimum* investment because of uncertainty, opportunity loss is a calculation of the *cost of uncertainty*. Therefore, the *expected* opportunity loss is the "best bet" that can be made concerning what this cost of uncertainty actually will be. It is, in other words, the optimum *estimate* of the cost of uncertainty.

As has been shown, the investment that minimizes the estimate of the cost of uncertainty is also the investment that maximizes the expected monetary value (EMV) of the investment. As has also been shown, the EOL is sensitive to changes in the probabilities of the various economies. This completely identical performance of EOL and EMV at first glance makes the use of opportunity losses appear to be redundant. Such is not the case, however, because the EOL not only provides the optimum investment decision, but also provides the "price" the investor is paying as a result of the presence of uncertainty. In other words, if the analyst could eliminate the uncertainty concerning the economies, he could reasonably expect to gain a larger return on his investment, and the amount he would expect to gain is precisely the amount of the expected opportunity loss.

Even though the analyst has already minimized the effect of uncertainty by choosing the lowest expected opportunity loss, some cost of uncertainty nevertheless remains and is precisely measured by the EOL. If this uncertainty could be eliminated, the expected value of the investment would increase by a known amount (by the EOL). Certainly, the investment manager would be willing to pay anything up to this amount in order to receive perfect information concerning the economies because he would be reimbursed by his additional return on investment. Therefore, the minimum expected opportunity loss (the expected opportunity loss of the "best" security) is equal to the expected value of perfect information (EVPI). In the example, perfect information concerning the economy for the coming year would have a value to the investor equal to 1.0% of his investment if he assumed the probabilities shown in Table 5-10 because the EOL of the best investment in this situation is 1.0%.

Unfortunately, it is not often possible to find sources of perfect information, but the manager could reasonably spend a portion of the money available for *perfect* information in order to buy *imperfect* information: information that is helpful but is not a complete solution to the decision problem. Naturally, he would be willing to spend less money for imperfect advice than for perfect information, and the precise amount he would spend would depend upon the degree of imperfection as well as the amount of money available from the expected opportunity loss. A large proportion of the more advanced uses of decision theory is devoted to the problem of determining the precise amount of money that should be used to purchase various imperfect pieces of information. Although this subject is beyond the scope of this book, the applicability of the problem to the field of investments is obvious, for a number of sources of imperfect information are available. The particular application discussed here does, however, show that the value of information stems from both economic and analytic considerations.

AN APPLICATION OF CONTINUOUS PROBABILITIES

The discussion of probabilities up to this point has been restricted to situations where only a finite number of alternative developments could occur. The market would be either good, neutral, or bad. The economy would be either Economy I, Economy II, or Economy III. The performance of the stock would be either good, neutral, or poor. Unfortunately, many realistic situations exist where an infinite number of alternative results could occur. For example, if the expected return on a stock is 15% with a standard deviation of 10%, the actual return can be expected to fall between 5% and 25% roughly two-thirds of the time. But an infinite number of values are possible for the actual return next year. In this situation, the return on the stock is called a random variable. The analyst needs a different approach to treat this type of problem.

Consider one of the simplest cases of a random variable, where any value between two numbers may occur, and the likelihood that any particular number within this range will occur is equal for all such numbers. This situation is called a rectangular distribution and can be graphed as Figure 5–3, showing that any number between one and three is equally probable and that no other number may occur.

Figure 5–3

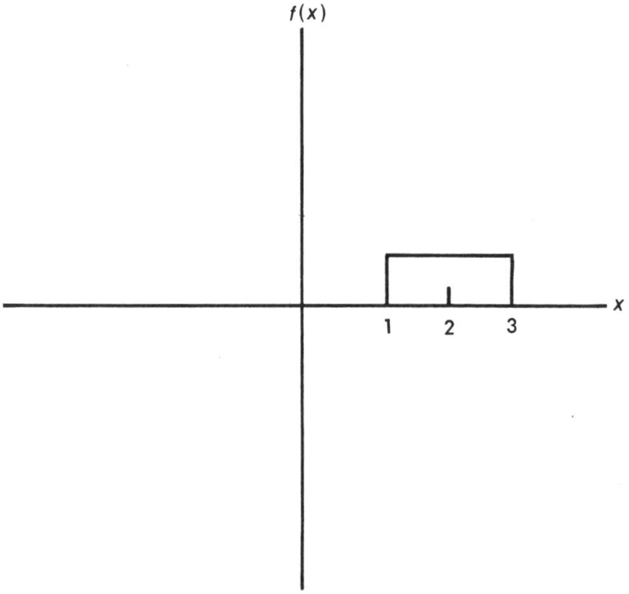

Probabilities are defined to be *desired* events divided by all *possible* events. In cases where the number of possible events could be counted, this definition is simple enough. But when the possible events include *all* numbers between one and three, a simple enumeration of events becomes impossible because there are an infinite number of such events. Therefore the set of events must be partitioned into the desired versus the undesirable outcomes while weighting each of the events by their likelihood of occurrence. The distribution (rectangular, in this case) performs this weighting. Partitioning the weighted events is accomplished by finding the area under the distribution that falls in desired regions of x and then dividing the result by all possible events, which in this case is the entire area under the distribution.

Assume for a moment that the top of the rectangular "box" is one unit high (its vertical coordinate is "one"). How can the probability that the random variable will assume a value greater than zero be calculated? It obviously does not need to be calculated because if all possible values must fall between one and three the probability of a value greater than zero must be 1.00 (must be 100% probable). Nevertheless, it is useful in mathematics to start with the very simple and then generalize to the realistic problem. How could the probability that x will be greater than zero be found *analytically*?

The rules for probability when the number of events cannot be counted indicate that the area under the curve in desired regions of x must be found and then divided by the total area under the curve. The desired region for x in this case is $x > 0$. The area of the rectangle in this region is two units of length times one unit of height, or two. The total area under the distribution is two. Dividing the former by the latter produces $2 \div 2 = 1.00$ as the probability that x will be greater than zero.

Generalizing to a more realistic case, what is the probability that x will be greater than 2.5? The area under the distribution in the desired region is 0.5 times 1.0, or 0.5. The total area is 2.0. The probability is therefore $0.5 \div 2.0 = 0.25$. Note that the height of the distribution does not affect the probabilities. If, for example, the rectangle were two units high, the desired area would become 0.5 times 2.0 = 1.0 and the total area would become 2.0 times 2.0 = 4.0. The probability would therefore be $1.0 \div 4.0 = 0.25$, as was just calculated using a height of one.

THE NORMAL DISTRIBUTION

The rectangular distribution is useful to introduce some of the concepts of probability theory, but the normal distribution is much more useful in practical applications. All of the concepts just learned can be transferred to this new distribution, although the shape of the curve is different. The normal curve for the stock's return discussed at the beginning of this section is shown in Figure 5-4.

Figure 5-4

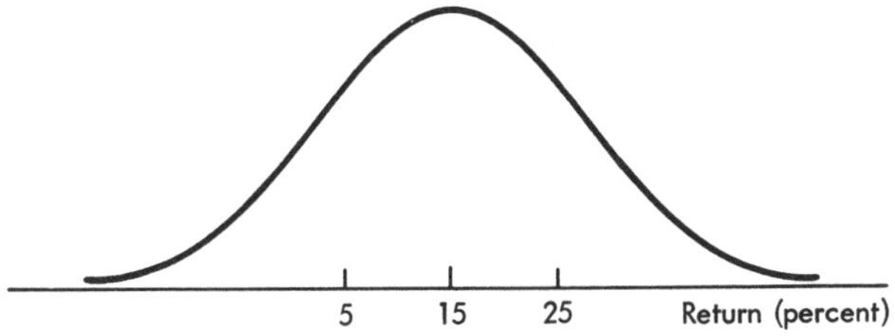

The peak of the curve is at the mean of the random variable being analyzed (15% in the example). The curve is bell-shaped and starts to flatten out sharply on each side when it gets one standard deviation away from the mean. In this example, this flattening occurs at 5% and at 25%. The vertical axis of the curve is normally not shown because (just as in the case of the rectangular distribution) it is not important.

The normal curve is used in the same way as the rectangular distribution. In the example, the probability of, say, a return greater than 30% can be computed by dividing the area under the curve to the right of 30% by the total area under the curve.

The simplest way to explain the use of the normal curve in deriving probabilities is to work through a simple but reasonably practical example. Assume that the stock in the earlier example and a bond that will produce a certain return of 10% are being compared as investment alternatives. The stock has a higher expected return, because its mean return is 15% compared to the bond's 10%. Unfortunately, this stock also has a higher risk, with a standard deviation of 10% compared to the bond's (hypothetical) standard deviation of 0%. Deadlocks in discussions of this kind of risk-return tradeoff can sometimes be avoided by asking for the probability that the stock will outperform the bond. This probability can be computed as the area under the curve that is greater than 10% divided by the total area under the curve, as depicted in Figure 5–5.

Figure 5–5

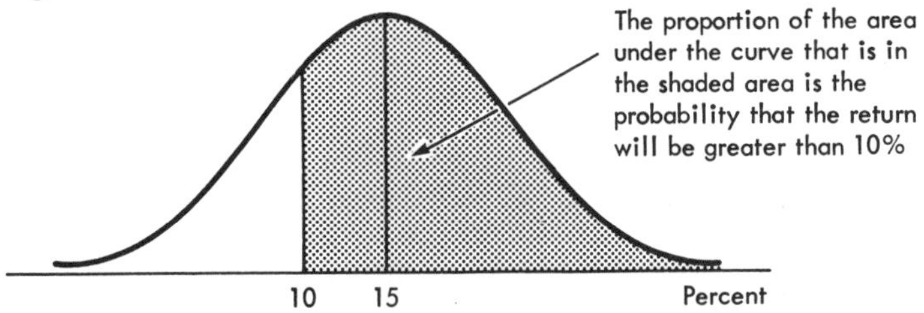

This area can be found by looking up the probability in a table of normal probabilities. However, these tables are expressed in terms of probabilities and σ, so that any particular application must be converted to units of standard deviation before the table can be used. In this example, 10% is 0.5 standard deviation away from the mean because it is 5 percentage points from the 15% mean and σ is 10 percentage points. The desired probability is therefore found to be 0.3085 in a normal probability table under $\sigma = 0.5$. The table has partitioned the normal curve into two sections (shaded and unshaded, in effect) and has indicated that the *smaller* of those two sections is 0.3085, which in the example, is the probability that the return is *less* than 10%. The probability that the return will be greater than 10% is therefore 1 − 0.3085 = 0.6915.

Another practical use of the normal distribution involves computing from a known probability to an unknown mean. For example, assume that the portfolio manager has estimated that it is 80% probable that the stock market will outperform the assumed 12% total return next year from an investment in bonds. Assume further that empirical studies of the market have shown its standard deviation to be 10%. What return on the market must the portfolio manager regard as most likely if his reasoning is consistent with this standard deviation? Because the most likely return in a normal distribution is the mean return, the problem (shown graphically in Figure 5-6) is to find the mean.

Figure 5-6

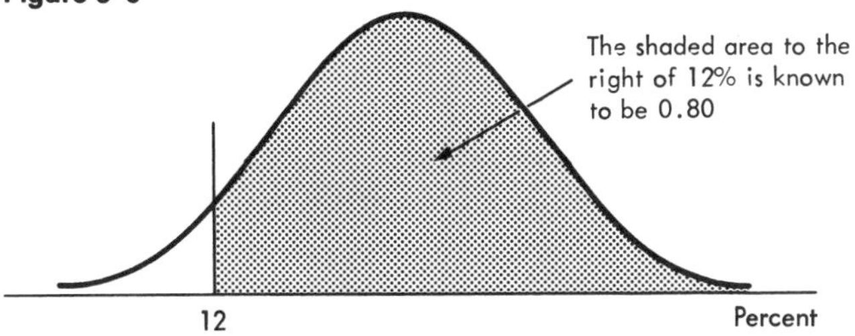

Looking in the table of normal probabilities for the probability level of 0.80, we find no entry this high. The other side of the distribution is 0.20, the probability of achieving less than 12%. This entry is found where $\sigma = 0.84$. The 12% value is therefore 0.84σ from the mean. Multiplying 0.84 times σ ($\sigma = 10\%$) gives 8.4%. The mean is therefore 8.4 percentage points greater than 12% and must equal 20.4%. As a result, the portfolio manager must believe that the most likely return on the market is 20.4% if he is 80% confident that the market will outperform the 12% anticipated bond result.

Those applications certainly do not exhaust the ways that the normal distribution can be useful to the professional. Care must be taken, however, to avoid using these techniques based on a normal distribution when the problem deals with data that do not have a normal distribution. In addition to the techniques described, a number of other distributions are available for use in various practical applications. Several of these are mentioned in the next chapter.

ADDITIONAL READINGS IN PROBABILITY THEORY

Feller, William. *An Introduction to Probability Theory and Its Applications, Vol. I.* New York: John Wiley & Sons, Inc., 1957.

This book is a solid mathematical treatment of the elementary aspects of probability (436 pages). The material has less immediate practical value than the following text and requires a mathematical orientation on the part of the reader. It is valuable to the reader already familiar with probability theory, however, because it clarifies the mathematical aspects of the theory. (Volume II treats the mathematical problems of continuous probability distributions and requires a much higher level of mathematical expertise than is required in actual business applications.)

Schlaifer, Robert. *Probability and Statistics for Business Decisions.* New York: McGraw-Hill Book Co., 1959.

This book is the classic text in the field of statistical decision theory (669 pages). It is readable and practical, but the level of presentation will hardly insult the reader's intelligence. Numerous examples are used and are directly related to business situations. The introduction and part one treat the nature of subjective probabilities. Part two covers the various simple probabilities. Part three uses Bayesian theory to analyze the results of samples. Part four covers the value of additional information, and part five deals with the classical approach to statistics.

Chapter 6

Hypothesis testing, or how certain are patterns in the real world?

Although financial analysis involves processing vast amounts of data, questions often arise whether samples of data taken from a universe or population are representative of the population itself. Statistical techniques have been devised to answer these questions that involve testing the null hypothesis, that is, determining with what level of confidence the opposite of what you are trying to prove can be rejected. Parametric tests deal with data drawn from a population with known characteristics, which usually means that they are normally distributed. Nonparametric tests deal with data not normally distributed. Two parametric tests are the *t* test, which measures whether the difference between the arithmetic means of two samples is significant and whether they are representative of the population, and the *F* test, which answers questions concerning the equality of variances. The principal nonparametric test is the Chi Square test, which tests data to see whether they match an already established idea of what they should look like. Illustrations are given for applications of these tests in financial analysis.

SCIENTIFIC METHOD AND STATISTICAL TESTING

The *method* of statistics is quite often overlooked or at least underemphasized when quantitative techniques are first applied to a new field. This statement is probably no less true of the quantitative applications in investments than of any other field. In the tentative, testing phase of quantitative applications, the use of tools without a systematic technique quite often leads to a piecemeal approach to problems and to results of limited value. In quantitative analysis, just as surely as in investment or economic analysis, methodology tends to predetermine the answer, because the line of attack chosen by the analyst can reasonably be expected to provide the most significant step toward the development of the particular answer to be obtained.

The body of knowledge now referred to as classical statistics originally developed as a device by which scientific theories or tentative hypotheses about the nature of reality could be subjected to empirical testing. The basic pattern of the scientific method is procedural in nature, going from basic observation of data to the formation of a hypothesis and then checking that hypothesis against additional observations in the world of experience. The strength of the technique lies in the impossibility of theorizing in contradiction to available facts or about unobservable matters, i.e., matters not subject to empirical verification. Agreement with observed reality is the fundamental criterion of science, and the perpetual modification of tentative theories therefore lies at the heart of the scientific method. The value of the results achieved, however, depends upon two factors:

1. The power of the new creative hypothesis.
2. The ability of the analyst to obtain data to be used for verification.

Both the power and the limitation of statistics lie in this latter area, for the methods of statistical theory are highly useful tools for the *verification* of hypotheses but can never jump beyond this application into the *formation* of theory.

With the techniques provided by the efforts of previous thinkers, the analyst is able to determine the validity of an analysis of the great masses of available data. But, strictly speaking, he is not able to analyze the data directly because he must have some plan or concept in mind in order to direct his efforts. Without the formation of a coherent, useful, and original theory or hypothesis, statistics could not provide any information other than the "boiled-down" results of numerous observations. This "summary presentation" is not statistics at all, but rather arithmetic on a massive scale.

Classical statistics *begins* with a scientific hypothesis and then attempts either to verify or to refute it. Unfortunately, however, it is impossible in a scientific sense ever to prove anything to be absolutely correct. As a result, statistical technique is forced into the position of making probability statements about the possibility of being correct. Actually, the probability statements of classical hypothesis testing take the opposite of the hypothesis or theory and attempt to show that it is very likely to be wrong. If, for example, a theory says that the P/E ratio of a stock is higher than average if the growth in the stock's earnings is above average, statistics would reverse this theory and deal with the following statement: "It is not true that a stock's P/E is higher if its earnings growth is higher." An attempt is then made to reject this statement. This "reverse methodology" is called the attempt to reject the *null hypothesis* (H_0) and can never be totally successful simply because it is impossible to observe every instance pertaining to a universal "law." It is considered satisfactory if the null hypothesis (H_0) can be rejected with some confidence that the rejection will not later prove to have been in error. The "level of confidence" as a result has become a dominant statistical theme and quite naturally has been expressed in terms of probabilities. The hypothesis is tested by actually observing a number of examples of the population and then using statistical inference to move from statements about the examples to statements about the population in general.

Classical statistics, then, is a methodology that formally states a currently accepted theory concerning the nature of the world and then attempts to prove that the scientific evidence makes it highly improbable that the theory is true. This approach is really much less mysterious than first appearances would indicate. After all, if an analyst were to argue that the commonly accepted notion that "high-multiple stocks outperform low multiple stocks" was an incorrect theory, he would probably state the theory and then show facts tending to refute it. This approach would certainly be more direct than the alternative of stating some opposing view and then trying to establish the new theory without refuting the currently established thinking on the subject. Classical statistics simply states the current hypothesis and attempts to refute it. Therefore, classical statistics is by nature only a "bubble burster," a destroyer of illusions. The theory to be tested (and possibly rejected) is the null hypothesis, and the level of confidence is the desired accuracy in rejecting the null hypothesis. For example, if a 95% level of confidence is chosen, 5% of the null hypotheses rejected will, in fact, be true. This possibility of error cannot be eliminated because a possibility always exists that the particular data selected were misleading. The advantage to statistics is that such errors can be controlled and kept within acceptable limits. Frequently used levels are 95% and 99%, although some scientific applications require substantially higher certainty.

Once a student moves beyond the most basic aspects of statistical analysis, he discovers that the value of the use of statistics is not determined by the models evaluating the data, but rather by the usefulness of the hypotheses put forward by the analyst. Formal statistics is not a decisive technique when used simply to summarize data or "pulverize" information in a wild search for some hidden meaning. Hypothesis testing when properly used clearly specifies the theory to be tested and the test procedure, providing a clear and decisive acceptance or rejection. The value of an acceptance or rejection of a theory is completely dependent upon the value of the theory being tested. Statistics cannot provide theories for testing (only a valuable insight by an analyst can do that), but statistics can be of great value in relieving the burden of verification from the analyst and so allowing more time for the formation of concepts that may prove useful in investment operations.

The subject of hypothesis testing is divided into two broad areas of application—parametric tests and nonparametric tests. The parametric tests assume that the data being tested are drawn from some population having known characteristics and usually that the population is normally distributed. The nonparametric tests do not assume normality and as a result can be applied to a broader number of practical situations. In fact, a number of these tests can be applied when the data are only ranked and have no numerical value at all.

The advantage of the nonparametric tests is that they require fewer favorable characteristics in the problem being analyzed. Unfortunately, actual problems (especially in the investment field) have a pronounced tendency to defy formulation in classical terms. Data frequently are not normally distributed, often are only a ranking of preferences, and sometimes consist only of the classifications "good" and "bad," or "buy" and "sell." In such cases, the assumptions of the parametric tests obviously are not met, which means that these models cannot be used because they are not relevant to the problem at hand. The only recourse at that point is a nonparametric test. If the data *do* fit a parametric model, then *this* approach should be used, because the parametric tests (when their assumptions are met) produce less chance of an error in classifying the null hypothesis as true or false. In this chapter, only two of the parametric tests will be discussed: the t test (also called "student's t") and the F test.

THE t TEST

The t test is applied in a number of problems, the most important of which deals with finding a probability concerning the means of statistical populations. For example, one possible t test could be applied to the following problem. A portfolio manager receives an account from a new client and is interested in testing to see if the ability of the former manager in handling equity investment is significantly superior to a random selection of stocks. Because this particular account is invested 100% in equities, it presents a unique opportunity to "sample" the other manager's performance. He finds the project to be worthwhile and proceeds by building a "control" account that can be used to show the results of completely random performance. This step can be done by taking a random sample (say, by using random number tables until the desired number of issues has been selected) of stocks of investment quality, because these stocks represent the population from which the previous manager was making his decisions. All of the stocks in the actual account being analyzed have about the same total market value, so that the manager has two samples of data: x_1 (the account, a sample of the previous manager's performance) and x_2 (the random sample).

The random sample of stocks provides information concerning the performance of investments that were not under any investment management. The account provides information concerning the performance of investments under a previous manager's control. If it can be shown that these two groups of data are essentially identical, then it follows that the control of the previous manager was equivalent (in terms of performance) to having no investment management at all.

Two problems immediately present themselves in this study. First, because the data in the samples are unwieldy, it would be useful to find a representative number typical of each set of stocks. The average, or arithmetic mean, can be used for this purpose. The manager therefore is interested in whether the average results of the account's stocks equal the average results of the random sample.

If we agree to call the average performance of the prior manager μ_1 (mu) and the average for all stocks μ_2, we can state mathematically that he is interested in whether $\mu_1 = \mu_2$. Note that μ_1 and μ_2 are not the sample averages. This point is subtle but important: μ_1 is not the average performance of the stocks in the account, but refers to the average performance of the first manager of the account. The account merely provides one sample of this manager's performance, and its average may be different from the true average performance capability of the manager. μ_1 is the *true population average* that the sample average $\bar{x}_1$ is estimating. μ_2 is the true population average estimated by $\bar{x}_2$, where $\bar{x}_2$ is the average of the random sample of stocks.

Another problem is that, because the data are only samples, it is impossible ever to prove *absolutely* either equal or unequal performance. It is only possible to prove results in terms of some level of confidence, which always leaves some small probability of an incorrect decision. In this particular problem, the null hypothesis is $\mu_1 = \mu_2$ and the portfolio manager decides that a 95% confidence level is sufficient. If the other manager performs better than the random sample and also if he can reject the null hypothesis at the 0.95 confidence level (indicating that the difference in performance is a *significant* difference), then he will consider the other manager to have established a performance better than random. He will, however, still have a 5% chance of this conclusion being wrong due to the possibility that the data may not represent the true performance picture. The next problem is that of finding a method by which the hypothesis that $\mu_1 = \mu_2$ can be subjected to a precise testing procedure even though the subject matter is probabilistic in nature.

In this problem, the equality of the means of two samples is being tested, which is an ideal use for the t test. Because the portfolio manager is assuming in his null hypothesis that the two samples are being drawn from the same population, he assumes that the variances of the two samples are approximately equal. In addition, it can be shown that the means of reasonably large samples drawn from any population are normally distributed. The assumptions of the t test are therefore at least closely approximated, and the next problem is the actual calculation of the t statistic.

Let:

n_1 = the number of items in sample one (the account)
n_2 = the number of items in sample two (the random sample)
$\bar{x}_1$ = the mean of the values in sample one
$\bar{x}_2$ = the mean of the values in sample two
s_1^2 = the variance of the values in sample one
s_2^2 = the variance of the values in sample two.

Then the t statistic can be found by the following formula:

$$t = \frac{\bar{x}_1 - \bar{x}_2}{\sigma_{\Delta\bar{x}}}.$$

The numerator is simply the difference between the means of the two samples. The denominator is an estimate of the amount by which the two means might be expected to differ. It is the standard error of the numerator. For our purposes, it is possible simply to regard it as a number calculated by the following formula:

$$\hat{\sigma}_{\Delta\bar{x}} = \hat{\sigma}\sqrt{\frac{n_1 + n_2}{n_1 n_2}}.$$

where $\hat{\sigma}$ is an estimate of the variation in the performance of stocks and is determined by the formula:

$$\hat{\sigma} = \sqrt{\frac{n_1 s_1^2 + n_2 s_2^2}{n_1 + n_2 - 2}}.$$

In actual calculation of the value of t, the analyst would first compute $\hat{\sigma}$, which would provide an estimate of the variability of the performance of stocks—the standard deviation of the "stock universe" from which the data on performance were selected. Next, the value of $\hat{\sigma}_{\Delta\bar{x}}$ could be found, which is a measure of how great a difference between the two means could be expected simply on the basis of chance variation. It is the standard deviation of the possible values of $\bar{x}_1 - \bar{x}_2$. In other words, the manager would not expect $\bar{x}_1$ to equal $\bar{x}_2$ exactly because the data simply are not that perfect an indicator of performance. He would, however, expect $\bar{x}_1 - \bar{x}_2$ to be reasonably close to zero if no real difference exists in the performance of the other manager and the performance of a random sample. The statistic $\hat{\sigma}_{\Delta\bar{x}}$ is a precise measure of how great a difference between $\bar{x}_1$ and $\bar{x}_2$ might be expected. The difference $\bar{x}_1 - \bar{x}_2$ would be expected to be zero give or take $\hat{\sigma}_{\Delta\bar{x}}$ about two-thirds of the time if the assumption of equal performance is correct. The manager can then compute t as $(\bar{x}_1 - \bar{x}_2)/\hat{\sigma}_{\Delta\bar{x}}$, which is the amount by which the two samples actually differ divided by the amount by which they would be expected to differ if there is no essential difference in performance characteristics. The value of t is the difference in means divided by the "range" of difference that we would expect to result from our having taken random samples. If t equaled 0.5, then the difference would only be one-half of what might be expected simply on the basis of chance variations in the data. The difference in this case would hardly be significant. If t equalled 4, however, the difference in performance was four times the amount that might reasonably be attributed to chance, and the difference might very well be significant.

As an example of the calculation of t, working through the example that has been used may be helpful. Assume the following results from the samples:

Other manager		*Random sample*	
n_1	12	n_2	15
$\bar{x}_1$	15%	$\bar{x}_2$	10%
s_1	3%	s_2	2%

Note that n_1 is the number of stocks, $\bar{x}_1$ is the average performance, and s_1 is the standard deviation of the performance of the stocks under control of the other manager. The same letters with the subscript "2" refer to the comparable data for the random group of stocks. Also, note that the standard deviations s_1 and s_2 are much lower than an experienced analyst would expect from any set of stocks; they are set at an unrealistically low level for purposes of this example. Larger standard deviations make it much more difficult to establish a significant difference in performances.

Using these initial data, it is possible to calculate $\hat{\sigma}$, the estimated standard deviation in the performance of stocks in general:

$$\hat{\sigma} = \sqrt{\frac{n_1 s_1^2 + n_2 s_2^2}{n_1 + n_2 - 2}} = \sqrt{\frac{12 \cdot 3^2 + 15 \cdot 2^2}{12 + 15 - 2}} = 2.59.$$

Next, $\hat{\sigma}_{\Delta\bar{x}}$ can be computed:

$$\hat{\sigma}_{\Delta\bar{x}} = \hat{\sigma} \sqrt{\frac{n_1 + n_2}{n_1 n_2}} = 2.59 \sqrt{\frac{12 + 15}{12 \cdot 15}} = 1.00.$$

The value of t can now be found as the difference between the two means divided by the expected difference stemming from the random nature of the data:

$$t = \frac{\bar{x}_1 - \bar{x}_2}{\hat{\sigma}_{\Delta \bar{x}}} = \frac{15 - 10}{1.00} = 5.00.$$

The result of this rather complex set of calculations is a single number—the value of t in this particular test. At this point the value of t is still of no use to the portfolio manager whatsoever. He was attempting to find the actual probability of being in error if he rejected the null hypothesis. But the probabilities of error have already been worked out and stored in tables for any particular value of t. As a result, once t has been found, the problem of deciding whether or not the null hypothesis can safely be rejected is solved by simply locating a number in a table. A portion of a t table is reproduced in Table 6–1.

Table 6–1

	Risk		
Degrees of freedom	*0.10*	*0.05*	*0.01*
1	6.314	12.706	63.657
5	2.015	2.571	4.032
10	1.812	2.228	3.169
20	1.725	2.086	2.845
25	1.708	2.060	2.787

A number of important points can be drawn from this table. First, all of the entries in the table are values of t, and if the t that the manager calculated is *larger* (disregarding the sign) than the value in the table, the null hypothesis can be rejected. But which table value should be used? This value depends upon two things: (1) the level of risk the analyst is willing to accept (0.05 in the example, i.e., he wished to be 95% certain); (2) the degrees of freedom involved in the particular test being made.

"Degrees of freedom" is a rather complicated topic but essentially refers to the number of observations involved in the data used in the test. If more observations are used in the sample, the "value" of the results is greater, and the confidence in the results can naturally be increased. The phrase "degrees of freedom" is used instead of "number of observations" because it frequently happens that the mathematicians will destroy the value of one or more observations when they set up the formulas being used in the statistical test. The phrase "degrees of freedom" refers to the number of observations minus the number of the observations lost by using any particular formula. In the case of our example, the d.f. equals $n_1 + n_2 - 2$, showing that two observations were rendered useless because the formula for the two-sample t test was used in order to find the value of t, leaving the balance of the observations in the samples available for service as degrees of freedom.

This information concerning the use of the t table is sufficient to permit the final solution to the problem of the portfolio manager. In this example, the confidence level was set at 0.95, implying a 0.05 risk level. The number of stocks in the two samples was 12 and 15, so that the number of degrees of freedom $(n_1 + n_2 - 2)$ equals 25. The appropriate value of t can therefore be found in the table in the 0.05 column and the 25 d.f. row: this value for t is 2.060. Consequently, in this particular study, the value of t would be less than 2.060 95% of the time if in fact the performances were equal. Because the manager found a value for t of 5.00, the logical conclusion is that such a large value for t would not have occurred if performances were equal, and so the null hypothesis (of equal performance) is rejected. This conclusion, of course, is the same as accepting the alternative hypothesis that they are unequal. Because the computed t is greater than the table value of t, the manager can therefore reject the null hypothesis with 95% confidence.

Several additional points concerning the nature of t are useful. For example, the fact that the t table entries become smaller as more degrees of freedom are involved indicates that larger samples have more power than small ones. More observations increase the chance of success of rejecting the H_0 when it should in fact be rejected. In addition, the size of the t table entry decreases as the level of risk increases, indicating that it is easier, for example, to reject the null hypothesis if a risk of 0.10 is acceptable than if a risk of 0.05 is the maximum permitted. It is more difficult to prove the validity of a 95% confidence than it is to prove a 90% confidence.

The behavior of the *table* values of t therefore shows that larger samples will produce fewer errors than smaller samples and also that it is easier to reject an hypothesis if a greater risk of error is allowed. But the ability to reject an hypothesis (to "prove" something) depends not only upon the table value of t but also upon the calculated value. In other words, for any given degrees of freedom and confidence level, larger values of the *computed t* would make rejection easier. This statement leads to the interesting question of how the variables used in the calculation affect the value of t. As the difference between means becomes greater, t becomes larger. This observation is reasonable, because it is more likely that performances differ if our sample means show a greater difference, other things being equal. Also interesting is the fact that as the standard deviations of the performance of the stocks in the "portfolio" (s_1 and s_2) become smaller, t becomes larger, which means that the same difference between average results $(\bar{x}_1 - \bar{x}_2)$ is more significant if less chance variation exists in the populations being sampled. In the example, it would have been more difficult to prove a difference in performance had s_1 and s_2 been, say, 10%, simply because the 5% difference in means $(\bar{x}_1 - \bar{x}_2)$ would have a greater possibility of having been caused by the (now much larger) random fluctuations in the data.

Regardless of the particular application that may have caused an analyst to compute a particular *t* statistic, the same *t* table is used. The *t* table is therefore valuable in any application involving a *t* test of any kind, and our example covered only one particular application. All of the commonly used *t* tests deal with population means, but a number of variations are possible. For example, a population mean can be tested to see if it equals a specific value, two populations can be tested for equal means with an alternative hypothesis that one specified population has a higher average value, one population can be tested to see if it is greater than some specified value, etc. In spite of the diversity in applications, however, the *t* test can always be reduced to the calculation of a simple formula that can be found in any elementary statistics text. In addition, all *t* tests always use the same *t* table and are always formulated in terms of a null hypothesis that may be rejected at some stated level of confidence.

THE *F* TEST

The *F* test, like the *t* test, is parametric, for it assumes that the populations being tested are normally distributed. And just as the *t* test has many applications, so does the *F*. But while *t* tends to deal with the means of the groups being studied, the *F* tends to be concerned with the variances. The only application of the *F* test that will be considered here is concerned with the equality of variances.

In the example of the *t* test, the portfolio manager assumed that the variance of the portfolio was a good estimate of the variance in the previous account manager's buy selections *and* that this variance was equal to the variance in stock performance in general. This assumption was necessary for the *t* test to be applicable. Unfortunately, this assumption may prove to be invalid, so that the manager would be well advised to test whether the variances of the two populations may be assumed to be equal $(\sigma_1^2 = \sigma_2^2)$ before applying the *t* test. If it is established that $\sigma_1^2 \neq \sigma_2^2$ with 90% confidence, then there would only be 10 chances out of 100 that the *t* test would be valid. In this case, of course, the *t* test would have to be abandoned. Discretion being the better part of valor, the manager decides to determine the probability of

$\sigma_1^2 = \sigma_2^2$. No direct method of discovering this probability is available, so he calculates:

$$F = \frac{\text{The variance of the group of stocks having the larger variance}}{\text{The variance of the group of stocks having the smaller variance}}.$$

This value will be a single number and, of course, will be a value equal to or greater than one. But F, like t, has no direct value to the portfolio manager; he wants the probability. The probabilities associated with F have been computed and are available in tables, a section of which is reproduced in Table 6–2.

Table 6–2

Degrees of freedom in sample 2 (0.05 risk)	Degrees of freedom in sample 1 (0.05 risk)		
	1	*2*	*3*
1	161	200	216
2	18.51	19.00	19.16
3	10.13	9.55	9.28

The value of the computed F is compared to the appropriate value in the table; if it is greater than the table entry, the H_0 is rejected (which means that $\sigma_1^2 \neq \sigma_2^2$). The problem is now reduced to locating the proper value in the table. Because the manager is working at the 90% confidence level, 10% risk is acceptable. However, because he has two alternative hypotheses ($\sigma_1^2 > \sigma_2^2$ and $\sigma_1^2 < \sigma_2^2$), he has a 5.0% level of risk *per alternative* and so the 0.05 table is used. But which number in the table is to be chosen? This depends, once again, upon the concept of degrees of freedom. In this particular test, one degree of freedom is lost from each of the two groups being tested. The number of degrees of freedom (d.f.) for each group is therefore the number of observations in that group minus one. The $(\text{d.f.})_1$ locates the proper column, and the $(\text{d.f.})_2$ locates the proper row, thus isolating the single number in the table to be used for the test.

In the example of the portfolio manager's problem, $n_1 = 12$; $n_2 = 15$; $s_1 = 3$; $s_2 = 2$. Because variance is equal to the standard deviation squared, the variance of the other manager's account was $3^2 = 9$ with degrees of freedom of $12 - 1$, or 11. The variance of the "random" control sample was $2^2 = 4$ with degrees of freedom equal to $15 - 1$, or 14. Because the other manager's account had the greater variance, it is used as the numerator in the F ratio and we have

$$F = \frac{9}{4}.$$

The numerator has 11 degrees of freedom; the denominator has 14 degrees of freedom. The value of F^{11}_{14} at the 5% level is 2.56. Because the computed value for F of $9/4 = 2.25$ is not greater than the table value of 2.56, the null hypothesis cannot be rejected and the assumption that the variances are equal is not statistically invalidated. Once again, under the assumption of equal variances, the t test is valid.

CHI SQUARE

The chi square (χ^2) distribution is the leading example of the nonparametric tests. It can be used in a number of applications, only one of which will be considered here. The applications do, however, all have a common concept characteristic of χ^2; they test the data to see if they match an already established idea of the way the data *should* appear. If the test shows significant deviation from the *expected* results, then the theory that caused the analyst to expect a certain behavior in the data must be discarded. This ability of χ^2 to check theories to see if they are an adequate model of the real world makes the χ^2 test very valuable in the investment profession, where untested theories are found in abundance. This power of χ^2 as a "bubble-burster," coupled with the fact that it does not assume normality in a world unfortunately abnormal, probably makes the tests using χ^2 the most underrated simple statistical application in the world of finance.

Assume that an analyst has discovered a stock having excellent prospects and a P/E of 13. He wishes to recommend the stock in the Investment Committee meeting but knows that several members favor high-multiple stocks on the grounds that low-multiple issues offer lower prospects for strong capital appreciation. This theory, of course, does not necessarily eliminate the purchase of this one stock; it merely covers the overall approach toward stocks in general, leaving room for exceptions. Nevertheless, the analyst believes that the approach would be applied in this particular case and that the only hope for a purchase lies in discrediting the theory at least to the extent that it will allow minor exceptions (e.g. this stock). The theory would lead the committee to *expect* a certain performance from high and low multiple issues, and it is logical to see if the *actual* performances matched these expectations. The analyst knows that a $P/E < 15$ is considered low, and a $P/E > 25$ is considered high by the committee. He also knows that a compound annual rate of return $< 5\%$ is poor while $> 15\%$ is good. Examining the stocks normally analyzed by the staff, he locates the cheap and expensive issues in the past and checks their performance, placing each stock as in Table 6–3.

Table 6–3

	Good performance	*Poor performance*	*Total*
Low *P/E*	8	14	22
High *P/E*	12	13	25
Total	20	27	47

Thus far, the results aren't too convincing to anyone. The analyst was hoping for the results in Table 6–4.

Table 6–4

	Good performance	*Poor performance*	*Total*
Low *P/E*	25	0	25
High *P/E*	0	22	22
Total	25	22	47

The committee would expect a tendency toward the results in Table 6–5.

Table 6–5

	Good performance	*Poor performance*	*Total*
Low *P/E*	0	25	25
High *P/E*	22	0	22
Total	22	25	47

The fact that the pattern desired by the committee did not occur is hardly evidence that the theory is false, and the analyst is to be congratulated for not presenting this argument to the committee. Instead, he decides to test the hypothesis that no relationship at all exists between *P/E* and the performance in order to see if the two ideas were completely independent. Because he has already filled out a contingency table, he decides to use a test for independence. If the "expected" results were *independent,* it is possible to place the expectations in parentheses in Table 6–6.

Table 6–6

	Good performance	*Poor performance*	*Total*
Low *P/E*	8 (9.35)	14 (12.65)	22
High *P/E*	12 (10.65)	13 (14.35)	25
Total	20	27	47

These figures were easily derived. The 9.35 was found by first locating the "percentage" (more accurately, the proportion) of *all* of the stocks that performed well. This was 20 ÷ 47 = 0.425. In other words, 0.425 of all stocks analyzed could be expected to perform well, without regard to their *P/E* ratios. If *P/E* is assumed to be unrelated to performance, it would therefore be natural to expect 0.425 of all low *P/E* (or high *P/E*) stocks to perform well. Because there are 22 low *P/E* stocks, 0.425 of these 22 stocks would be expected to show a good performance. The arithmetic is 0.425 × 22 = 9.35. Once this number is found, the remaining values are very easy to compute because 9.35 plus one of the unknown numbers must be equal to one of the row or column totals. For example, 9.35 plus the expected number of high *P/E* good performance stocks must equal 20. Only 10.65 will satisfy this requirement. The 10.65 is merely 20 − 9.35 because the total of 9.35 and this number is already known from the table to be 20. The other two values are found by subtracting the expected value from the appropriate row total. The expected number of low *P/E*, poor performance stocks when added to the expected number of high *P/E*, good performance stocks must obviously equal the total number of low *P/E* stocks considered in the study (22). The indicated arithmetic is 22 − 9.35 = 12.65. The expected value of the high *P/E*, poor performance stock is found through the same line of reasoning, with the resulting arithmetic of 25 − 10.65 = 14.35.

Once the expected values are known, the amount by which the data deviate from the expectation can be found easily. The problem is whether the deviation is *significantly* large. No one would expect a *perfect* match even if the assumption of independence were true, but at what point do the data deviate to such an extent that they disprove the hypothesis? To answer this, χ^2 must be computed.

Let

x_{ij} = the actual value in row i and column j.
$\bar{x}_{ij}$ = the expected value in row i and column j.

Then:

$$\chi^2 = \sum_i \sum_j \left[\frac{(x_{ij} - \bar{x}_{ij})^2}{\bar{x}_{ij}}\right].$$

(Recall that Σ_j means "sum all of the j observations" (columns). $\Sigma_i \Sigma_j$ means "first total all of the columns and then add all of these totals together.") The result is a single number that is the χ^2 value in the particular test. It can then be compared to a χ^2 table to determine the validity of the hypothesis, as in Table 6–7.

Table 6–7

Actual	*Expected*	$x_{ij} - \bar{x}_{ij}$	$(x_{ij} - \bar{x}_{ij})^2$		$\frac{(x_{ij} - \bar{x}_{ij})^2}{\bar{x}_{ij}}$
8	9.35	−1.35	1.82		0.195
12	10.65	1.35	1.82		0.171
14	12.65	1.35	1.82		0.144
13	14.35	−1.35	1.82		0.123
				Total	0.633

This value of χ^2 can be compared to the χ^2 table, a portion of which is shown as Table 6–8.

Table 6–8

Degrees of freedom	*Risk*		
	0.10	*0.05*	*0.01*
1	2.71	3.84	6.63
2	4.61	5.99	9.21
3	6.25	7.81	11.34

If the value of the computed χ^2 is greater than the table value, then the actual deviation of the data is significantly greater than the amount of deviation that could be expected under the assumption that P/E and performance are not related. The hypothesis that P/E and performance are independent would therefore be rejected.

The appropriate column of the table is found by selecting the level of risk considered to be acceptable. In the example, the analyst chooses a 10% level of risk in order to make it relatively easy to reject the assumption of independence, because he is asserting the truth of the independence hypothesis and wishes to make the test as capable of working against him as possible. At the 90% level, independence will be rejected much more easily than would be the case at, say, the 99% level of confidence. The appropriate row in the table is found by selecting the correct number of degrees of freedom. The d.f. is (the number of rows in the contingency table less one) times (the number of columns in the contingency table less one). In this particular case, d.f. =

$(2 - 1)(2 - 1) = 1$ d.f. Looking at the χ^2 table, the appropriate value is 2.71. Because 0.633 is certainly not larger than 2.71, the null hypothesis is not rejected and the data do not provide any evidence that would justify the conclusion that P/E is related to performance. The χ^2 technique used in this example can be applied to a very broad variety of problems, including contingency tables of any size. χ^2 also has other applications not related to contingency tables, but all applications relate to the problem of evaluating the significance of the deviation of observed data from expected results.

METHODOLOGY AND ETHICS

The previous example showed, among other things, a particular case of how business ethics enters into statistics. The choice of the confidence level in the example was made in such a way that the analyst's position was not shown favoritism. This example, plus the fact that this section is the close of the chapter dealing with statistical method and the discovery and verification of scientific truth, make a few comments on the relationship between statistics and business ethics appropriate.

Statistics has been assailed for years for being a device by which lies might be "proven" to be the truth. Graphs are shown in advertisements without a scale to show the appropriate numbers. Graphs occur in annual reports with the bottom two-thirds chopped off so that a rise in sales from $65 million to $100 million goes from the bottom of the chart to the top. "Independent laboratories" prove anything superior to everything. The government has at times been accused of misusing numerical data. All of this is occurring at the same time that statistical technique is providing invaluable assistance in the natural and social sciences and is becoming indispensable in such diverse fields as quality control, auditing, and market research.

Unfortunately, almost anything *can* be "proven" by statistics, but only if statistical technique is deliberately and systematically misused in order to serve nonscientific motives. Although statistical *data* can be manipulated by statistical *technique* to "prove" anything, the use of the statistical *method* will produce scientific truth, and very possibly may be the *only* means by which scientific truth can be developed.

The point to this section, and perhaps to this entire chapter, is that statistics as a discipline does not permit the introduction of self-interest in its method. It sets up an hypothesis and then attempts to reject that hypothesis, with the burden of proof always on the new, unestablished theory (the analyst's theory). When statistical manipulations are reduced to tools to be used to "back up" an untenable position, the misrepresentation is not only unethical from the standpoint of the financial analyst, it is an act of dishonor in man's attempt to develop a scientific view of the world.

ADDITIONAL READINGS IN HYPOTHESIS TESTING

Chou, Ya-lun. *Statistical Analysis.* New York: Holt, Rinehart & Winston, Inc., 1969.

This book treats the problems of point estimation, interval estimation, and tests of hypotheses in Chapters 9 and 10 (78 pages). These pages clearly define the procedure necessary to execute each particular technique, and each type of problem is specifically identified as a separate section in the table of contents. This clear organization, coupled with an unusually usable set of tables, makes the text a valuable reference handbook when computational or definitional problems are encountered. The description of the procedure of testing (pages 304–13) is entirely verbal and is a statement of method that can be very profitably read by any analyst in about one hour.

Jedamus, Paul, and Frame, Robert. *Business Decision Theory.* New York: McGraw-Hill Book Company, 1969.

This book deals with hypothesis testing and estimation from the standpoint of minimizing the dollar cost of error to the firm (239 pages). This work considers the possibility of replacing the classical statistical idea of an arbitrary level of confidence (such as 95%) with a level of confidence that will minimize the sum of the cost of uncertainty and the cost of obtaining information. This approach points out that uncertainty has a true dollar cost to management because it produces some chance for erroneous decisions and errors therefore *must* eventually occur. It is reasonable to assume that management should be willing to attain only that level of confidence that will bring costs to their lowest point, because a desire for additional confidence would produce exorbitant expenses in gathering information. No quantitative background beyond the probability and hypothesis testing chapters of this book is needed. The entire text can be covered in two weekends and will restructure the reader's thinking concerning the nature of risk and business information.

Siegel, Sidney. *Nonparametric Statistics.* New York: McGraw-Hill Book Company, 1956.

This book is a presentation of the nature of the nonparametric techniques and a description of 27 specific nonparametric tests (239 pages). A verbal description of their characteristics, an example of their application, and a step-by-step statement of their calculation are included. The calculations are extremely simple, the emphasis is on practical application, and numerous examples are drawn that are simple enough to be understood by the nonexpert. The entire book is excellent and shows how quantitative precision can be achieved in the analysis of problems that at first appear to be completely qualitative.

Chapter 7

Regression, or how to express the relationships among variables

A common task of the financial analyst is to simplify a mass of data into a simple statement and then to see whether a relationship exists between two variables. Linear regression is a technique for determining whether and by how much a change in one variable will result in a change in another variable. Multiple linear regression permits the prediction of an unknown variable that depends upon several known variables. Illustrations are provided in estimating stock betas and in the field of econometrics.

BASIC CONCEPTS

The logical manipulations in the chapter on algebra have some direct practical value, but the problem for a financial analyst is not fundamentally the execution of operations in mathematical terms. The really basic problem in quantitative applications is the reduction of a fantastic mass of data into a manageable set of simple statements. Simplification is the first job of a research analyst or portfolio manager, and this task is the subject matter of elementary statistics. But basic statistics and algebra combine to provide the foundation for the study of the *relationship* between variables. Algebra permits the manipulation of functions such as

$$y = a + bx$$

but does not provide the analyst with the technique by which he can discover whether two variables have such a relationship. Even given the function, the analyst is unable to decide upon the values to use for a or b and so cannot use the equation for practical applications. Statistics, however, permit the researcher to reduce data on two variables to the equation by using the tool called simple regression.

Returning to the rather time-worn example of P/E and G (growth in

Figure 7–1

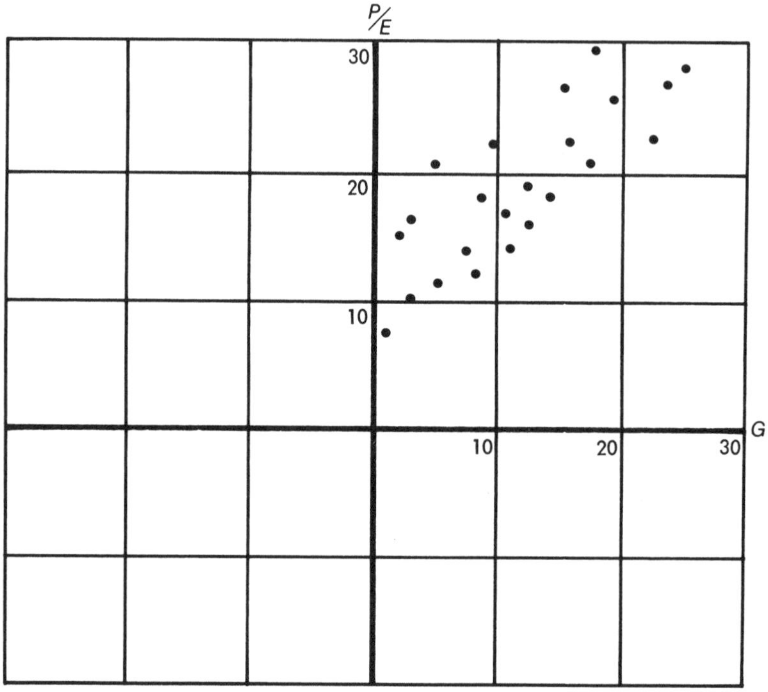

earnings), assume that an analyst suspects that these two aspects of individual stocks are closely related. He believes that high P/E's are associated with high G's, and low with low. Being aware of the use of graphs, he decides to "picture" a set of 23 stocks in which he is interested. He therefore plots 23 pairs of $(G, P/E)$ values on a graph, and each pair, naturally, is represented by a point, as shown in Figure 7–1. All of the pairs fall in the upper right-hand quarter of the graph (quadrant I) because all of the issues in which he has an interest have a positive growth rate and a positive level of current earnings, although such a relationship is not necessary for either the graph or the regression technique.

The most conspicuous thing about this graph is that the "swarm" of points appears to have a pattern. They tend to form a "channel" running diagonally across the paper. The easiest way for the analyst to simplify this "swarm" is to draw a straight line through the "middle" of the points, as shown in Figure 7–2.

The line describes the pattern of the observations (points) without the "clutter" in the original system. By using this graph he is able to take a stock he is analyzing, estimate its growth rate, and then go over on

Figure 7-2

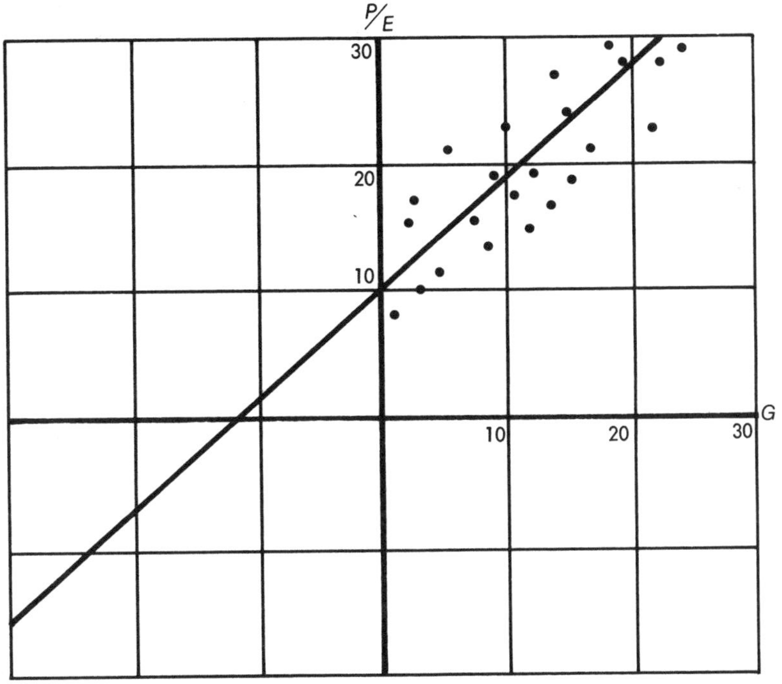

the G axis to this growth rate, up to the line, and read the P/E from the vertical axis. This P/E is the expected "general" area around which he would anticipate the market's valuation of the stock to fluctuate. The technique is workable and can be used by any analyst.

Assume now that an analyst using this graphic technique showed the "scatter diagram" to a statistician. The first thing that he would hear, of course, would be that the equation for a straight line is

$$y = a + bx$$

or, in this case,

$$P/E = a + bG.$$

Inasmuch as the analyst already had his line, the statistician may well argue, "Why not use its equation to derive the P/E for the stocks instead of this over on G, up to the line approach?"

Actually, the analyst had already found a and b when he drew the line on the graph. The value of a is the "intercept"—the value of the P/E when $G = 0$ algebraically or the point at which the line crosses the P/E axis geometrically. The analyst could find a by simply looking at his graph. Now b is the amount of additional P/E gained when G goes up one. It can be found from the graph by going over one on the G axis and observing how much P/E goes up. An example might be: G up one, P/E up 0.8. The value of b is therefore 0.8. Algebraically, it is the rate of change in P/E; geometrically, it is the slope of the line drawn by the analyst.

Performing these simple examinations, the researcher finds that

$$P/E = 10 + 0.8G$$

and this equation can predict P/E just as well and certainly much faster than the cruder graphic method. He has moved from a graphic to an analytic approach, trading one model in for a superior one.

INCREASING PRECISION

Some problems still exist in the way the analyst is attacking the problem. First, he is still wasting a great deal of time because he must draw the scatter diagram so that he can "fit" his line and observe the values of a and b. Second, when he fits his line, he is using freehand methods and will be slightly inaccurate as a result. Because he has already taken the first step in the analytic approach, he could very easily use algebraic techniques to avoid these difficulties by applying the method of least squares.

To find a and b by least squares, all that is needed is to plug values into the following two equations:

$$\Sigma Y = Na + b\Sigma X$$
$$\Sigma XY = a\Sigma X + b\Sigma X^2,$$

where

Y is the dependent variable (P/E in this case),
X is the independent variable (G in this case),
N is the number of observations (number of points in the scatter diagram).

Because all of the symbols in the two equations can be converted into numbers except a and b, the analyst has a system of two equations in two unknowns, which he can then solve algebraically.

In order to use this analytic approach, the analyst only needs to calculate for each observation:

$$Y = \text{the } P/E$$
$$X = \text{the growth rate}$$
$$XY = (P/E)(G)$$
$$X^2 = G^2$$

and then add all of the observations together, giving ΣY, ΣX, ΣXY, and ΣX^2, and then "plug" these into the "normal equations" along with N (the number of observations). Solving the equations then gives a and b.

This approach will give the *precise* equation that will minimize the amount by which the line "misses" the points in the diagram as shown in Figure 7–3.

This technique, then, permits the investment analyst to use the "best" equation, or function, that describes the relationship underlying the data on two variables and minimizes the error in a line drawn freehand. It reduces literally dozens of numbers to a simple formula. In addition, it reduces the "essence" of the scatter diagram to a simple mathematical expression. But the least squares line is a *model* of the diagram. It does not reproduce every aspect of the graph. And some of these aspects are very important to the analyst. For example, the presence of the "pattern" first indicated to the analyst that a relationship existed. Second, the "width" of the channel made by the points indicated the accuracy of the line in describing the relationship. If analysis is to replace graphs, measures of these factors are necessary.

Figure 7–3

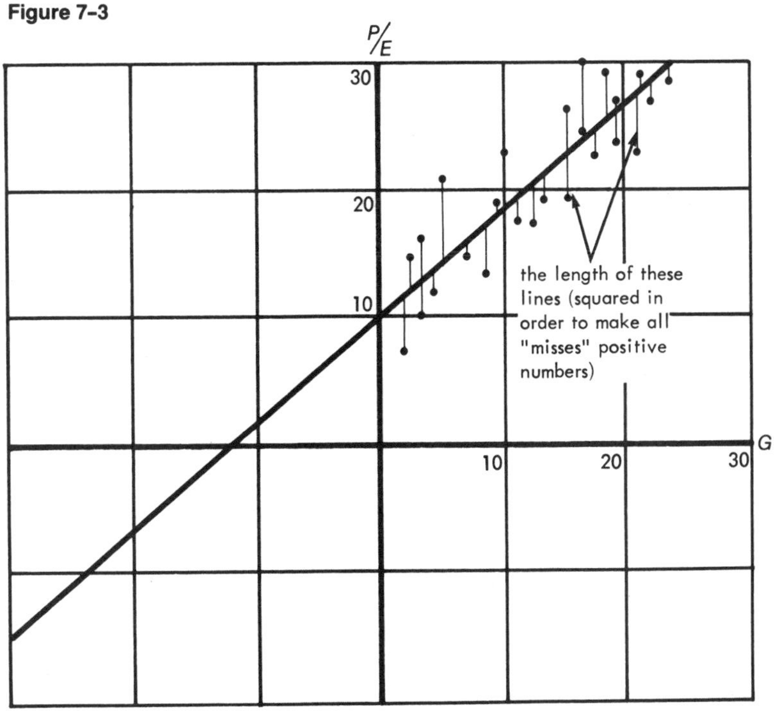

STANDARD ERROR OF ESTIMATE

Even if a relationship exists, an analyst is not especially interested in it unless it produces practical results. If a regression line can tell the analyst the *P/E* of a stock given the growth rate, give or take a little because of the limitations of the data, then the analyst is interested in just *how much* this "give or take" figure is. For example, Figures 7-4 and 7-5 show a relationship.

Figure 7-4

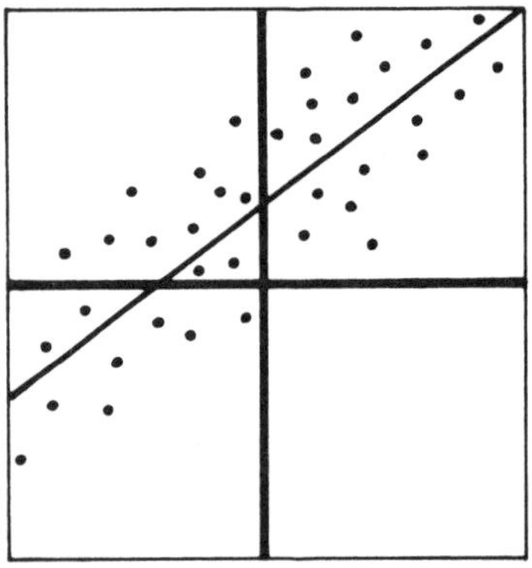

Figure 7-5

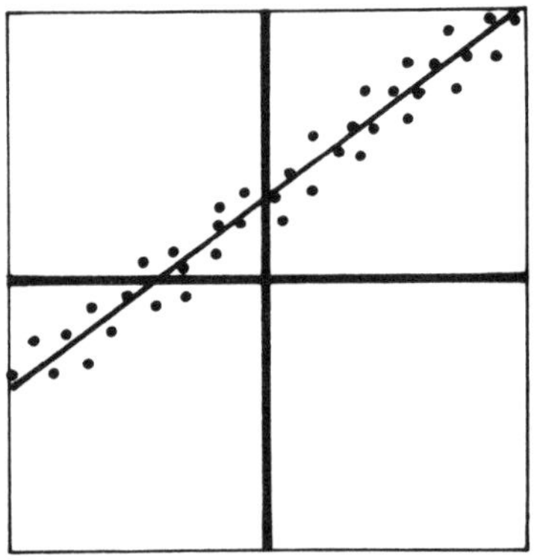

The first graph, however, has a very wide channel, while the second graph closely approximates the regression line. The value of the regression is obviously greater in the second graph, because the line will more closely characterize the data. The model will not have lost as much information in this case—it will have captured the "essence" of the base data. What the analyst needs is an analytic measure of the size of this channel.

The standard error of estimate ($s_{y,x}$) provides this information. This figure is the standard deviation of the points around the regression line. As a result, if a great deal of "scatter" exists, the $s_{y,x}$ will be very large, indicating a high standard deviation of the points from the line. If the line fits the data well, $s_{y,x}$ will be small. The importance of $s_{y,x}$ in measuring the "channel" can easily be seen in Figures 7-6 and 7-7.

The wider scatter in the first graph caused a "broader" channel (a larger $s_{y,x}$). Notice that not all of the points are included in the channel, just as not all observations in a sample fall within one standard deviation of the mean. In general, about 68% of the points would be expected to fall within the lines. If we doubled the width of the channel, about 95% of the points would be included. The line of regression can be regarded as a sort of "mean" around which there is a standard deviation, which in this case is called the standard error. This idea corresponds to

Figure 7-6

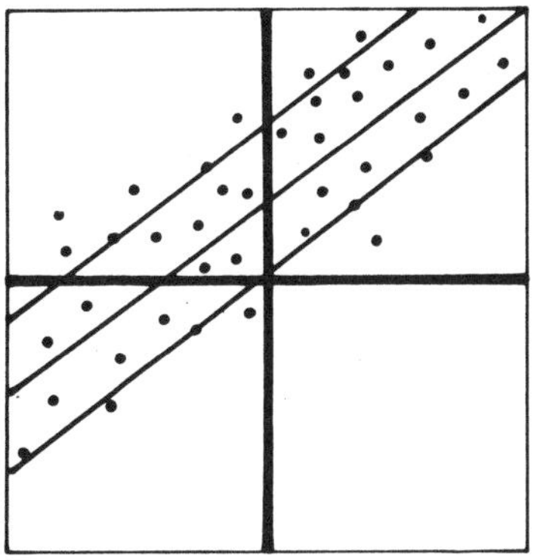

Figure 7-7

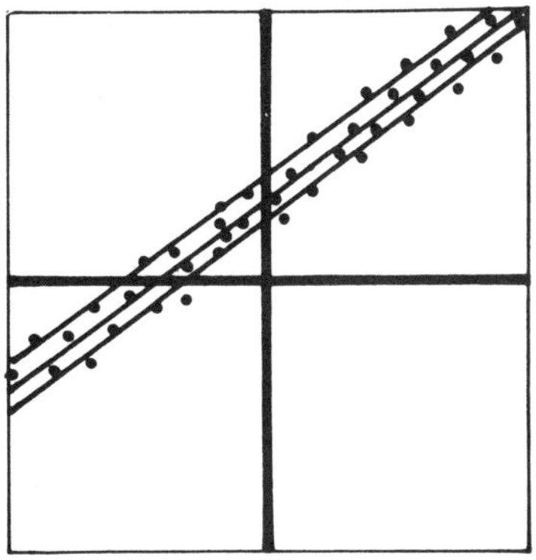

the intuitive idea of the line on the diagram being the most likely *P/E* "give or take a little" and the idea of the regression line being a "best estimate."

The standard error is measured as the distance from the regression line to one of the "bracketing" lines of the channel. This distance in any one study, of course, is always the same regardless of where it is measured because the two lines are parallel to the regression line (see Figure 7-8). The length of this line can be read from the vertical axis (*P/E* axis in the example). Therefore, an $s_{y,x} = 1.2$ in the example would mean that about two-thirds of the time the actual *P/E* would fall within 1.2 of the value of the *P/E* calculated from the growth rate. The unit of measurement (*P/E* in this case) for $s_{y,x}$ is always the same as for the variable being predicted because both are read from the vertical axis.

In order to calculate $s_{y,x}$ without resort to a scatter diagram, the following formula is used:

$$s_{y,x} = \sqrt{\frac{\Sigma(y - \hat{y})_i^2}{N - 2}}$$

where for each observation:

y = the item being predicted (*P/E*, for example)
$\hat{y}$ = the predicted value for the y, found by using the regression equation and the observation's value of x (growth in the example)
$(y - \hat{y})_i$ = the amount by which the equation "missed" the actual value of the observation,

and for the study as a whole:

$\Sigma(y - \hat{y})_i^2$ = the total of the squared deviations of the observed y

Figure 7-8

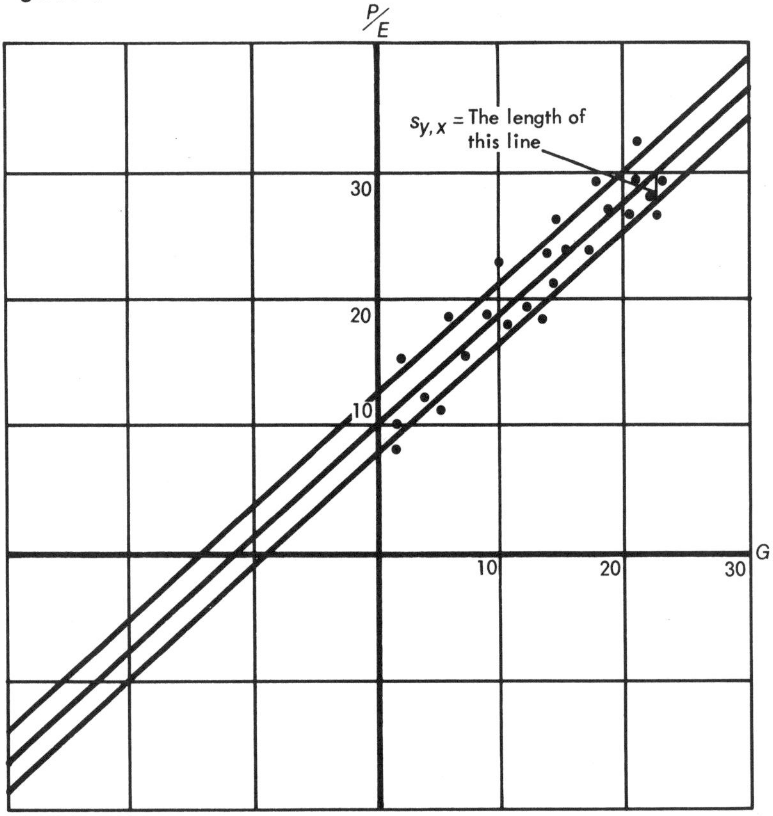

from the value $\hat{y}$, predicted by the equation for each observation. All of the $\hat{y}$ values will fall on the regression line.

N = the number of observations being totaled.

$\frac{\Sigma(y - \hat{y})_i^2}{N - 2}$ = the average squared deviation from the regression line (the "variance" from the line). The denominator is $N - 2$ instead of N because of rather complicated concepts involved in the theory of statistical inference. $N - 2$ can most easily be thought of as the number of observations adjusted to eliminate bias.

THE COEFFICIENT OF CORRELATION

All of the work related to the regression model up to this point has assumed that the two variables being considered actually do have a relationship. In the example, P/E has been assumed to be a function of G. Obviously, in many cases, the data may indicate that the fundamental relationship indicated by theory has not been substantiated by real events. In the scatter diagram, the absence of a relationship would be shown by the absence of any pattern in the points. Analytically, a measure of how well the variables are related is provided either by the coefficient of correlation or the coefficient of determination.

The coefficient of correlation r is simply an index number that can be used to gauge the extent to which two variables are related. If $r = 0$, no tendency exists for one variable to vary with the other, i.e., no linear function ties the two variables together. If $r = +1.0$, the value of y can be perfectly predicted from a knowledge of the value of x. In addition, when x rises, y rises also. In this situation, two variables are said to have a perfect direct relationship. If $r = -1.0$, the value of y can still be completely predicted from a knowledge of the value of x, but when x rises, y falls. In this case, the two variables are said to have a perfect inverse relationship.

This behavior of r permits the analyst to use the absolute value of r, denoted $|r|$, as a measure of relationships. A high $|r|$ indicates a high degree of association between the variables, while an $|r|$ close to zero indicates that whatever relationship is present in the data may very well have been caused by chance. The real value of r, however, is in more advanced statistical applications. When an analyst is attempting simply to gain an intuitive feel for relationships, the coefficient of determination has a much more obvious interpretation and is therefore more frequently used.

The coefficient of determination, R^2, is the percentage of the variance in y that is "explained" by x. The reason that R^2 is a helpful statistic may be made clearer by the following illustration.

Assume that you have been required to guess the value of some y (the P/E of some unknown stock at the end of next year, for example). In addition, assume that you are not permitted to use any other variable in guessing. About all that you could do would be to look at the past P/E's of stocks and guess the mean of these numbers as the actual value that will occur next year. You will probably be wrong, but you haven't been permitted to use very much information, either. How wrong will you be? The variance of the P/E's of a large group of stocks around their mean P/E is a good measure of the size of the error in your guess. If these stocks have a variance of 6 in their P/E's, your estimate will be more accurate than if they have a variance of 15.

Now assume that you are permitted to know the growth rate of the earnings of the company and that you are familiar with regression theory. Instead of simply guessing the mean P/E, you can now guess the value of the P/E associated with the company's earnings growth. Now how wrong will you be? The width of the channel in the scatter diagram measures the amount of error that would be likely, and analytically the amount of error is measured by $s_{y,x}$.

If the error in this new problem, which can be measured by $s_{y,x}$ or by $s^2_{y,x}$ is less than the error in the original problem as measured by the variance of P/E around the mean, then you will have reduced the extent of your error. But this statement is the same as saying that a knowledge of growth rates is helpful in predicting P/E's, which could only be the case if the two variables are related. How can you measure how much error has been eliminated? The error remaining after the regression has been performed divided by the original error (the original variance) is the *fraction* of the error wiped out by the use of the regression model. Mathematically, this is:

$$R^2 = \frac{\Sigma(\hat{y} - \bar{y})^2 \leftarrow \text{The variance of the predicted values of } y}{\Sigma(y - \bar{y})^2 \leftarrow \text{The variance of the actual value of } y}.$$

The mathematical relationship between R^2 and r is easily pointed out by showing the formula for r:

$$r = \sqrt{\frac{\Sigma(\hat{y} - \bar{y})^2}{\Sigma(y - \bar{y})^2}}.$$

r therefore equals the square root of R^2.

USING REGRESSION TO ESTIMATE BETAS

Quite a body of financial literature has been developed in recent years describing the nature and use of "beta coefficients". The most frequently used technique for estimating the beta coefficients published and used by the profession is linear regression.

A beta coefficient (or simply "a beta") is a number that can be used to describe how sensitive a stock is to movements in the market as a whole. The Standard & Poor's 500 stock index usually is used to approximate the movements of the overall market. A beta of 1.0 indicates that the stock is exactly as volatile as the market, that is, a 1% move in the S&P can be expected to produce a 1% move in the stock and a 10% rise in the S&P is associated with a 10% rise in the stock. The relationship works both ways, for a 10% decline in the S&P would be associated with a 10% decline in the stock.

A beta of 2.0 would indicate that the stock is twice as sensitive as the market. A 10% rise in the S&P would, in this case, be associated with a 20% rise in the stock. A beta of 0.5 would indicate a relatively stable stock that would rise only 5% when the S&P gained 10%. Obviously, if the beta of a stock is known and the stock is closely related to the market, the analyst can understand a great deal about the stock's price behavior. Unfortunately, the beta of a stock is never known; it can only be estimated.

The input to the linear regression model that is used to estimate betas is the historical percentage changes in the S&P 500 (as the x variable) and the historical percentage changes in the price of the stock (as the y variable). For example, an analyst might use the quarterly percentage changes in the price of GM and the S&P for recent past years as input. This exercise would produce observations that could be pictured in the scatter diagram in Figure 7-9.

Figure 7-9

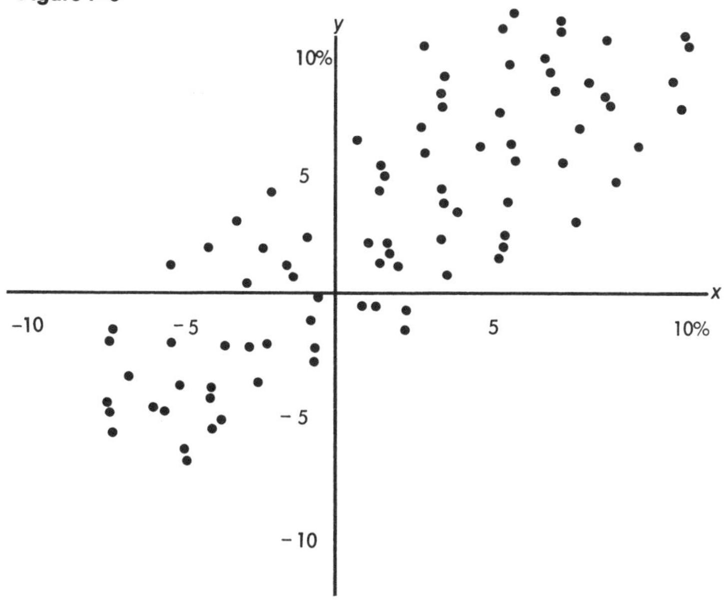

This diagram is now easily recognizable as a regression application. All that is needed is to draw the line through the data swarm and estimate the width of the channel. A wide channel would indicate that the movement of the S&P does not explain a large amount of GM's movement. A narrow channel would indicate a good predictor and a close relationship. The width of the channel, of course, is the standard error of estimate, and R^2 or r can be used to describe the extent of the relationship.

Although the standard error and correlation coefficients are very easily applied to the estimation of betas, the regression equation $y = a + bx$ requires some additional explanation. The regression lines in Figure 7-10 portray the market action of Widgets, Inc., (a stable stock) and XYZ Corp. (a volatile stock).

Notice that the slope of the regression line for the stable stock, Widgets, Inc., is 0.5, while the slope of XYZ's regression is 2.0. The slope of the regression line (the b in the regression equation) is the beta

Figure 7-10

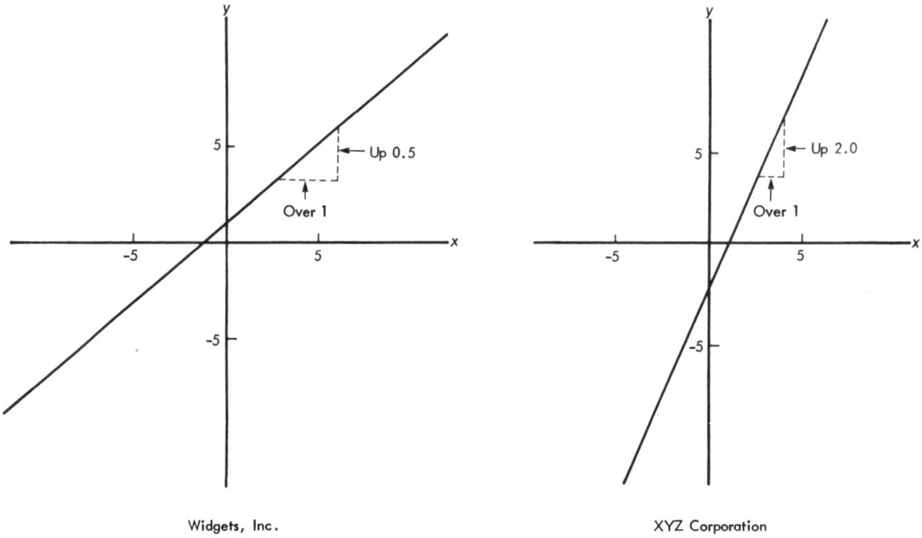

coefficient. A *b* of 2.0 in the regression means that the stock's beta was 2.0 during that time period.

Notice also that the regression line for Widgets, Inc. does not have a zero *y* intercept. The percentage increase for Widgets, Inc., when the market has zero change is, in fact, about 2%. Therefore, Widgets, Inc., gained 2% per quarter over and above the gain achieved by virtue of the change in the market. This 2% is the *a* in the regression equation and is frequently referred to as the "alpha" when betas are being discussed. A positive alpha is, of course, a desirable characteristic for a stock to have. As can be seen in the diagram of XYZ Corp., a negative alpha is pictured as a negative number on the *y* intercept. In the regression equation, a negative alpha is shown as a negative value for the *a* in $y = a + bx$.

This application of regression can be extended in several ways. First, an analyst could aggregate companies into an industry index or an economic sector index and then estimate the beta of the industry. Second, it is possible to track the percentage changes in the market value of a portfolio and then compute the regression values for the portfolio as a whole. The beta would then indicate the sensitivity of the portfolio to changes in the market. The alpha would show the portfolio return over and above the return achieved by market action alone. The R^2 shows the part of the portfolio's price movement that can be explained by movement in the market as a whole. This approach toward portfolio evaluation is now integral to most current work in performance measurement, because it allows the analyst to differentiate between market-induced performance and performance independent of broad market action. The return independent of the market, or alpha, is called the "risk adjusted" return and can be regarded as the incremental return added to the portfolio results through the efforts of the portfolio manager.

A word of caution is necessary at this point, however. The use of regression to estimate betas has been subjected to extensive testing and a number of problems have been discovered. For example, a company's beta can and does change over time. The beta during the historical period used for input to the regression model may not be the same as the stock's beta during the future period in which the analyst is interested. Also, a different beta may be obtained using monthly or weekly percentage changes instead of quarterly changes, even if the same historical time period is being used. Other problems relate to how long a time period should be used and how betas change over time. These problems have created a situation in which the portfolio manager can never be certain that the stated beta of his stocks is accurate. In addition, the beta of individual stocks typically explain only 20% or 30% of the stocks' movement, although portfolio betas typically explain 80% or 90% of the entire portfolio's sensitivity. Betas therefore need to be used with great caution on the individual company level but seem to have more value in connection with portfolio risk analysis.

MULTIPLE LINEAR REGRESSION

Expanding the regression concept

Multiple regression is one of the most valuable techniques available to the financial analyst because it permits a number of variables to be used to predict some unknown variable. For example, the growth rate, debt to equity ratio, and yield of stocks might be used to predict the stocks' P/E. Multiple regression is simply an extension of simple regression. In simple regression, the analyst can find an equation of the form $y = a + bx$ that describes (more or less) the relationship between the two variables being studied. Applications for the two-variable case are often encountered, but quite frequently the financial manager has reason to believe that the value of y is heavily influenced by more than one thing. In this case y is a function of more than one x. Actually, in the extremely complicated financial world, $y = f(x_1, x_2, \ldots x_n)$ is almost always a model significantly superior to $y = f(x)$.

The most logical extension of simple regression, therefore, is multiple regression. Instead of using x to locate or "retrieve" the value for y, it is possible to use $x_1, x_2, \ldots x_n$. The mathematical technique is more complicated, but the concepts involved are essentially the same. The analyst still is attempting to discover the particular linear function that will predict or describe y. A number of past observations of the x's and of y still are required before the model can provide meaningful information. The model still provides an equation as an answer, and the equation still can be used in the same way. The similarity in form between the two equations can be seen by the following examples:

$$y = 10 + 0.8x; \qquad y = -0.10 + 0.6x_1 + 0.4x_2.$$

Note from the examples that the use of subscripts makes the expression simpler than using completely different letters. Subscripts are used extensively in multiple linear regression, as could be expected from what was said in the section on notation about simplification when many variables are introduced.

What multiple regression does, in effect, is to state that, because y is related to several x's, it is reasonable simply to add the values of the x's in order to get the value of y. It goes one step further, however, "adjusting" each x before adding the adjusted figures. The "adjustment" is a weight applied to each variable, and the real purpose of the model is to select the "best" weights to use in the equation, which produces, naturally, the "best" such equation.

In mathematical notation, any variable with a zero subscript is defined to equal the number "1." For example, x_0 by definition equals 1. In a regression equation such as $y = b_1x_0 + b_2x_1 + b_3x_2 + b_4x_3$, the b's represent the particular weights chosen by the model, and the weighted x's are then added to "retrieve" the value of y.

The next question is how the model treats the qualitative idea of "best" in mathematical terms. Regression uses the data provided by the analyst concerning the values of y that occurred, given certain values for the x's. It evaluates the weights (the b_i) that could have been used for the x's in order to predict the values of y. The set of weights that would have produced the *predictions* of y closest to the *actual* values of y is then selected. As a result, the equation produced is the linear combination of the x's that most accurately predicted all of the values of y provided as input to the model. The equation might therefore be expected to produce about the same quality of predictions for new values of y. If anyone could graph the equation (in four-dimensional space because there are four variables), he would find that it is the straight line that bisects or best fits the swarm of data points that were input to the model, which is analogous to the way that $y = a + bx$ fits the points in a scatter diagram in two dimensions.

An example

The principles of regression can be understood much more easily if they are presented within the framework of a concrete example. It is not the purpose of this chapter to explain how to compute a multiple regression equation. Such computations can be performed either by "canned" computer programs or by a statistician. Rather the intent is to explain the use of multiple regression and to provide an understanding of the results.

The following problem has been fabricated in such a way that the results appear to be reasonable. Remember, however, that the example is not the result of actual data. Extending the example used in the chapter on simple regression, let

y = P/E of any stock being analyzed.
x_1 = Growth rate of the stock's earnings.
x_2 = 1 − the debt to equity ratio of the company. (Simply called debt/equity in the chapter.)
x_3 = The yield of the stock.

The equation that this study produces would have the form

$$y = b_1x_0 + b_2x_1 + b_3x_2 + b_4x_3.$$

(Note: Recall that $x_0 = 1$ by definition.)

The objective of the analyst is to study the relationship between: (1) the growth rate, debt/equity ratio, and yield of stocks; and (2) the P/E the market is willing to assign given any stock's value in these three areas. Naturally, an analyst would not undertake this analysis if he did not already believe that x_1, x_2, and x_3 were factors that were, in fact, involved in the determination of the price-earnings ratios of stocks.

Input requirements

In order to utilize the multiple regression model, the researcher obviously needs to provide a certain amount of data as input. In the case of this particular example, the data consist of the P/E, growth rate, debt/equity ratio, and yield of a number of stocks. Data for only one stock will not be sufficient, because this information would be equivalent to providing only one point for a scatter diagram. Drawing the best line "fitting" only one point is impossible. In fact, because two points are needed to draw a line on a plane representing two variables, when the study has a surface representing four variables at least four points will be needed. In the example, the study would require at least four stocks.

Actually, however, more than four stocks are needed for this study to be valid because the points must form a swarm having at least some scatter around the regression line. In the most primitive terms possible, the regression line is supposed to be a mathematical expression representing general, broad relationships in the data, and enough observations must be present to allow the relationships to become recognizable and to be subjected to statistical examination. The minimum number of observations (stocks, in this case) must exceed the number of variables in the study, but as many observations as possible should be used because each additional observation increases the reliability of the results and the accuracy of any future predictions that might be made.

The correlation matrix

In the section on simple regression, r was used to describe the degree of relationship between the two variables. It ranged between -1.00 and $+1.00$, with 0.0 showing no relationship and ± 1.00 showing perfect positive or negative correlation. The r statistic is retained in multiple regression but is expanded a bit because multiple regression involves more than two variables. Nevertheless, *any pair* of variables can have a coefficient of correlation, so that what develops is a *matrix* of r's, called the *correlation matrix.*

In order to understand the correlation matrix, it is necessary to identify uniquely the two variables to which each r relates. Using subscripts for this purpose, let:

Subscript		*Variable*
1	=	y
2	=	x_1
3	=	x_2
4	=	x_3

In this notation, $r_{1,2}$ would be the correlation coefficient of the variables y and x_1; $r_{3,4}$ would deal with x_2 and x_3. It is now possible to present a hypothetical matrix of the r_{ij} that might result from the study of P/E's:

$r_{1,1} = 1.00$	$r_{1,2} = 0.99$	$r_{1,3} = 0.95$	$r_{1,4} = 0.96$
$r_{2,1} = 0.99$	$r_{2,2} = 1.00$	$r_{2,3} = 0.93$	$r_{2,4} = 0.93$
$r_{3,1} = 0.95$	$r_{3,2} = 0.93$	$r_{3,3} = 1.00$	$r_{3,4} = 0.98$
$r_{4,1} = 0.96$	$r_{4,2} = 0.93$	$r_{4,3} = 0.98$	$r_{4,4} = 1.00$

Each of the values in this matrix is a simple correlation coefficient and has exactly the same interpretation as in simple regression. For example, $r_{3,1} = 0.95$ is the correlation coefficient for variables 3 and 1, and 0.95 is precisely the same value for r that would be obtained if a simple regression were run for these two variables without any consideration of the other variables whatsoever.

The structure of the matrix

This array points out several interesting facts. First, the correlation of a variable to itself is 1.00. This statement is reasonable, for if the value of a variable is known, its value can then be predicted with perfect accuracy. Because the main diagonal of the matrix is the correlation between variables 1 and 1, 2 and 2, etc., this diagonal is all ones. Second, $r_{1,2} = r_{2,1}$, and $r_{3,4} = r_{4,3}$, and so forth. Therefore, the upper right triangle of the matrix equals the lower left triangle. Third, because the meaning of each r_{ij} is fixed by its location in the matrix, the coefficients can be presented without showing the variables with which they deal. The first row deals with the first variable and the first column also deals with the first variable, etc. The coefficient in the second row and the third column is, obviously, the value of $r_{2,3}$. The correlation matrix can therefore be written as

$$\begin{pmatrix} 1.00 & 0.99 & 0.95 & 0.96 \\ 0.99 & 1.00 & 0.93 & 0.93 \\ 0.95 & 0.93 & 1.00 & 0.98 \\ 0.96 & 0.93 & 0.98 & 1.00 \end{pmatrix}$$

Because the upper right triangle equals the lower left triangle, the correlation matrix R is frequently written as

$$\begin{pmatrix} 1.00 & 0.99 & 0.95 & 0.96 \\ & 1.00 & 0.93 & 0.93 \\ & & 1.00 & 0.98 \\ & & & 1.00 \end{pmatrix}$$

without the loss of any information.

The R matrix provides a table of the results of a number of simple regressions even before the *real* multiple regression is begun. Interpreting this particular R in terms of the variables used in the example, the relationships are high in every case, but the debt/equity ratio variable has the lowest relationship to P/E and the worst relationships are found in growth to debt/equity ratio and growth to yield. The results of the study are already interesting, for it begins to look like growth may be a being-unto-itself that is more closely tied to the P/E than to any other variable. But this analysis is as far as "r" can go. To proceed, the analyst needs a measure of the "explanatory power" of *all* of the x's, not just one at a time.

The coefficient of determination

R^2, the coefficient of determination, serves the purpose of measuring the extent to which all the x's taken as a whole serve as an "explanation" of y. Its meaning is the same as in simple regression, for it still measures the percentage by which the overall fluctuation in y can be removed (or "predicted") by the use of the regression equation. The R^2 statistic has a direct interpretation as the percentage of y's variation eliminated (or "explained") by the values of the x_i variables. If the regression equation is the result of a simple regression, it measures the explanatory power of x; but if the equation is a *multiple* regression, it measures the total explanatory power of *all* of the x_i. If $R^2 = 0.95$, then 95% of y's movement could be predicted by the regression equation. R^2 obviously is a very useful measure of the value of the regression. Its chief drawback is that its ability to provide a synopsis of the results has caused it to be used as a *sole* indication of the results without regard for other aspects of a regression study. R^2 is a key measure of the value of the equation that the model produces, but it should be used in conjunction with other statistical results provided by the technique.

The coefficient of determination, R^2, is frequently presented with subscripts to indicate the particular variables included in the model. The dependent variable y (the variable being predicted), is denoted by the first subscript and is followed by the x's (independent variables). The y is separated from the independent variables by a period (or sometimes by a comma). Hence, $R^2_{1.234}$ would be a way of writing the coefficient of determination in our example of P/E ratios. Alternative ways of expressing R^2 are fairly numerous: $R^2_{y.123}$ meaning R^2 for y *given* x_1, x_2, and x_3 is one possibility; another is $R^2_{y.x_1x_2x_3}$, which is clearer but is somewhat cumbersome.

Reviewing, it can be seen that R^2 is a kind of a "percentage" measure, thus indicating the proportion of the fluctuations or "scatter" in y that can be explained by the changes that occurred in x_i. If y goes all over the chart, but x_i is the only reason for this wandering, x_i "explains" *all* of y's movement and the index is 100% (expressed as $R^2 = 1.00$). If a study were conducted initially involving ten independent variables and an equation using only three of the x_i were finally selected, the resulting R^2 might be $R^2_{y.345} = 0.87$, which would be an 87% "explanation" of y by the variables x_3, x_4, and x_5. If all of the x_i explained absolutely none of the fluctuation in y, then R^2 would equal 0.00. The subscript notation used for R^2 also can be applied to the standard error, giving $s_{y.123}$, the "expected" miss in the predictions of the equation, i.e., the size of the "channel" in the scatter diagram that showed y predicted by x_1, x_2, and x_3. As a specific example, a $s_{y.123} = 0.12$ would normally mean that the predicted value of y missed the actual value of y by 0.12 or less about 68% of the time.

A measure of the value of *b*

In statistics, almost everything is a "give or take a little" type of problem. For example, when the statistical idea of the "probability of missing" was applied to the problem of predicting y, the concept of the standard error proved to be helpful. Statisticians openly accept the limitations of the regression model as a predictor. In effect, the technique produces an equation that itself is a model of the actual relationships found in the real world. Because of the inherent limitations in any consideration of data having a random element, the equation may not be the absolutely correct equation even if the relationship in the real world satisfies all of the assumptions of the model. The problem is that, in an equation like $y = a + bx$, the technique is estimating the actual value of b that describes the situation in the real world, and this estimate may well be wrong. However, it is possible to determine statistically how *likely* it is to be wrong.

Recall from algebra that in the equation $y = a + bx$, b is the weight given the predicting variable. Geometrically, it is the "slope" of the line that best describes the data in a scatter diagram. It tells us how much "extra y" is received for each "extra x" put into the equation. The amount of error in the coefficient of x (b, in other words) can be measured by a statistic called $\hat{\sigma}_b$ (the standard error of the coefficient). The "σ" is a familiar symbol that is always related to the measurement of variation. It indicates what type of measure this new statistic is, a "give or take this amount or less about 68% of the time" type of number. The b, of course, indicates that it is the variability of b that is being measured. The ˆ (hat) indicates that the $\hat{\sigma}_b$ is an estimate of the true condition in the real world.

As a concrete illustration of this statistic, assume that $\hat{\sigma}_b$ is 0.03 for the coefficient (b_1) of x_1 and the actual value of b is 0.85. The regression model appears to have generated an equation describing the "real world" relationship very well, for it appears that the 0.85 value is accurate within about $\pm$ 0.03. In the example of regression being used in this chapter, x_1 is the earnings growth rate of a company. A value of 8 for x_1 would mean an 8% annual rate of growth. The coefficient (b_1) of 0.85 would therefore mean 0.85 of the 8 could be added to the *P/E* of the company. The value of $\hat{\sigma}_b$ shows that the 0.85 could be as low as 0.82 or as high as 0.88. This range is fairly narrow, which justifies the conclusion that the equation is valuable. Instead of 0.03, if the model showed that $\hat{\sigma}_b = 0.65$, the true value of b_1 would be anywhere between 0.85 $\pm$ 0.65 (this is a [0.20 − 1.50] range). The predictions of the model would obviously be far less accurate, for a 1% increase in the growth of a company could increase its *P/E* by anything between 0.20 and 1.50 *P/E*.

The $\hat{\sigma}_b$ statistic actually can be used in a much more precise way by calling upon the t statistic discussed in the chapter on hypothesis testing. A value for t in simple regression can be computed by the following formula:

$$t = \frac{b}{\hat{\sigma}_b}$$

where $\hat{\sigma}_b$ is equal to

$$\sqrt{\frac{\dfrac{\Sigma(y - \hat{y})^2}{n - 2}}{\Sigma x^2 - (\Sigma x)^2/n}} .$$

In multiple regression, a t can be computed for each b_i being estimated. As shown in the earlier chapter, the calculated value of t is of no direct benefit to the analyst. By using the t table with $n - 2$ degrees of freedom, however, it is possible to accept or reject the null hypothesis that $b_1 = 0.0$ at any desired level of confidence. If it cannot be shown by this test that b_i is not equal to zero, then the variable x_i (growth rate, for instance) must still be assumed to have no relationship to the item being predicted (P/E, in this case), because a $b_1 = 0.0$ means that an increase in growth will add 0.0 to the value of the P/E. If all changes in the growth rate have a zero effect on the P/E, the two variables are obviously not related. Using t to reject the null hypothesis that $b_i = 0.0$ is therefore a statistical method to establish with some confidence the fact that a relationship exists.

After the t associated with any given variable x_i and its coefficient b_i has been found, it can be compared to the table value of t (found by using $n - 2$ degrees of freedom and the desired risk level). If the calculated t exceeds the value of t in the table, then the value of b_i cannot be explained by chance alone. The only alternative explanation is that, say, growth (x_1) does affect the value of P/E (y). If this relationship is found to be true for all of the variables x_i, then the regression equation can reasonably be expected to produce better predictions than would result from simply guessing the value of y without referring to the values of the predicting variables x_i.

Confidence limits for b_i also can be computed using the t statistic. Confidence limits are a range or an interval within which a value might be expected to fall, say, 95% of the time. Because b is estimated by the model and therefore may be subject to error stemming from chance variation, it is frequently valuable to provide an interval within which the true value of b_i in the real world can be expected to fall. This interval is $b_i \pm$ (the value of $\hat{\sigma}_b$ times the table value of t at $x - 2$ degrees of freedom and the desired risk level).

The numeric value of $\hat{\sigma}_b$ is a very useful indication of the value of a regression, since a b_i that has a high $\hat{\sigma}_{b_i}$ is a number that relates two variables but is one in which the analyst cannot be confident. In studies involving a number of variables, high correlations among the predicting variables may cause the confidence in the b_i as measured by the $\hat{\sigma}_{b_i}$ to be very low even though the equation has a high R^2. This problem often can be avoided by taking more observations or by removing one or more of the predicting variables.

Confidence interval for predictions

The true value of b_i in the real world is often called β_i, in which case b_i is said to be an estimate of β_i. The confidence level for b_i is therefore the interval that is expected to contain β_i 95% of the time. The idea of a confidence interval, a range within which a number can reasonably be expected to fall, is a useful concept to apply to the predictions of the value of y provided by a regression equation. The regression provides a value for y that can be used as a prediction of y assuming certain values for the x_i in the equation. But the accuracy of this prediction is certainly not indicated in the single value for y that the equation produces. In the example, a predicted P/E of 17.0 for a stock does not indicate whether the actual P/E can be expected to be between 16.9 and 17.1 or between 14.0 and 20.0. It would be much more valuable if the model provided an interval within which y could be expected to fall 95% of the time. The single value of y (such as $P/E = 17.0$) would be the midpoint of this interval, but the "spread" of the interval would serve as an indication of the value of the prediction.

Multiple regression provides this information, and the results are once again found by the use of the t statistic. The value of the interval is the predicted value of y (which is $\hat{y}$) $\pm$ the table value of t (with $n - 2$ degrees of freedom and the desired risk level) times $\hat{\sigma}_{\bar{y}}$ (the standard error of y). The mathematical calculations need not be discussed here, for the important point is that the confidence interval is more valuable in predictions than the single estimated value for y produced by the regression equation.

AN EXAMPLE OF APPLICATION

A study of some hypothetical regression output may show the relationships between the various statistical measures that have been discussed. An example of a simple regression is:

$$y = a + bx,$$

where

x = growth rate (percent per year)
y = P/E ratio.

Analysis of a group of data yielded the following results:

Statistic	*Value*	*Explanation*
a	7.0	*P/E* ratio is 7.0 when growth rate is zero.
b	0.85	*P/E* ratio rises 0.85 for each 1% increase in annual growth rate.

Statistic	*Value*	*Explanation*
$\hat{\sigma}_b$	0.03	In 68% of the cases studied, the value of *b* fell within the range 0.82–0.88 (that is, 0.85 ± 0.03).
$s_{1.2}$	0.12	The actual *P/E* ratio will differ from our estimate by 0.12 or less 68% of the time.
$r_{1.2}$	0.99	The correlation is extremely high.
$R^2_{1.2}$	0.97	Variations in growth rate explain 97% of variations in *P/E* ratio.

Substituting the definitions of the variables (x and y) and the values of the parameters (a and b) into the original regression equation, we write

$$P/E \text{ ratio} = 7.0 + 0.85(\text{growth rate}).$$

An example of a multiple regression might be

$$y = a + b_1x_1 + b_2x_2,$$

where

x_1 = growth rate (percent per year)
x_2 = debt/equity ratio
y = P/E ratio.

In this case, the analysis yielded the following results:

Statistic	*Value*
a	10
b_1	0.60
b_2	0.40
$\hat{\sigma}_{b_1}$	0.07
$\hat{\sigma}_{b_2}$	0.10
$s_{y.12}$	0.09
$R^2_{y.12}$	0.99

Substituting the definitions and values as before, we write

$$P/E \text{ ratio} = 10 + 0.60(\text{growth rate}) + 0.40(\text{debt/equity ratio}).$$

Interpreting this regression, we see that the x_i explain almost all of the P/E because $R^2 = 0.99$ (and 1.00 is perfect). If growth rate and debt/equity ratio are zero, the P/E is 10. It is unlikely that the two variables will be zero, however, so that a certain amount of additional P/E must be given for each unit of increase in the growth rate or debt/equity. How much should be added? The total P/E is increased 0.60 for every unit of increase of growth and 0.40 for every unit of increase in the debt to equity measure being used. These are the coefficients (b_i) in the equation.

What was gained by going from a simple (growth, P/E) regression to a multiple regression? By including debt/equity in the explanation of the behavior of P/E, the model increased R^2 from 97% to 99% and so achieved a slightly better explanation. In addition, the scatter around the predicted values for y (the P/E) dropped from 0.12 to 0.09, thus permitting a more accurate prediction of y.

If adding the debt/equity ratio to the simple regression (thus making the study a multiple regression) added a reasonable amount of information to the study, what effect would adding the yield have? Including yield in this particular study added only 0.001 to R^2, the coefficient of determination, and reduced s, the standard error, by only 0.0009. In effect, yield can be eliminated from this hypothetical study because of a lack of confidence in the existence of a correlation, although more precise reasons for dropping yield can be developed using partial correlation as discussed in the next section. As a result of rejecting this variable, the analyst would conclude that the "best" explanation of the P/E ratio is found by the use of growth rate and the debt/equity ratio. In other words, P/E is best described as a function of the growth rate and debt/equity. And if this particular function is used, the regression indicates it is not statistically useful to include the yield at all as a predictor of the value of a stock's P/E.

PARTIAL CORRELATION

The extremely valuable results achieved in the last 400 years or so as a result of the use of the scientific method can, to a very large extent, be ascribed to the concept of the "controlled experiment." The scientist attempts to eliminate the influence of all aspects of his problem except the particular variables with which he is dealing in order to obtain reliable measurements and thus provide a firm foundation for his conclusions. As an example, a physicist rolling a ball down a slope would not be expected to conduct his experiment on an extremely windy day unless he specifically wished to include the effects of wind as a factor in his experiment. Unfortunately, the basis of this scientific method, the *controlled* experiment, is not available to the investment analyst. Businessmen and economists attempting to analyze their problems scientifically are not able to control outside influences and as a result are forced to accept analyses that suffer from a great deal of unavoidable imprecision.

It would certainly be useful to be able to calculate the relationship between two items in a scientifically controlled environment, but this is impossible. The analyst, however, does have an alternative at his disposal. It is possible to determine statistically the relationship between, say, P/E and growth as it *would* have been *if* the price-earnings ratio had not been affected by an outside influence of, say, yield. In effect, the variable that constitutes the outside influence is controlled statistically instead of by the physical design of the experiment. The variable statistically controlled is in effect eliminated from the correlation under consideration by the nature of the statistical technique. This technique is called partial correlation.

The symbol for a partial correlation is familiar from previous applications. The correlation coefficient r is used, but it now has subscripts attached in such a way that the meaning is clearly distinguishable from a standard correlation coefficient. The only new aspect of the notation for partial correlation is the location of a period in the subscripts. All variables in front of the dot are included in the correlation, while all items after the dot are (in a certain statistical sense) held constant. Therefore, if $r_{12.4} = 0.88$, variables number 1 and 2 are correlated to a fairly high degree if variable number 4 is not allowed to influence the study. Another example would be $r_{y1.2} = 0.95$, indicating that y and the first x have a very high relationship if the second x is not allowed to interfere with the investment analyst's "experiment."

As an example, assume the two independent variables, growth rate and debt/equity, are used to predict P/E:

$$r_{y1.2} = 0.91.$$

This statistic shows the correlation between P/E and growth, ignoring the effect of the debt/equity ratio. In other words, the technique of partial correlation has held the debt/equity ratio constant and then measured the correlation between the two variables being considered, P/E and growth in this case.

Partial correlation permits one variable to be held constant in the statistical sense because the analyst is unable to hold it constant in the real world. The correlation resulting from this removal of an unwanted factor need not be the same as the simple correlation. In fact, if the factor removed *does* have an influence on the apparent relationship, the "adjusted" correlation will *necessarily* vary from the simple one. The simple correlation of P/E to growth is 0.99, but the correlation net of the variations induced by the debt/equity ratio is 0.91. Therefore, some of the variations in debt/equity are causing both P/E and growth to react, and this tendency for both variables to react to a common cause quite naturally forces them to appear to be more highly related than actually is the case.

The impact of unwanted changes in an extraneous variable is shown even more graphically in $r_{y2.1}$, the correlation of P/E to the debt/equity ratio net of the impact of growth. This value is 0.71, down from 0.96 for the simple correlation coefficient for P/E and debt/equity, indicating that a great deal of the apparent relationship between P/E and debt/

equity actually stems from the fact that both are sensitive to changes in the value of another variable—the growth rate.

The partial correlation coefficients are computed from the simple correlation coefficients through the use of a fairly simple formula and are automatically provided by most computerized regression programs.

ADDITIONAL TOPICS IN REGRESSION

Multiple regression actually includes a broad variety of additional techniques too complex to be treated in detail here. A brief statement of some of the more commonly used extensions is presented so that the analyst will be able to recognize the approaches taken either in professional articles he may encounter or in the results of studies undertaken by his firm's quantitative analysts.

Statistical tests of r

The correlation coefficient, r, is a statistic used to estimate the actual relationship between the variables being studied. The actual relationship in the real world is called ρ (rho) and r may incorrectly estimate ρ because of sampling error. If this happens, the analyst might maintain that a relationship was present when in fact it was not. The *possibility* of this occurring is unavoidable, but it is possible to determine the *probability* of error, that is, it is possible to test r at a given level of confidence to see if a relationship does in fact exist (to see if ρ is not zero). A t test is used for this purpose, and the result might be, for example, that one can be 95% confident that the two variables are related.

The use of F tests

The analysis of variance can be applied to multiple regression. In this technique, a value for F is computed for each independent variable in the equation. This F indicates whether or not the analyst can be confident (at some specified level, say, 90%) that the variable being predicted is in fact dependent upon the value of the given independent variable. Obviously, if the test shows that this level of confidence is not present, then the variable should not be used as a predictor. This technique tests the significance of the independent variable *net of the impact* of the other variables, that is, tests the significance of the correlation that is measured by the *partial correlation coefficients*. A predictor with a high correlation coefficient may be completely insignificant when considered in combination with other predictors. This type of result seldom can be seen by a direct traditional analysis of the data and may be useful to the analyst in rejecting relationships as invalid that on the surface appear to be quite real.

Stepwise regression

The use of the F test to determine the confidence that can be placed upon the value of any predicting variable is the basis for a powerful extension of regression technique. Stepwise regression permits the analyst to start with a large number of variables that might have predictive value and then use the model to select the particular variables that appear to provide the best prediction.

Using this technique, for example, an analyst might select ten variables that could conceivably influence the price-earnings ratio of stocks and present the values of these variables for a large number of stocks to the model. Stepwise regression would then proceed by calculating the F for each of the ten variables. This approach, of course, is a measure of the significance of each variable as a predictor of P/E ratios. If any of the variables is significant, the *most* significant one is used to produce a regression equation. Next, the significance of the variables is *recalculated* to determine their predictive value, *given* that the current regression equation is used. If a significant improvement can be achieved by including another variable in the equation, the best variable is selected and the regression equation is recalculated to include the new predictor.

The technique proceeds by simply evaluating the variables and adding them into the predicting equation if it is desirable to do so. The one exception to this rather straightforward process stems from the fact that whenever a new variable is included in a regression equation, the significance of other predictors already present may decline substantially. For example, assume that the growth rate of earnings was related to the percentage of earnings retained after dividends and the P/E ratio was related to the accumulation of earning assets in any given company. What would happen if the stepwise regression procedure at the first step used the growth rate as a predictor and at the second step added the percentage of earnings retained as a second predictor? The significance of the growth rate would decline substantially because a high proportion of its predictive power would now be transferred to the variable just added to the equation. If this loss of explanatory value is so large that the growth rate variable is no longer significant, the regression equation is obviously unsatisfactory.

Stepwise regression solves this problem by checking all of the variables in the equation after a new variable has been added in order to be certain that they remain significant. Insignificant variables are systematically ejected from the equation before any attempt is made to enter any new variable. Once the equation is corrected, the process of evaluating and inserting additional variables is resumed.

The model proceeds stepwise, evaluating possible predictors, inserting the best of these into the equation, removing variables in the equation that may have become insignificant, and then returning to the evaluation and insertion of new variables. The process is completed when all of the significant variables presented to the model have been included in the regression equation, and all of the insignificant variables have been excluded. The model will automatically evaluate the variables presented by the analyst and select those most useful in predictions. This entire process is performed in one computer run without any need for additional information at any intermediate step. In effect, the analyst inputs the set of all possible predictors, and the model outputs the most useful regression equation. In addition, all of the statistical information associated with a standard regression is automatically provided *for each step* executed in the procedure.

Nonparametric correlation

The techniques described in this chapter are parametric; they assume a normal distribution. In a number of cases, this assumption may be severely violated. If so, nonparametric methods for computing correlation coefficients and partial correlation coefficients are available, complete with statistical tests for their significance. Unfortunately, however, the prediction equation cannot be produced by nonparametric methods because these techniques are based upon ranking the data instead of using the actual numerical values.

Nonlinear regression

The regression equation considered in this chapter is linear (i.e., straight line). Curvilinear (curved line) regressions are also possible. For example, the logarithm of a variable can be presented to the model instead of the variable itself. The computations used by the model remain exactly the same, but the resulting regression equation is a linear equation in the log of the variable, which is clearly nonlinear in terms of the variable *itself*. It is possible to use the square of a variable, the cosine of a variable, the product of two variables, etc., to produce regression equations. These changes in the original variables are called transformations, and the output of the regression model is still linear in terms of the transformed variables. It is only nonlinear in terms of the original variables.

A truly nonlinear regression (i.e., one that is nonlinear in terms of the coefficients being estimated) is seldom encountered in actual practice.

Joint regression occurs when the variable being predicted is a function of two or more variables that cannot be separated, that is, $y = f(x_1, x_2, \ldots x_n)$ but is not a function of the form $y = f_1(x_1) + f_2(x_2) +, \ldots, f_n(x_n)$. In this case, the equation that describes the behavior of y as, say, x_1 changes will itself change for each of the different values of x_2. This shifting of values produces a sticky statistical problem that is complicated even when the set of observations is very large.

ECONOMETRICS

Regression theory has proven to be a most useful statistical technique in economic analysis. This usefulness stems from the value of regression in estimating the relationships among variables, thus providing economists with a tool for empirical verification of relationships postulated by various economic theories. For example, an economist might try to predict the price of a commodity, using its per capita production and per capita real disposable personal income. Or he might try to estimate the relationship between output for a particular product and the labor and capital inputs for that product.

The financial analyst can, of course, gain a great deal of insight into economic relationships and how these economic linkages affect the capital markets by studying the results of econometric analyses. That type of material, however, is more relevant to a text on economics than to one on statistics, so that this section simply discusses some of the problems with the regression model that were discovered by economists when they attempted to apply it to economic problems. These limitations are important to analysts because they indicate why the results of regression studies should be viewed with caution.

Autocorrelation is a problem frequently encountered by financial analysts when their input to the regression model is a set of time series. The term "autocorrelation" refers to a problem in the "predictions" of the input y's using the x_i variables. The problem arises because a prediction error in, say, the first quarter of 1975 will tend to be associated with a similar prediction error in the second quarter of 1975. For example, if the analyst is using regression to determine whether his predictors for the stock market actually relate to market movement, he might develop a regression equation that gave the market predictions shown by the dotted line in Figure 7–11.

Notice that a low prediction in one quarter tends to be followed by a low prediction in the next quarter. An error on the high side tends to be followed by another high error. This relationship illustrates the problem of autocorrelation, which is that successive errors are correlated to each other. In this situation, ordinary regression is not strictly appropriate because it underestimates the amount of error in the regression

Figure 7-11

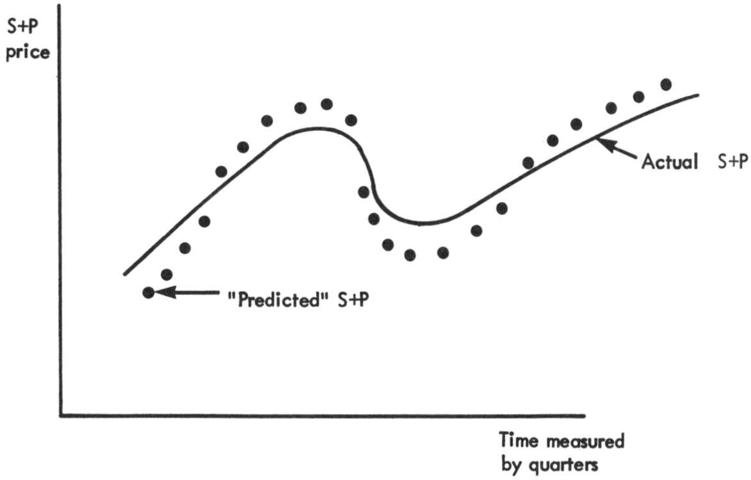

equation estimates. Usually, autocorrelation is an indication that an important predicting variable has been left out of the study. The most straightforward solution to the problem therefore is to locate the missing variables. An alternative is to use a more complex, econometric estimation technique instead of standard regression.

Multicollinearity is another problem frequently encountered by analysts. When a number of the variables included in the study are very highly correlated to each other, it is difficult for the regression model to tell them apart and determine the separate effect that each has on the variable being predicted. As a result, the standard error of the regression coefficients ($\hat{\sigma}_b$), which measures the reliability of these coefficients, may become very large and, in turn, make the coefficients of the variables in question fail their t test for significance. The problem can be avoided by eliminating one of the highly correlated variables from the study, or in some cases by adding more observations as input to the regression. If the $\hat{\sigma}_b$ are satisfactory, multicollinearity is not a problem, that is, the correlation of variables is not in itself damaging unless unsatisfactory values of $\hat{\sigma}_b$ result.

Heteroscedasticity occurs when the prediction errors resulting from the use of the model do not have the same variance (the same degree of reliability). For example, a model attempting to describe the sales of a company during a period where those sales climbed from $1 million to $85 million would have less error (measured in absolute dollars) at the low sales level than the high sales level. If standard regression technique is used, all observations are given the same weight, which in reality underweights the earlier and smaller observations relative to the later years of larger dollar sales.

Errors in variables pose a severe problem for analysts. The variables input to the regression are not known exactly, but only with some measurement error. Economic variables are estimated by the government from surveys, market movement is estimated by using a market index, interest rates are estimated from a sample of securities, etc. Standard least squares regression does not allow specifically for this type of error and may produce misleading results.

Other problems that have been explored include errors correlated with predicting variables (which biases the results) and predicting variables that are themselves random variables not known with certainty (which causes the amount of error in the regression study to be underestimated).

In light of all of these problems and all of the confidence estimates produced by the regression model, how is the analyst to proceed in a particular regression study? Only general suggestions are available to answer this question. In fact, empirical investigation using regression theory still requires a great deal of ingenuity and "feel." Perhaps the most important single point made by the statistical researchers is their emphasis upon the t test of the regression coefficients instead of R^2. The t test determines whether a coefficient (and its variable) is reliable enough to use in the equation. To pass the t test, the regression coefficient must have an acceptably small standard error ($\hat{\sigma}_b$). In other words, we must be fairly certain that we have estimated the influence of the variable with a reasonable degree of accuracy. Reasonably good coefficients mean a reasonably good equation. Only after the $\hat{\sigma}_b$ are considered acceptable does the statistician evaluate R^2 to discover the percentage improvement in prediction power. After all, if the estimated values for the regression coefficients (b_i) are not reliable, it doesn't matter how well the unreliable equation "explained" the input data, because it cannot be expected to predict the future data.

Financial analysts tend to place far too much emphasis on the level of the R^2 statistic. Because the regression equation will be used to predict the future, why choose an equation with an R^2 of 0.90 that has very unreliable coefficients assigned to the predicting variables rather than an equation with an R^2 of 0.50 and reliable coefficients? In the former case, no reliable prediction is possible, while in the latter case a true 50% reduction in error has occurred. Analysts may have drifted toward a demand for high R^2 because of the very high level of interdependence typically found in financial and economic data. In this operating environment, any attempted regression that has properly chosen predictors is likely to produce a "good" R^2 value. In order to choose between two alternative equations, the analyst frequently is forced to choose between an R^2 of 0.80 and an R^2 of 0.88. Such choices between equations are much sounder if based on the reliability of the coefficients.

The quality of a regression also can be evaluated by carefully examining the behavior of the residuals. Any "pattern" in the errors (the extent by which the regression failed to predict the input variable, or the $(\hat{y} - y)$ values) indicates a problem in the regression model. Therefore the errors should be arranged in various ways to see whether such patterns exist. For example, the residuals could be arranged in order of time, where successive residuals indicate the "forecast" of the input data in successive quarters of data history. A pattern such as that in Figure 7-12 reflects the autocorrelation problem discussed earlier.

Figure 7-12

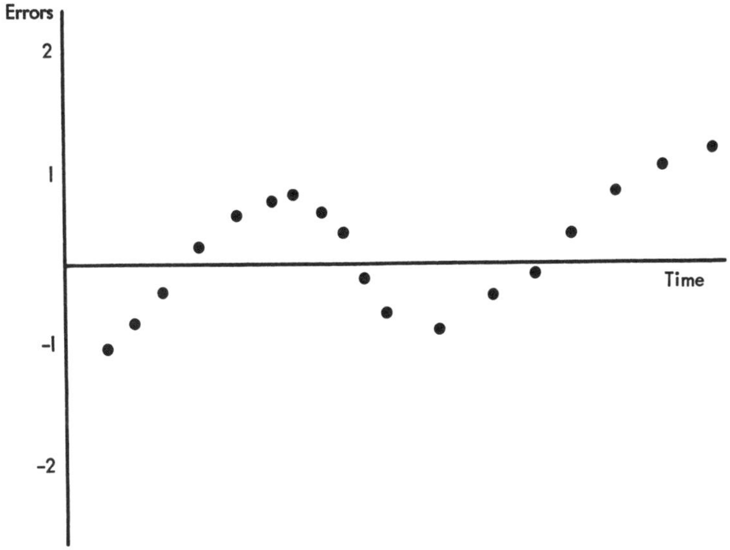

Another possibility is to arrange the residuals in order of increasing numeric values of the dependent (predicted) variable. For example, if P/E ratios were being predicted using growth and an index of price stability as predictors, the graph shown in Figure 7-13 could be constructed. This reflects the problem of heteroscedasticity.

The errors arranged in order of increasing values of a dependent variable such as growth might show a pattern like that in Figure 7-14. In this situation, the errors are correlated to one of the predicting variables. Any of these problems with the residuals indicates fairly serious problems in the regression equation. Avoiding these problems by using an alternative model is usually worthwhile even if a lower R^2 results. Econometrics is primarily concerned not just with identifying these and similar problems in regression applications but also with

Figure 7-13

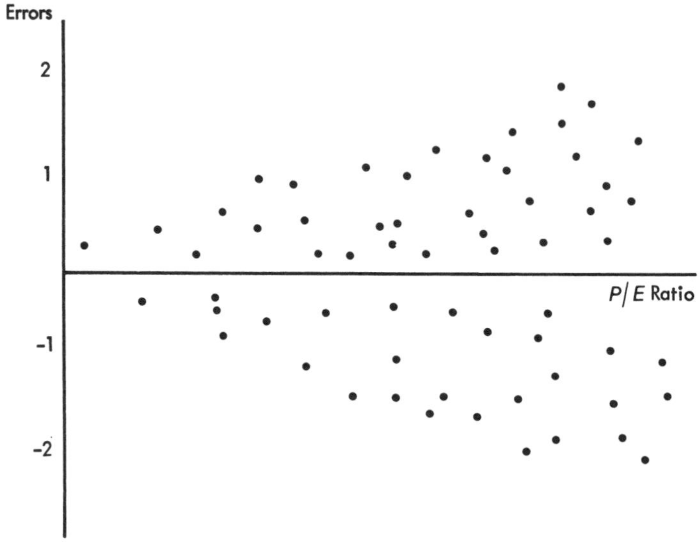

Figure 7-14

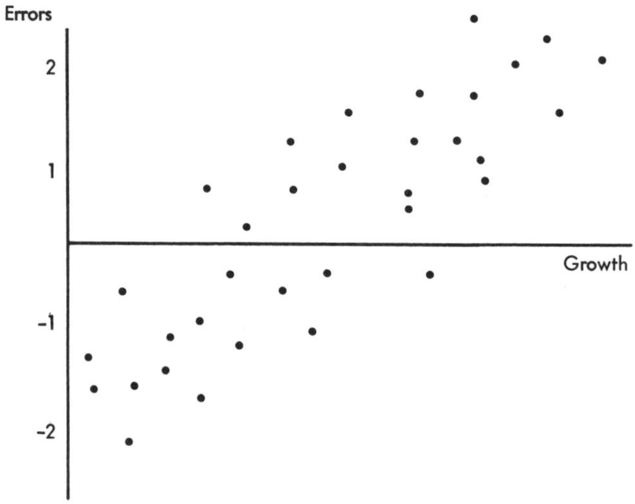

developing more advanced models that will apply when basic regression technique is not adequate.

ECONOMETRIC MODELS OF THE ECONOMY

Economics has become so basic to the input to the financial analyst, and econometrics has become so important to the research of the economist, that the analyst should be familiar with at least the nomenclature and basic structure of statistical models of the economy. The structure of these models depends very heavily upon complicated multiple regression analysis. The same basic line of attack can be applied to any multiple-equation model of a financial problem.

An econometric model starts with a set of *structural equations,* or equations that describe the structural or causal laws in the economy. There are two types of structural equations—*empirical* and *definitional.* For example, the equation

$$C = 0.8Y$$

shows that consumption (C) is a function of income (Y). The 0.8 would be an estimated value discovered by the use of some type of regression technique. The equation is *empirical* because it has been formulated from an examination of empirical relationships. On the other hand, the equation

$$Y = C + I$$

states that income is defined as the sum of consumption and investment (I). It is a *definitional* equation and does not depend upon empirical relationships.

A realistic model contains many variables, but these variables can be divided into two types: *endogenous,* or predicted by the model, and *exogenous,* or provided to the model so that the predictions of the endogenous variables can be made. As in any system of equations, a solution showing the numeric values of the variables being "predicted" is possible only when the number of equations equals the number of variables being predicted. A system having as many equations as endogenous variables (variables to be predicted) is called a *complete model.* In the two preceding equations, consumption and income are endogenous variables and investment is exogenous. Because two endogenous variables and two equations are given, the example constitutes a complete system, although an unrealistically simple one.

It is possible to use algebra to manipulate this system in the following manner. Because $C = 0.8Y$ and $Y = C + I$,

$$Y = 0.8Y + I.$$

Therefore, $0.2Y = I$ and

$$Y = 5I.$$

Because $Y = C + I$, $5I = C + I$, and

$$C = 4I.$$

This alternative way of describing the system,

$$Y = 5I$$
$$C = 4I,$$

is called the *reduced form* of the model, which shows each endogenous variable directly as a function of the exogenous variable. The reduced form is handier if predictions are to be made using actual values of the exogenous variables; the structural equations are more useful if the economic relationships are being studied. Various econometric regression techniques can be used to estimate the values of the coefficients in the equations using either the structural or the reduced forms, but the reduced form generally can be estimated with simpler techniques.

In addition to exogenous variables, lagged variables are frequently used in these models. Lagged variables are previous values of economic variables, for example, profits last year or output last year. These variables affect the variables being predicted, but at the time of the prediction their value is known with certainty. Some lagged variables can be included in the predictions of the model. For example, profits might be predicted by the model (and hence be an endogenous variable) while "profits last year" might be a separate, lagged variable known with certainty at the time of the prediction. An econometric model and a set of assumptions for exogenous variables for a number of future years can be used to generate a set of forecasts for each year, using previous forecasts as values for the lagged variables. This approach is sometimes helpful in evaluating the long-run effects of alternative policies.

Large models of the economy can provide valuable insights into how various segments of the economy interact. In addition, actual predictions of economic variables can be made if assumptions are made concerning the values of the exogenous variables. Such predictions, of course, are subject to three different kinds of error. First, the model could be right (correctly formulated and well estimated) and the equation still will predict the economic variable only with some error. Second, the model may be right and the assumptions for the exogenous variables (such as government policy) may be wrong. Third, despite the best efforts of the researchers, the model may, to some extent, have failed to abstract all of the essential economic relationships relevant to the future operation of America's economic machinery.

SUMMARY

Multiple regression has been shown to be a technique by which an analyst can explore the relationship between variables in a fairly precise quantitative manner. In addition, if variables are shown to be related, a regression equation can be used to assist in the prediction of future values. The model requires past observations of the variables involved in order to have sufficient information to be able to make reasonable assertions, and it is best to have many more observations than variables. The variables that might be chosen as input to the model are selected because some theoretical consideration leads the analyst to suspect that a relationship exists. The output of the model has been described in some detail, but it is always related to the measurement of the relationships, predictions that can be made on the basis of these relationships, or the accuracy of these predictions.

ADDITIONAL READINGS IN REGRESSION

Regression has received attention on all levels of mathematical sophistication. Simple regression is included in most introductory statistics courses and (probably because of the intriguing visual characteristics of the scatter diagram) can be found in almost all journals. Multiple regression is almost invariably treated in the elementary statistics texts, even though the instructors never seem to have time to include it in the course. On the other hand, variations of the basic regression model or advanced consideration of the probabilistic meaning of the statistical tests usually included with the basic analysis have filled a number of advanced texts.

The reason for the remarkable volume of material available in this area undoubtedly stems from the practical nature of the regression technique. Properly used, it can provide concrete predictions for real world values and also indicate the accuracy of those predictions. The literature is simply an extended analysis of the meaning of the phrase "properly used."

Klein, Lawrence R. *An Introduction to Econometrics.* Englewood Cliffs, New Jersey: Prentice-Hall, Inc., 1962.

This work is an extremely readable, essentially verbal, statement of the particular economic problems to which econometric methods have been applied (270 pages). The particular econometric techniques discussed are only very minor variations of simple and multiple regression. The text is therefore very valuable as an introduction to actual applications of regression analysis. The emphasis throughout the work is on finding the set of variables that will predict the unknown variable and then setting up the predicting equation. The solution of the equation, (finding the actual numerical value of the coefficients) by actually performing the regression analysis is never discussed. The material is an excellent introductory presentation of the interaction of statistical with economic theory and should be read by every financial analyst.

Duesenberry, J. S.; Froman, G.; Klein, L. R.; and Kuh, E., eds. *The Brookings Quarterly Econometric Model of the United States.* Chicago: Rand McNally & Co., 1965.

This book is a collection of regressions performed in order to predict various economic variables (738 pages). The chapters can be read independently, and each is an example of the process by which practical applications of regression are performed. The actual results of the studies are included, but the mathematical characteristics of the regression technique are not discussed. Because the use of regression by financial analysts is naturally more oriented toward the methodology of its application than toward its statistical characteristics, an examination of a few chapters from this book can substantially expand the reader's concept of the power of the statistical method.

Chou, Ya-lun. *Statistical Analysis.* New York: Holt, Rinehart and Winston, Inc., 1969.

This book is a standard elementary statistics textbook (736 pages). Chapters 19 and 20 (78 pages) present a reasonably clear statement of the method of calculating regressions and their associated statistical tests. The chief value of this material to a financial analyst would be its use as a handbook that can clarify the meaning of various statistics included in computer output he might receive or articles he might read.

Ezekial, Mordecai and Fox, Karl A. *Methods of Correlation and Regression Analysis.* 2d ed. New York: John Wiley & Sons, Inc., 1941.

This work provides an excellent presentation of both the elementary and somewhat more advanced aspects of regression (477 pages). The material is well illustrated with practical examples, and the calculations needed for any given technique are shown in detail. A great deal of verbal discussion on method and on the nature of each technique is included, adding significantly to the reader's intuitive understanding of the models. The first 347 pages provide practical techniques that can assist the analyst in everyday regression studies. The remaining material includes a discussion of joint regression, measuring correlation when the predictor is qualitative, and regression when a system of equations is being estimated.

Draper, N. R. and Smith, H. *Applied Regression Analysis.* New York: John Wiley & Sons, Inc., 1966.

This work is a somewhat more advanced presentation that could be helpful to an analyst already familiar with regression theory because it includes a number of variations in technique (such as dummy variables) that increase the range of applications without altering the computational aspects of the model itself.

Johnston, J. *Econometric Methods.* New York: McGraw-Hill Book Company, 1963.

This book discusses regression theory from an advanced standpoint (296 pages). The first part of the book covers the standard multiple regression model, and the second covers various modifications to the model that can be made when certain assumptions of the basic model do not apply. A knowledge of the simpler aspects of matrix algebra is required, but the material can be read and understood if a knowledge of the more powerful models is needed.

Latané, Henry A. and Tuttle, Donald L. *Security Analysis and Portfolio Management.* New York: The Ronald Press Company, 1970.

This book covers a very broad variety of investment topics with an unusually high degree of clarity (732 pages). The diverse set of investment problems are covered within the context of a single methodological framework that nevertheless remains remarkably free of dogmatic fealty to particular applications of models. The framework recommended is very flexible and can easily be used by practitioners without forcing their established techniques to be abandoned. Although the recommended methodology is quantitative, the presentation is verbal.

Regression and correlation are discussed in Chapter Nine (29 pages), but other chapters are very useful as follow-up reading to the presentation of other quantitative tools. Chapter Eight (33 pages) discusses applications of the mathematics of finance and also elementary statistics. Chapters 18 and 19 discuss the applications of probability theory to security analysis (53 pages), and Chapters 23 and 26 cover risk and the portfolio model problem (65 pages). The breadth of quantitative applications in the book make it difficult to decide where it should be listed in this book, and the choice of the regression chapter is purely arbitrary. If time limits the reader to only one selection from the list of additional readings, this book is the logical choice for the investment analyst or portfolio manager.

Chapter 8

Portfolio models

Linear programming is designed to examine a large number of combinations of data and from these select the best combination possible when the selection is affected by a number of restrictions. Linear programming can be used to select a set of stocks for a portfolio that will have predetermined desirable characteristics. Modifications of this technique are discussed. More complex mathematical procedures have been used in the development of portfolio theory. The Markowitz Mean-Variance Model, the Sharpe Diagonal Model, the Cohen and Pogue Multi-Index Model and the Treynor-Black Model are discussed. Finally, the Efficient Market Hypothesis and the Capital Asset Pricing Model are reviewed.

USING LINEAR PROGRAMMING TO FIND THE BEST MIX

Linear programming (LP) is an "optimizing" model, and its output is a maximization of all of the possibilities that the analyst presents to the technique. If he presents 45 alternatives, LP selects for him the "best" one. Actually, an infinite number of alternatives are given to the black box, and the best of all possible results is automatically returned. This capability obviously makes LP a useful tool, and it may profitably be used on any problem that the technique will accept. However, the computations used inside the model restrict the type of problem that it can solve. In other words, not every infinite set of possible solutions can be given to an LP model in the expectation of finding the "best" result. In order to understand the type of problem that LP is capable of maximizing, the following example of a legitimate application is given.

Assume that a portfolio manager has just received $100,000 cash and must now invest these funds in one or more of the 20 stocks that the research department currently has on the buy list. Naturally, he wishes to obtain the "best possible" return (defined as income plus capital appreciation) on this particular account's investment capital. As a result of a report distributed throughout the portfolio section, he knows the analysts' estimates for the expected return of all 20 stocks during the next year and has no further information upon which to gauge the investment desirability of any of the issues. Obviously, the portfolio manager can purchase a very large number of possible "mixes" of the 20 stocks, and he must attempt to select the best of these mixes. LP is capable of doing this precise thing: given all possible "mixes" of anything, it selects the best. In this particular, very simple example, both the analyst and the LP would choose to invest all funds in the one stock having the highest return because no consideration of diversification, risk, dividend yield, etc., has been included in the definition of the problem.

From this example, it can be seen that finding a use for LP is actually an attempt to discover a problem that requires finding the *best mix* of a number of items. Such problems are very frequent in business because the essential nature of an executive decision is the balancing of simultaneous resources, problems, or objectives. For example, in the investment area, what is the best mix of stocks to maximize return on invested capital? What mix of stocks will minimize the total price-earnings ratio in the account? If a relative value approach is being used by the research department, how can the portfolio manager maximize the relative performance of his accounts?

In most, if not all, of the above examples, the solution is obvious. Buy the stock with the highest return, or buy the stock with the best relative value. Why bother with LP when the answer is obvious? Because the obvious answer is not realistic. The portfolio manager buying only one stock would not be diversifying the risk. Any businessman is subject to a large number of restrictions, or constraints. His decision concerning the best mix is usually sharply restricted; it cannot exceed certain bounds.

In the real world, the number of rules that cannot be broken is in most cases very large. For example, a portfolio manager may have a diversification requirement imposed by the investment committee, a dividend yield requirement on the total portfolio imposed by the client, a yield requirement on each stock in the account imposed by policy, a risk limit stemming from a top-level policy decision, four stocks that cannot be sold for tax reasons, client-requested purchases that must be made, and so forth.

The presence of numerous constraints "clouding" the situation forces the analyst to accept "reasonable" solutions instead of optimum solutions. But LP can consider all such limitations and still produce the single mix that is the best of all possible mixes. LP is more realistic than human decisions in many cases because it can consider all of the very real aspects of the situation and still produce the best solution. At the same time, the solution still is fundamentally the result of human analysis, because the businessman always determines precisely what is to be maximized and what constraints really deal with the particular problem being presented to the model.

Actually, the analyst defines precisely what the best solution really is, and the computer determines the answer that the description implies. Once an analyst defines the problem for the LP run, he also defines a specific solution at the same time.

AN EXAMPLE OF USAGE

Assume for a moment that a portfolio manager has just received a new account which currently consists of only $100,000 cash. The portfolio manager has an LP computer program available and also has a statistician who can help him prepare the input data. The manager knows that only five stocks are currently on the buy list, and he is looking for the amount of money he should place in each issue ($0 invested in a particular stock being possible). This definitely is a "mix" type of problem, so he first takes a look at the nature of the mix with which he is concerned.

First, he decides that he wants the mix that will give him the best overall return on the account's investment for the next, say, five years. He is trying to choose the best set of values of x_i in the following list for the contents of the portfolio:

$\$x_1$ of stock A
$\$x_2$ of stock B
$\$x_3$ of stock C
$\$x_4$ of stock D
$\$x_5$ of stock E,

and he is going to use the percentage rate of return on each of these five stocks to determine the mix. Call r_i the rate of return for stock i. Then r_ix_1 would stand for the total annual dollar return from stock A. Similarly, it is possible to form this term for stock B, C, etc.; and the total of the dollar returns from each stock in the portfolio will equal the total return from the portfolio as a whole. It is therefore legitimate simply to add the five terms together in order to find the total return, and the total return is the quantity to be maximized.

As a result of the analysis of the portfolio return, the LP model is asked to maximize

$$r_1x_1 + r_2x_2 + r_3x_3 + r_4x_4 + r_5x_5,$$

where r_i is the expected annual rate of return for stock i, say, 8% on Widgets, Inc. Each x_i is the total number of dollars that should be invested in stock i. The rates of return (r_i) are known because they are provided by the research department, but the amounts to be purchased

(x_i) are not known. Determining their value is the reason for using the LP model.

This statement does not involve a great deal of mathematics, for only two changes in notation have been made. The item that is unknown has been given the name x_i, and the returns have been called r_i. The total return on the portfolio has then been stated in terms of r_i times the amount that is invested in each stock. The "r and x" expression is only another way of expressing the total return of the portfolio, total return being the sum of the returns on each stock that is purchased. The difficult part of this procedure, of course, is not the mathematical expression itself but the problem of casting the particular non-mathematical problem into the quantitative mode necessary if the LP model is to be used.

With the item to be maximized fully defined (its technical name is "objective function"), the next logical step for the portfolio manager is to list the restrictions to which he is subject in his investment of these particular assets. For example:

1. The total portfolio yield must exceed 4%.
2. The total portfolio P/E must be less than 14.
3. The total portfolio risk must be less than 10% possible loss for the coming year (using the analysts' estimated figures).
4. No more than 40% of the portfolio may be invested in any one stock.
5. The total investment must not exceed \$100,000.
6. A stock cannot be sold short.

The last two constraints are obvious, but the computer cannot detect through intuition even the simplest limitations. After the list of limitations has been completed, the manager and his statistician then convert the constraints into their mathematical representation so that it will be possible to prepare their input:

1. The total portfolio yield must exceed 4% of \$100,000, or \$4,000. By placing y_i = yield on stock i, the term $y_i x_i$ equals the annual dividend return in dollars for stock i. Because the portfolio return equals the sum of the $y_i x_i$, the statistician can write

$$y_1x_1 + y_2x_2 + y_3x_3 + y_4x_4 + y_5x_5 \geq \$4,000.$$

2. By defining m_i as the P/E ratio of stock i, the term $m_i x_i$ equals the value of stock i weighted by its P/E. The sum of these terms is the weighted value of the entire portfolio, that is, (P/E) times (100,000). It is possible to write

$$m_1x_1 + m_2x_2 + m_3x_3 + m_4x_4 + m_5x_5 \leq 1,400,000.$$

3. Setting v_i equal to the variation, or downside risk in stock i given a market down, say, 15%, the term $v_i x_i$ stands for the risk-weighted

commitment to stock i. The sum of these terms equals the total dollar risk in the portfolio as estimated by the research analysts. This can be written as

$$v_1x_1 + v_2x_2 + v_3x_3 + v_4x_4 + v_5x_5 \leq \$10{,}000.$$

4. Because each x_i (each stock) must be less than 40% of \$100,000, in other words, \$40,000, we have

$$\begin{aligned} x_1 &\leq \$40{,}000 \\ x_2 &\leq \$40{,}000 \\ x_3 &\leq \$40{,}000 \\ x_4 &\leq \$40{,}000 \\ x_5 &\leq \$40{,}000. \end{aligned}$$

5. Because the total investment in all five stocks must not exceed \$100,000,

$$x_1 + x_2 + x_3 + x_4 + x_5 \leq \$100{,}000.$$

6. Because only a positive amount of stock can be purchased in this account,

$$x_1 \geq 0 \qquad x_2 \geq 0 \qquad x_3 \geq 0 \qquad x_4 \geq 0 \qquad x_5 \geq 0.$$

With this quantitative description, the problem can be presented to LP, and the result will be a precise statement of the number of dollars to be invested in each of the five stocks. In addition, the model will provide the total expected return on the portfolio, given that the investments were made in the way recommended.

FORMULATING OBJECTIVES AND CONSTRAINTS

From what has already been said about the nature of linear programming, it can be seen that the most difficult part of the model is actually nonquantitative in nature. The major problem in establishing an LP model is the managerial problem of specifying the objective to be maximized and the limitations that are present in the real world as constraints upon the set of acceptable solutions. This selection of a desirable characteristic (objective) and real world restrictions are obviously not mathematical in nature, for mathematics is concerned neither with desires nor with real world conditions. Mathematics only manipulates symbols; managers must see to it that those symbols represent his desires and his reality.

The portfolio model used as an example of LP shows this principle very clearly. As already presented, the model has been given the objective of maximizing the expected total return on the portfolio over the next year. The "desired characteristic" was chosen because of a decision by the portfolio manager, not because of any mathematical consideration. The expected return over the next five years could have been chosen just as easily. In fact, the objective does not need to relate to "return" at all. An income-oriented account may have an objective of maximizing current income subject to the constraint of a "satisfactory" total return. If a portfolio manager accepts present value theory for stock valuation, the objective might be the maximum present value of the future dividend stream of the stocks available for investment. If relative value is the favored approach, the estimated deviation from "equilibrium" or "normal relative to the current structure of the market" might be chosen as the characteristic to be maximized. A very conservative manager might choose to minimize the downside potential of the account or possibly maximize the probability that the account will not decline. The choice of objectives is at the discretion of the manager, not the model, as these alternatives show. The LP technique will produce the portfolio most "desired" only after the manager has defined what he regards as "desirable," and different objectives produce different portfolios when using LP.

The constraints also are entirely under the control of the manager constructing the model. They can be realistic or unrealistic, depending upon the validity of his personal view of real-world conditions. LP will not violate his constraints under any circumstance, and he can choose to limit risk or to limit the minimum level of plant before depreciation for each company whose stock is considered. The model will accept both requirements as valid even though requiring some minimum level of plant before depreciation is a "strange" specification at best. The mathematical technique does not judge the constraints or "second guess" the manager; it simply produces the most desirable portfolio. The value of that portfolio is a function of the value of the manager, not the value of LP.

Constructing reasonable constraints can be a difficult matter, however, for the specifications must be firmly grounded in financial theory. Two major types of constraints can be applied to the portfolio example. First, limits must be placed on any portfolio as a result of the manager's knowledge of sound portfolio theory. Second, limits must be placed on particular portfolios to represent their individual needs and peculiarities. Examples of general constraints are limits on *P/E*, limits on risk, and limits requiring diversification. Examples of individual constraints are limits requiring a minimum yield, limits treating capital gains taxes, and limits restricting the sale of family-owned businesses.

Even though many constraints are general in nature, the precise values chosen for the constraints can be tailored to the needs of individual accounts. For example, the constraint limiting maximum acceptable possible loss may be set at 10% for the conservative account and at

20% for a more aggressive portfolio. Relaxing this restriction in more risk-oriented accounts permits the model to purchase more high-return stocks before having to "worry" about satisfying the risk requirement. This procedure permits the selection of a portfolio that has a higher estimated return but nevertheless does not go beyond the (now less severe) risk limitation of the (now more aggressive) investor. Relaxing the level of any constraint will usually result in a higher expected return (or more of the desired characteristic, however defined). In fact, the only time that "loosening" a constraint will *not* raise the return is when the constraint was already so loose that it did not restrict the selection of the highest return portfolio in the first place.

The return on the portfolio can be seen to be heavily dependent upon the constraints. If a high yield is required, the LP model must examine only the possible portfolios that produce the necessary immediate income. This may eliminate from consideration a number of portfolios that have a high total return. The result is a lower expected return on a portfolio that is constrained by a high yield requirement. The same line of thought applies equally well to very restrictive diversification or risk requirements, or to other constraints. For this reason, care must be taken to assure the necessity of each constraint and to set each constraint at the most relaxed level possible. Failure to do this will reduce the desirability of the portfolio by requiring it to conform to an unnecessary restriction.

All of the observations in this section point to one very important fact. The *value* of a mathematical model is not grounded in the *mathematics;* it is based upon the manager's ability to specify conditions of the real world. Mathematics merely points out the logical results of these specifications that must be realistic *given* that the original description of the world was realistic. If, for example, the original estimates of the return on each stock were "miserable," it is logical that the results of the LP portfolio that maximizes these "miserable" return estimates will not be outstanding. Because the LP model is usually run on a computer, this is an example of the fact that "computer selected" stocks are really selected by the criteria given to the computer by investment analysts and can produce results only as good as the estimates and constraints fed into the model.

RELATIONSHIP TO SYSTEMS OF EQUATIONS

The constraints limiting the various mixes that the LP model can consider have a very interesting relationship to the "screening" aspects of equations discussed in the section on functions. Recall that an equation such as

$$\text{Cost} = 10 + 0.8\,(\text{Production})$$

can be regarded as a mathematical way of screening out a number of inadmissible or undesirable pairs of (Production, Cost) values. A combination like (Production = 10, Cost = 8.2), for example, would no longer be possible. This "rule" for valid combinations is very similar to the "constraint" in LP stating that certain values are not permitted. In the example of an LP application, the first constraint was

$$\Sigma(y_i x_i) \geq \$4{,}000; \quad y_i = \text{yield}.$$

This statement requires that whatever the maximum solution of $\Sigma(y_i x_i)$ might be, the set of stocks purchased (the x_i) must have a total yield of $4,000 or greater. The constraint therefore "screens" a number of x_i combinations out of the set of possible solutions.

The nature of this use of inequalities as screens can be seen clearly if graphs are used to "picture" the various possible combinations. In order to use graphs, return for a moment to the two-variable case of Production and Cost, and assume that instead of an equality the following was known:

$$C \geq 10 + 0.8P.$$

The graph would look like Figure 8–1, where any C in the shaded region is still acceptable because it would be greater than $10 + 0.8P$. The line forming the lower boundary represents, of course, the equation $C = 10 + 0.8P$. If we consider the inequality

$$C \leq 10 + 0.8P$$

the graph would look like Figure 8–2.

Figure 8–1

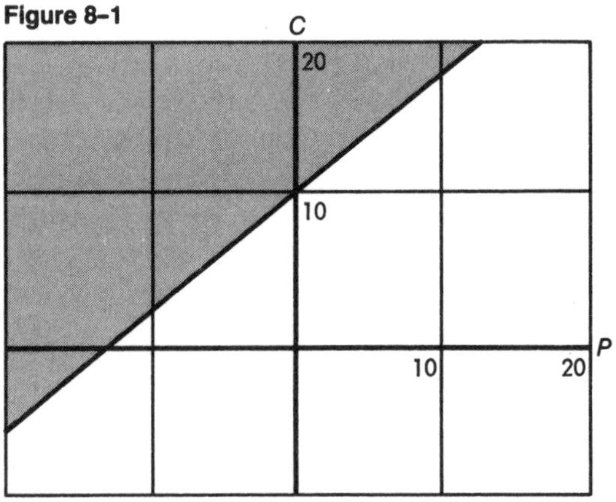

This chart shows that the other set of C values passes this inequality. The only set passing *both* inequalities is the set of (C, P) pairs that

Figure 8–2

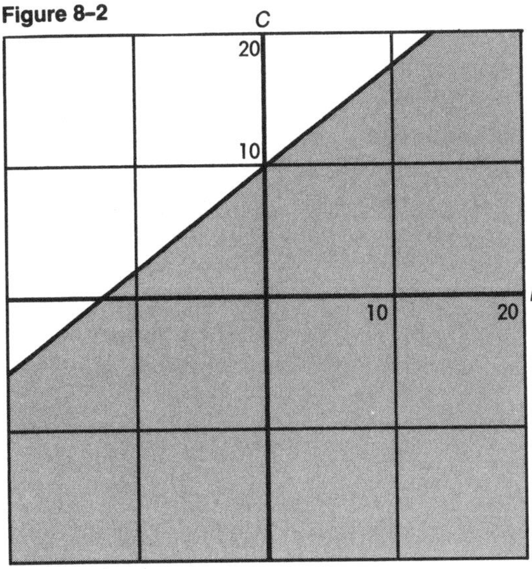

satisfies the *equation* $C = 10 + 0.8P$. This is reasonable, for if

$$C \geq 10 + 0.8P$$

and

$$C \leq 10 + 0.8P$$

are both true, the obvious conclusion is that $C = 10 + 0.8P$, which is graphed as the straight line, with all points above or below the line screened out.

Returning to the LP constraints, $\Sigma(y_i x_i) \geq \$4{,}000$ can be seen to screen a number of x_i combinations out of the solution in the same way as the graph screened certain Cost values, that is, the inequality sets up a "wall" in the solution space of x_i values. All x_i combinations on one side of the wall are excluded. If a number of constraints are introduced, a number of "walls" will "box in" the set of valid combinations of the x_i. This "boxing in" can be illustrated in the two-dimensional case by the graph in Figure 8–3.

The unshaded area represents the set of possible solutions that do not violate any constraint. Mathematicians have spent a great deal of time examining the characteristics of this set, and the proof that LP will work depends upon these qualities. Only a few points are of interest here, however.

The most important point that can be seen from this graphic presentation is the fact that once the analyst "boxes in" the permitted solu-

Figure 8–3

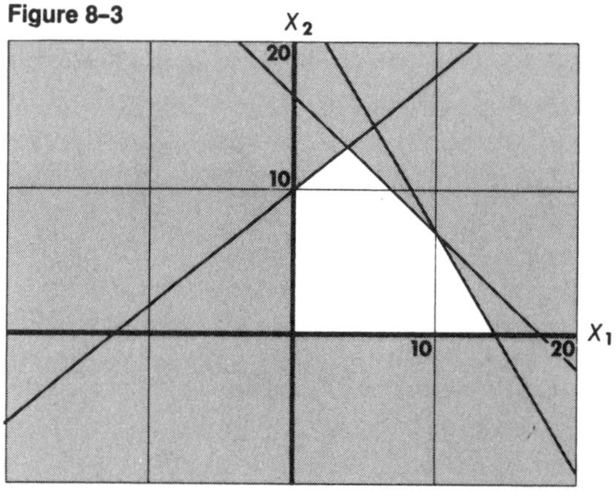

tions, the LP solution technique (called an algorithm) can examine the set of possible combinations and locate the "best."

The second conclusion evident from the discussion is that it is quite possible to specify a number of constraints that screen the set of possible solutions so thoroughly that no solution is possible at all. In this case, no possible mix can be constructed that will satisfy all of the requirements, and the problem is said to be "infeasible." An example of an infeasible set of requirements might be a $P/E \leq 5$, a yield $\geq 15\%$, and a growth rate $\geq 25\%$ per year. In this case, the model need not select the best of many alternatives, for it could not locate even a single stock that could pass these constraints.

A third concept related to the graphic interpretation of LP is the problem of an "unbounded" solution. If the analyst formulates the problem in such a way that the set of acceptable solutions is not "boxed in" completely, the model will be unable to evaluate all of the alternatives and no optimum solution can be found. An example of an unbounded problem might be the selection of an optimum portfolio with no limit on the number of dollars that could be invested. LP would simply start buying stocks and never stop.

LINEAR PROGRAMMING FOR A PORTFOLIO MODEL

The actual use of linear programming for finding desirable portfolios begins by locating the set of stocks that might have useful characteristics in a portfolio. Because a larger number of stocks tends to increase the flexibility of the model by providing more alternatives but at the same time increases costs because each stock must be analyzed, some thought needs to be given to the number of stocks to be included. A typical stock universe may consist of 75 to 150 issues.

Once the particular stocks have been chosen, the objective function (characteristic to be maximized) and the constraints need to be determined. This step must precede the evaluation of the stocks because the nature of the constraints determines the stock characteristics that must be estimated. For example, if constraints relate to yield next year, expected return, expected return in a bad economy, and beta, then the analyst must provide these numbers. The choice of objective function is a matter of the desires of the model's user. For example, expected return next year may be maximized, expected decline in an adverse economy next year may be minimized, the extent to which the portfolio's stocks' current *P/E* ratios are below some valuation model's predicted *P/E* could be maximized, *P/E* based on earnings five or ten years in the future could be minimized.

The choice of constraints also is a matter of the user's interests. For example, one set of constraints might limit the maximum percentage of the portfolio committed to any one stock, and the maximum and minimum participation in each industry, and the maximum participation in each economic sector. A set of constraints can relate to anticipated price behavior, limiting the anticipated loss in each of a number of adverse scenarios and assuring satisfactory results in favorable scenarios. Undesirable financial characteristics of companies can be given an upper limit and desirable features given a lower limit. The possibilities for these general types of constraint are almost limitless. A final set of constraints can "custom-tailor" the model to the needs of individual accounts, allowing for unique yield requirements, the client's desires concerning individual companies, etc.

Once the model's structure has been established, the necessary numbers describing each stock are located or estimated by the analyst. The model can then be run on a computer and provide the following types of output:

1. The percentage of the portfolio to be invested in each stock.
2. The value of the objective function. If, for example, the expected return next year is being maximized, the expected return of the recommended portfolio is reported.
3. The "cost" of each constraint. A number of the constraints may not be "binding" the recommended portfolio and therefore are satisfied at zero "cost" in the sense that their presence has not reduced the value of the objective function. For example, when maximizing expected return with one of the constraints limiting *P/E* to 15 or less, the resulting portfolio is found to have a *P/E* of 12. The *P/E* constraint therefore was satisfied without having to reduce the expected return by not including some high *P/E*, high return stocks in the recommended portfolio. This result could be phrased as the constraint having zero "cost". The cost of constraints that *are*

binding is also reported; this concept is the subject of the next section.

SHADOW PRICES (COST OF CONSTRAINTS)

One of the greatest side benefits of a knowledge of the nature of the linear programming technique is a knowledge of the nature of the costs of constraints. The cost information provided by the LP model is frequently called "shadow prices." In the portfolio application of linear programming, typical constraints are yield, *P/E,* risk, and a restriction on the amount that can be invested in each industry. Each constraint will have a shadow price representing the cost of not relaxing the constraint. For example, assume that the optimum portfolio has an expected return of 12% and is constrained to a yield ≥ 4%. Assume further that the shadow price of the yield constraint is 2, which means that the total return on the portfolio could be increased by 2% if the required yield were relaxed by one unit (from 4% to 3%). This shadow price therefore provides a precise measure of the "cost" in lost return that results from the presence of the constraint.

Each constraint has a shadow price, and the same interpretation that was given to the cost of "yield" can be given to any constraint. If, for example, the "risk" constraint were set at 10% of current market value, and had a shadow price of 3, relaxing the risk level to 11% would increase the expected performance by 3%. In the case of restrictions on investment in each industry, one constraint is set for each industry. Each industry would therefore have a shadow price representing the loss in performance that results from being unable to purchase more stocks in that industry. This information can be of great value in revising the diversification limits on portfolios because it pinpoints the restrictions that are too costly to performance.

If the shadow price is zero, the "cost" is zero. A constraint with a zero "cost" is satisfied by the portfolio that would have been selected even if the constraint were not present. The constraint, to put it bluntly, is not constraining. It is a limitation that would have been met automatically even if it had not been present. The presence of such a constraint does not mean that the problem has been incorrectly stated, because it is usually impossible to determine ahead of time that particular requirements will be met automatically. If the portfolio must yield more than 4%, for example, this constraint must be included in the problem. But if the optimum portfolio selected without regard to yield happens to yield 4.5%, the constraint happens to be unnecessary because it would have been satisfied anyway. In this case, the shadow price of the yield constraint would be zero, but the restriction should nevertheless have been included in the problem because the results could not have been foreseen. One of the advantages of LP is that it informs the user of the restrictions that are met without cost (zero shadow price) as well as the ones that are expensive. This information pinpoints the "free benefits" in the problem.

Shadow prices are also provided for the variables in the problem. The interpretation of these cost figures parallels the meaning of the constraint costs. In the portfolio example, the variables (x_i) are the values of the stocks available for purchase. The shadow price of a stock indicates the amount by which the portfolio's return would decline if one unit of the stock were purchased. If, for example, the problem were formulated in terms of the percentage of the account invested in each stock and Widgets, Inc., had a shadow price of 0.1, then committing 1% of the account to Widgets would reduce the portfolio return by 0.1%. The cost of every stock is provided, and issues having high shadow prices obviously are candidates for sale if currently held in an account. The stocks actually chosen by the LP model for the portfolio, on the other hand, have a zero shadow price, indicating that their purchase would not lower the optimum return. This result is reasonable, because their purchase is *required* for the optimum return.

The particular meaning of shadow prices will vary depending upon the nature of the LP problem being solved. A linear programming extension of input-output analysis will not have shadow prices expressed in terms of stocks. But all shadow prices of all LP problems have in common the fact that they are the cost of constraints or the cost of forcing the use of an undesirable variable.

PARAMETRIC PROGRAMMING

The level at which the constraints are set already has been shown to have an effect upon the numerical value of the objective function. In the portfolio problem, relaxing the constraints raised the return. The reason why this relation holds true is that different values for the constraints cause the inclusion of different variables in the final solution. In the portfolio application, for example, relaxing the yield requirement permitted the purchase of more high-return stocks that had a low yield.

The relationship between the levels of the constraints and the solution can be systematically explored by means of parametric programming. The precise manner in which the constraints are to be relaxed is stated mathematically, and the solution variables for a wide range of constraint levels are automatically provided. A simple example of this technique would be to hold all constraints constant except for yield and then study the behavior of a portfolio as the yield requirement is increased from zero to infinity. If ten stocks were available for investment, the results of the study might show something like Table 8–1.

Table 8–1

Total return	*Dividend yield between*	*Purchase*
16%	0% and 2.4%	x_4, x_9, x_{10}
14%	2.5% and 2.9%	x_4, x_9, x_{10}
13%	3.0% and 4.3%	x_1, x_4, x_9, x_{10}
9%	4.4% and 5.2%	$x_1, x_3, x_4, x_9, x_{10}$
7%	5.3% and 6.5%	x_1, x_3, x_4, x_8, x_9
—	6.5% up	no feasible solution

The return associated with each of these possible portfolios is also provided. The yield constraint examined, of course, could refer to the level of acceptable risk just as easily. In fact, two or more constraints can be varied at the same time. The level of the constraints in problems of this type is called a parametric requirements vector, and the problem is called "parametric on the right hand side" or "RHS parametric."

An alternative form of parametric programming is "parametric on the objective function." This technique systematically varies the coefficients in the objective function. In the portfolio model, it would vary the expected returns of the stocks. The results of this type of study show how the portfolio would change as the estimated return of the stocks were changed.

INTEGER PROGRAMMING

Integer programming is a special form of linear programming where the values of the variables must be integers. For example, assume that a portfolio problem has been formulated in such a way that the x_i refer to the number of round lots of stock i that are to be purchased. This approach is not a substantial change from the original example, where x_i referred to the number of dollars of stock i purchased. By using round lots, the integer requirement that the value of x_i be 0 or 1 or 2 or . . . forces the optimum portfolio to avoid the purchase of odd lots (which, of course, are fractions of round lots).

The solution given by integer programming is not necessarily the solution that would result if a normal LP run were made and the results were simply "rounded off" to the nearest round lot. If optimum results are desired, the integer requirement must be built into the structure of the problem itself, not approximated after the model has been applied.

The value of integer programming is far greater than might at first be suspected, for it would be ridiculous to follow a "normal" LP solution requiring the purchase of 1½ plants or the addition of 4.35 employees to the staff. Another invaluable use of the technique only can be mentioned in this chapter. If an integer solution is required and the x_i are also required to be ≤ 1, the only two acceptable solutions for any variable are 0 or 1. This type of model can be used in studies related to optimal selection, for the selected variables are assigned a one and the rejected variables are assigned a zero. If the set of "yes-no," "on-off," or "good-bad" variables must be found subject to a number of real world restrictions, this technique is invaluable.

Examples of this "0-1" model can be found in capital budgeting, personnel selection, and research and development allocations. Applications in investment research have not been extensively explored, but the practical nature of the problems solved by this approach indicates that many problems in this field could be approached in this way. For example, what set of companies deserve coverage by the research department? What set of industries not currently considered should be added? Which industries should be assigned to analyst A? What set of accounts deserve weekly review by the portfolio manager? If only five stocks can be recommended in a meeting, which five should be included?

MARKOWITZ'S MEAN-VARIANCE MODEL

The approach found in linear programming can be broadened by including the consideration of investment risk directly in the specification of the portfolio model. Harry Markowitz defined risk quantitatively in terms of the variance of possible returns that a portfolio might achieve in the single time period that the portfolio model considers, forcing the use of more complex mathematical procedures than linear programming but inproving the treatment of the risk variable. For example, an investor having a five-year investment horizon could view risk as the variance or "spread" of a probability distribution that describes his expected five-year return estimate. From this distribution, he could compute his probability of losing money, his probability of failing to offset inflation (assuming he had an inflation rate estimate), or the probability of failing to achieve some personally important "target" rate of return.

The variance of the return possibilities that might be achieved in a single period is a meaningful measure of the risk associated with investing at the beginning of that period. The idea of investing solely for a single time period may be less realistic, for in reality an investor can buy or sell during the period and may use different investment horizons for different investments. Nevertheless, the single-period model is a useful model, although it does simplify the assumptions about the flexibility of an investor's actions. A practical problem develops in assuming that risk can be described by the variance or standard deviation of the return. One possible assumption is that the variance of an investment's historical returns over time (past volatility) is a good measure of future risk. Depending upon the circumstances, this assumption may or may not be valid, but it is not a problem that the Markowitz model considers and is not the type of risk that Markowitz quantified when he used the variance of the portfolio's return possibilities at the end of a single period in the future.

In order to allow the model to compute the portfolio having the highest return for the desired level of risk, certain inputs have to be provided by the analyst. Markowitz suggested using the return expected by the analyst for each security under consideration. This approach also requires as input enough information about the securities to make it possible to compute the portfolio variance. Obviously, high-variance (unpredictable) securities tend to produce high-variance (risky) portfolios. But a portfolio of relatively unrelated securities will have a fairly low risk because the results of the various investments will tend to cancel each other out. Unusually favorable returns on a few stocks will be offset by unusually poor results on others. On the other hand, a portfolio of highly related stocks will be riskier, because unusually poor results for each stock will tend to occur at the same time.

The risk (variance) of a portfolio, in other words, is a function not only of the risk (variance) of the individual securities in the portfolio, but also of the number of securities in the portfolio and the extent to which they are related. As an earlier chapter has shown, the coefficient of correlation (r) is a measure of the relationship between two variables. The Markowitz model therefore requires as input the analysts' estimates of the variance of all securities and the correlation coefficient (or its weighted counterpart, the covariance) of every security to every other security.

The expected return on any portfolio that might be formed from these input data can be calculated from the following equation:

$$R = \Sigma r_i x_i$$

where

R = Portfolio expected return
r_i = Expected return on security i
x_i = Proportion of the portfolio invested in security i.

The total variance of any portfolio that might be formed from these input data can be calculated from the following equation:

$$V = \Sigma\Sigma\sigma_{ij}x_ix_j$$

where

V = Portfolio variance
σ_{ij} = Covariance of security i to security j.

These formulas apply to any possible portfolio of the securities in question. The model, however, is designed to produce the "best" portfolio (the highest-return portfolio for some given level of risk). The model cannot do this using linear programming, because the variance is not linear. In fact, because the variance is of a quadratic form (involves the square of a quantity), the model uses quadratic programming. In most portfolio applications, the "best" portfolio is desired for a number of risk levels, which is provided by parametric quadratic programming. This programming is directly analogous to the parametric linear programming described earlier. The Markowitz results can be provided subject to a set of linear constraints exactly like the constraints described earlier in the section on linear programming.

One result of this quantitative approach toward the portfolio problem was a change in the approach toward portraying the portfolio problem in a two-dimensional way.

Figure 8–4

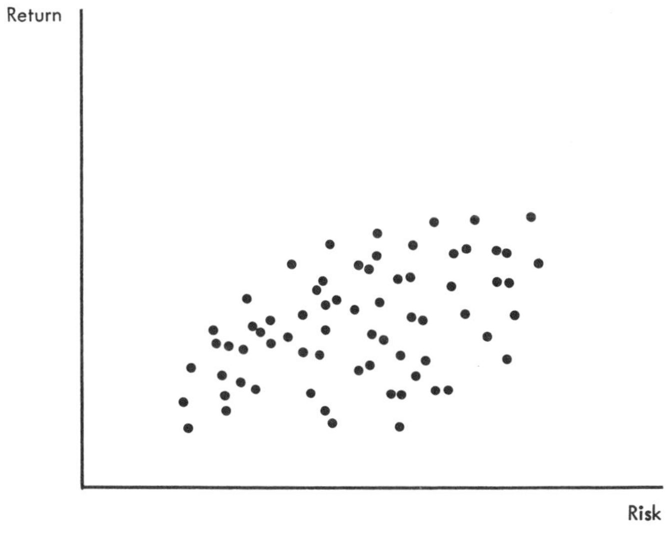

In Figure 8–4, each dot represents the expected return and expected risk of one portfolio. Risk is defined as the standard deviation of the expected return. The dots do not extend to the top of the graph because even the best portfolio is going to have some maximum return associated with it. The dots do not completely cover the lower right portion of the chart because not all portfolios are shown. Actually, because a new portfolio (dot) could be formed by owning $x\%$ of any portfolio and $(100 - x)\%$ of any other portfolio, the region of possible portfolios can be pictured with any degree of density that the analyst wishes.

Figure 8–5

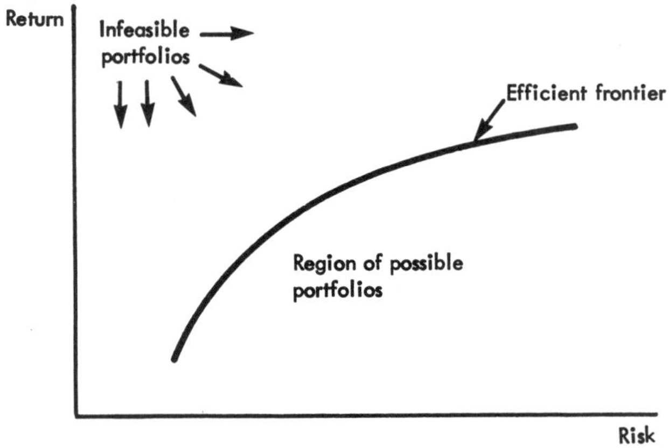

In Figure 8–5, the "efficient frontier" is the line separating feasible from nonfeasible portfolios. In other words, the efficient frontier represents the set of portfolios having one feature in common—each is the portfolio having the highest level of return at a particular level of risk. Portfolios on the efficient frontier are located by the Markowitz portfolio model, based on the analysts' input of data. The model uses the parametric programming technique to locate the optimal portfolio for each of a number of risk levels. The technique allows all of the constraints discussed in the section on linear programming to be used if desired. If used, the constraints will be satisfied by each of the optimal portfolios. Clearly, the Markowitz model retains the spirit of the linear programming approach to the portfolio problem and simply broadens the method to allow risk to be treated in terms of variance.

THE SHARPE SINGLE-INDEX PORTFOLIO MODEL

The fundamental practical problem of the Markowitz model is its input requirements. The model needs a computer for solutions to be generated. Institutions generally analyze between 100 and 200 securities, and the model would require more than 5,000 input estimates for only 100 securities. Because the cost and chance for error in estimating so many values for input to the model are high, some simplification was needed.

William F. Sharpe provided that simplification with his "diagonal model" or "single-index model." This approach assumes that the return for each security is correlated with the changes in some broad, general index of economic activity or of stock market prices (the latter has since become the standard variable). No security is correlated to any other security *except* for the correlation induced by their both being correlated to the broad index. Statistically, this statement is the same as saying that their *partial* correlation, net of the index, is zero.

This assumption greatly simplified the input process, for now only the unique return of each security and its relation to the index is needed, which is a substantial improvement over the requirements of Markowitz. This input is sufficient to allow the generation of efficient portfolios for each assumed level of risk and return. This approach draws attention to the use of alphas and betas to describe the market behavior of individual securities. The alpha is a unique return expected from an investment regardless of movements in the general index, and the beta is the sensitivity of the return on the security to the return the stocks represented by the market index. The simplification is mor than just a matter of reducing the number of input values, for analysts are probably able to provide better estimates of stock sensitivities to the market than correlations of, say, the return on GM to the return on IBM. Ordinarily, the analyst is more familiar with the relationships between price changes of his securities and the market, but less familiar with the price change relationships between pairs of stocks, particularly when they represent different industries or economic sectors.

Nevertheless, the difficulty experienced by the analyst in estimating alphas and betas for each security during the single future holding period evaluated by the Sharpe model caused both academicians and users to shift their emphasis away from analysts' input and toward the use of historical data. The input values rapidly became numbers generated by regressions of the historical returns on individual securities to the historical returns on the S&P 500 index (as described in the chapter on regression). Although this shift toward using past market behavior to estimate future behavior was a definite departure from the original Markowitz and Sharpe models, it appeared plausible under the assumption that "past is prologue".

This departure created several problems. First, all of the input numbers describing the volatility (and implicitly, the variance) of the securities' returns now come from historical market behavior. Therefore, the "variance" that the model implicitly identifies with investor "risk" is the historical variance of return over similar holding periods in the past. This historical variance of a security is the same variance to be expected during the future holding period *only* if the risk characteristics of the security remained unchanged over time. A number of studies of beta coefficients of stocks have shown that they change dramatically over time.

The alpha used initially by the model was the unique return estimated by the analyst to occur during the next holding period. When the shift to regression-generated historical numbers is made, however, the alpha becomes the excess (positive or negative) return achieved by the security in the past independent of past stock market movements. Because any security's historical market behavior is different from an analyst's evaluation and prediction of a security's future market behavior, the definition of the regression-generated alpha could be rephrased as "the past risk-adjusted market performance of an unanalyzed security." Very few analysts believe that a set of securities selected *without evaluation* could be expected to outperform other securities in the same risk class. But a non-zero regression-generated alpha says exactly that—and therefore it is not surprising that extensive testing by the academic community established that non-zero regression-generated alphas cannot be expected to persist over time. These studies, however, do not establish that analyst-estimated alphas are not valid.

As a result of these considerations, the Sharpe model can be considered a useful simplification of the portfolio problem, but one that still suffers from the main problem of the Markowitz model—the inputs must be accurate. The initial formulation of the model, using analysts' inputs, leaves the model's output as valuable as the analysts' input and makes the model useful as a way of seeing to it that analysts' estimates are, in fact, reflected in the construction of portfolios. If regression-generated historical input is used, the future alphas should be assumed to be zero and the betas will be only as reliable as the tendency for history to repeat itself. A compromise might be to use analysts' estimates of alphas and historical betas adjusted by current research and analysis.

MULTI-INDEX MODELS

The Sharpe model simplified the portfolio problem by assuming that each stock was directly related only to a single index. Some research suggests that this assumption is a severe oversimplification of the relationships among securities. Therefore, an alternative formulation assumes that all stocks in a given industry or economic sector are related to an index of that sector's market behavior. For each security, it would be necessary only to input the expected unique return (such as alpha) and the security's sensitivity to its sector.

In this approach, each security would be related only to a sector index. No security is related to any other security except for the relationship induced by the assumed relationship of each security to an index. In an example of such a model there might be an index of industrial stocks, an index of consumer stocks, and an index of financial stocks. These three indexes would be permitted to be correlated to each other. Any security would be permitted to be correlated to one and only one of these indexes. The correlation between, say, two financial securities would be zero except for the fact that both are related to the financial index. The correlation between, say, a financial security and an industrial security would be zero except for the fact that the financial security is related to the financial index, the financial index is related to the industrial index, and the industrial index is related to the industrial security.

A number of studies have been conducted to determine the relative effectiveness of full, single-index, and multi-index models. The results are somewhat varied, but in general single-index and multi-index models seem to provide roughly comparable results. The studies tended to rely heavily upon the input of historical data.

Implicit in the idea of the multi-index model is the assumption that a "stock market" is not sufficient to explain the structure of the movement of stock prices, but rather that stocks tend to move in groups, with all stocks in one group behaving in a similar way but with different groups behaving differently. A number of studies using the advanced statistical techniques of factor analysis and cluster analysis have tended to verify this description of market activity.

THE TREYNOR-BLACK MODEL

All of the preceding models have assumed that some incremental performance can be achieved by the use of information such as estimates by analysts. Incremental performance in this sense is performance beyond that achievable by investing in the market as a whole and adjusting the level of risk by purchasing U.S. treasury bills (T-bills). Because "buying the market" achieves a diversified return and is the best that could be done in the absence of valuable investment research information, it is reasonable to value information on the basis of its investment results compared to that of the market, adjusted for risk. The Treynor-Black approach goes further, expressing the entire portfolio problem in terms of unique insights and a "market portfolio." To the extent that analysts have a unique insight, the portfolio is committed to stocks found desirable, producing the "active portfolio." The remainder of the portfolio is invested in a set of stocks that approximate market behavior, called the "passive portfolio." Using analysts' estimates, the computerized model produces the percentage of the total portfolio that should be invested in each stock in the active portfolio and the percentage that should be invested in the passive portfolio.

The Treynor-Black model makes assumptions similar to those of the Sharpe model. Both begin by asserting that returns on stocks are correlated to the market return. Treynor-Black, however, directly treats the analysts' attempts to predict that portion of each security's return that is independent of the market. The analyst's estimate of the independent return of a stock will be correlated to the actual return that that stock will achieve in the future, with the correlation coefficient falling somewhere between zero and one. At zero correlation, the analyst's estimate has no value; at correlation of 1.0, he is a perfect predictor. The percentage of the active portfolio that is invested in any individual stock depends only upon this one characteristic—the correlation of the estimate of independent return to the actual independent return. The higher the correlation, of course, the greater the investment in the security.

The mathematical machinery used in developing the model established a number of interesting results under the assumption that the return on a security can be divided into two parts, one related to the market and one independent of the market and to some extent predictable by the analyst. In order to understand these results, a few definitions are needed.

1. *Market risk* is the risk in a stock caused by its being related to the market. This risk cannot be eliminated by diversification.
2. *Appraisal risk* is risk in a stock independent of the market but possibly predictable by the analyst.
3. *Riskless interest* is the interest rate on a riskless investment.
4. *Risk premium* is the additional rate of return over the riskless interest rate anticipated as compensation for bearing market risk.
5. *Appraisal premium* is the additional rate of return anticipated as a result of the analyst's activities.

The Treynor-Black approach indicates that:

1. The amount of market risk in stocks chosen for the active portfolio is not important because it can be adjusted by changing the percentage of the total portfolio committed to the passive portfolio or to T-bills. For example, a 10% commitment to an active portfolio containing stocks with a sensitivity twice that of the market has the same effect as a 20% commitment to an active portfolio having stocks with a sensitivity equal to that of the market.

2. The rate at which the portfolio can be expected to earn riskless interest depends only upon the market value of the portfolio, or upon the investor's equity in the portfolio if it is leveraged.
3. The amount of risk premium that the investor logically should anticipate is a function only of the market risk in the total portfolio and is not related to the investor's equity position or the structuring of the active portfolio.
4. The composition of the active portfolio depends upon appraisal premium and the appraisal risks associated with that premium. It does not depend upon market risk or market premium.
5. The security analyst can influence the performance of a well-balanced portfolio only by providing estimates of stocks' future independent returns that are correlated to their actual independent returns. The higher the correlation, the greater the contribution to performance. The analyst's performance is not related to the magnitude of the estimated returns, only to the correlation.

The Treynor-Black approach indicates that the portfolio problem should be attacked in three stages. First, the active portfolio should be constructed on the basis only of the expected correlation between the analyst's estimates of returns and the actual returns. Next, the risky-asset portfolio is formed by using a passive portfolio to adjust the total active and passive portfolios to the desired risk level. Third, the remaining funds are placed in risk-free T-bills.

THE EFFICIENT-MARKET AND CAPITAL-ASSET-PRICING MODELS

Portfolio theory originally developed as a "normative" discipline, as an attempt to provide an optimizing technique to assist in constructing desirable portfolios. Gradually, academic thought shifted toward "positive" theory, an attempt to explain how capital markets actually work. The findings of the new, "positive" theory are in many cases relevant to practical portfolio management. The enormous quantity of academic research that has been published on the behavior of stock market prices can be treated in the following four categories:

1. The weak form of the efficient-market hypothesis.
2. The semistrong form of the efficient-market hypothesis.
3. The strong form of the efficient-market hypothesis.
4. The capital-asset-pricing model.

The efficient-market hypothesis

Research in this area began by examining the pattern of movements of stock prices over time. Statistical tests of stock prices showed that they move randomly over time, that is, their future direction, up or down, could not be predicted using the past pattern of their behavior. This research indicates, for example, that three consecutive weeks of rising prices for a stock do not imply either that the next week will show another rise or that it will show a decline. Initially, these findings were met with some reservation because of the belief that the statistical tests might be too limited to evaluate effectively a number of the rather complex technical trading patterns then used by stock market technicians. Subsequently, direct computer tests of actual trading rules were conducted, and the results generally indicated that the rules were unable to benefit the investor when measured net of trading costs and relative to a "buy and hold" market strategy.

As the debates continued, it became clear that the "random walk hypothesis" questioned the value of "technical" analysis, not "fundamental" analysis, and that it was difficult to find empirical evidence supporting the belief that past prices could be used to predict future returns on securities or portfolios. By the mid-1960s, academicians and professionals seemed to have reached a consensus that past returns on a stock could not be used to predict future returns. This position, of course, did not imply that other variables, such as the company's financial position or the state of the economy could not be useful in predicting returns, so that the position taken by the fundamental analyst was not under attack. The scientific discipline of testing the data empirically to be certain that they are in agreement with theory (in this case, the technician's theories used at that time) established a practical result for the practitioner.

The natural question evolving from this situation was, for the academician, "How can it be that stock prices move randomly?" One increasingly popular answer is that the financial markets are efficient. Efficient markets, for all practical purposes, are held by this theory to reflect instantaneously all of the information relevant to their prices as soon as it becomes available. Because new information becomes available on a random basis, stock prices might well also move randomly. Theoretical results established that randomly occurring information necessarily will cause random movement of stock prices in a perfectly efficient market. This conclusion did not prove, of course, that the information flows were *causing* the randomness in stock prices. It showed only that an efficient market implied random prices, not that random prices implied a perfectly efficient market. Nevertheless, the idea certainly merited further research, and gradually the "random walk hypothesis" became known as the "weak form of the efficient-market hypothesis."

The semistrong form of the efficient-market hypothesis asserts that the link between efficient market pricing (prices based upon instantaneous discounting of information) and stock price movements does in fact exist. This form of the hypothesis asserts that all of the useful information available to all investors is used by these investors in deciding to buy or sell stocks, and that the investors' actions in the market-place will force the price of the stock to the level consistent with the information available. Therefore, the price always will equal the stock's "value," where "value" is interpreted as the price indicated by the available information.

Obviously, if the semistrong form is strictly true, even fundamental analysis would not be useful to the investor, because the current price of each stock would always equal its true worth. The semistrong form has not been widely accepted by investment professionals. The controversy seems to center upon the interpretation of the word "information." Data of the type available to analysts must be interpreted. This interpretation converts the data into information concerning the implied price change. With so much interpretation involved, many professionals believe that some divergence between price and value may occur.

The strong form of the efficient-market hypothesis asserts that all information relevant to pricing is reflected in the market even when that information is not publicly available. The problem with this theory is that it is not clear how information not publicly available could affect market prices. The implication of the hypothesis is that even insider activity in a stock would not produce an unusual profit.

The capital-asset-pricing model

While the efficient-market theory attacked the problem of stock prices from the standpoint of the action of buyers and sellers on information in the marketplace, the capital asset pricing model was being developed to explain investor behavior as an extension of the approach used in the mathematical portfolio models discussed earlier. This theory begins with a number of assumptions about how investors behave and then proceeds to deduce mathematically a number of findings about how they should invest. It is important to point out that the model treats investor expectations about returns in a single future time period. The model does not attempt to describe how investors have behaved historically or how stock prices have behaved in the past, but only how investors would behave in the next time period if they acted consistently with the model's assumptions. The most important of these assumptions are that investors view the investment problem in the same terms as that found in the Markowitz model (a risk-return trade-off), that all investors have the *same* expectations about the risk and return available from each investment, and that each investor can borrow and lend at a risk-free rate of interest.

Because the model assumes that all investors have formed the same expectations about risks and returns, the logical point to begin the analysis is to determine how an investor might choose between alternative securities or packages of securities (portfolios). This problem is attacked by using a standard approach developed in microeconomic theory—indifference curves. Recall that in the Markowitz formulation of the portfolio problem, every portfolio could be portrayed as a dot on a graph such as that of Figure 8-6, with the portfolio's expected return (E_p) on the vertical axis and the portfolio's risk or standard deviation of possible returns in the next holding period (σ_p) on the horizontal axis.

Figure 8-6

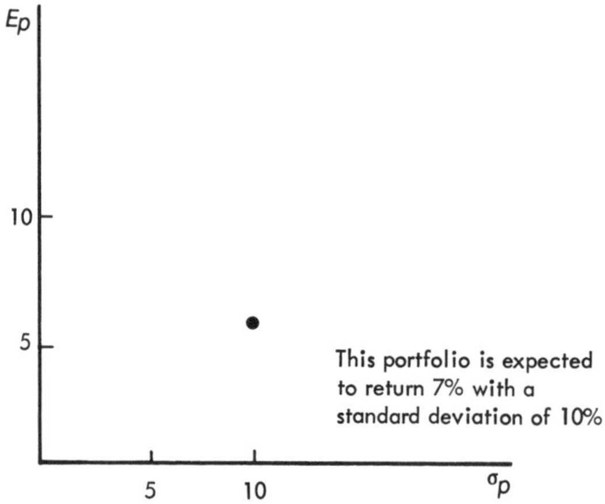

Any investor is going to demand a certain return at each level of risk, and he reasonably will demand a higher return to compensate for a higher level of risk. Therefore, we could draw a set of portfolios to which he would be indifferent as a line on the (σ_p, E_p) graph in Figure 8-7.

Figure 8-7

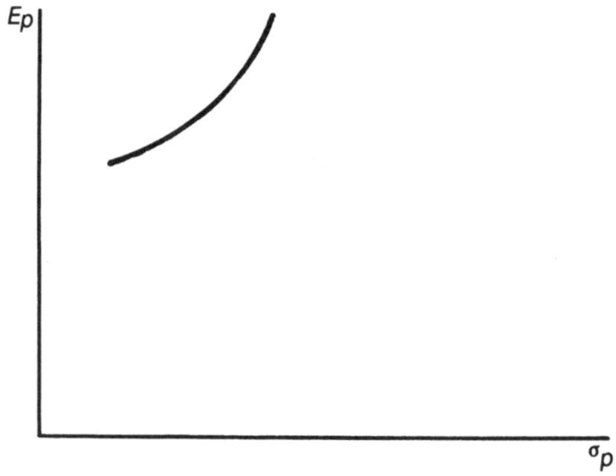

A line is plotted instead of a series of dots with one dot per portfolio because there is an infinite number of portfolios to which the investor is indifferent—an infinite number of possible risk-return trade-offs. The line slopes upward because the investor demands more return as risk increases or he will not remain "indifferent" to the risk-return combination. The line simply portrays the portfolio risk-return combinations that the investor willingly would trade one for the other. If no portfolios are available on this indifference curve, then the investor is forced to consider a set of portfolios offering a lower return at each risk level than that indicated by the original indifference curve. Graphically, this situation can be portrayed as a new line, as in Figure 8–8.

Figure 8–8

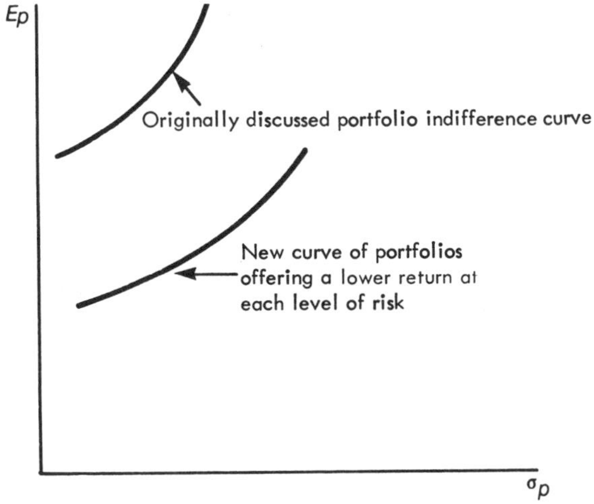

In fact, any portfolio can be considered as a member of a set of portfolios to which the investor would be indifferent, and hence the graph could be drawn as a completely dense set of indifference curves. Naturally, the investor prefers portfolios on higher curves to portfolios on lower curves, because higher curves have a higher return at every level of risk.

The Markowitz formulation of the set of portfolios showed—as in Figure 8–9—the available portfolios in the σ_p, E_p plane with the "efficient frontier" as the line describing the portfolios having the highest return at each risk level.

These two concepts can be combined by graphing the indifference curves and the efficient frontier together. High indifference curves fall in the non-feasible region. They represent the set of magnificent but unattainable risk-return tradeoffs. Low indifference curves fall in part below the efficient frontier, but, because better returns for the same

Figure 8–9

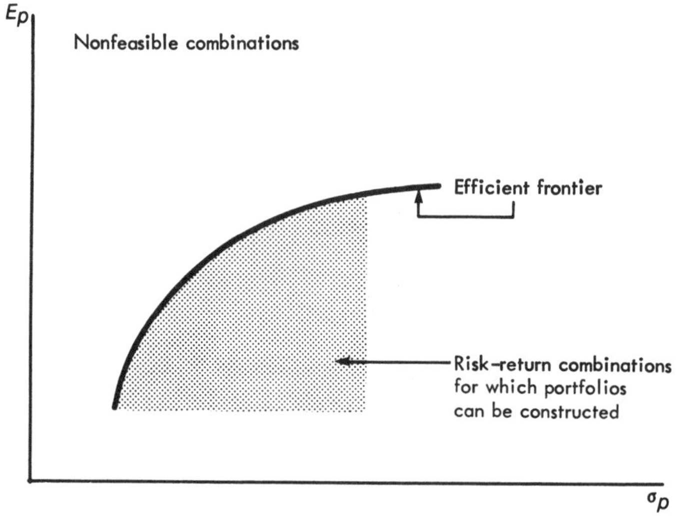

risk are available, they are less desirable portfolios even though they are attainable. One indifference curve, however, is tangent to the efficient frontier. It is therefore feasible, and, because no better portfolio (higher return at the same risk) is available, it is also the most desirable. The situation is graphed in Figure 8–10.

What happens when the investor can borrow or lend at the risk-free rate of interest? (For practicality, assume temporarily that treasury bills are risk free.) Because treasury bills (T-bills) have a positive return at zero risk, a portfolio of T-bills can be portrayed as a dot on the graph located exactly on the positive E_p axis (zero risk is zero σ_p), as shown in Figure 8–11.

Any investor, in this extended version of the theory, now has an option of a portfolio of risky assets, a portfolio of T-bills, or a portfolio that is a combination of risky securities and T-bills. But the last graph did not show the points that represent the return and risk associated with each of the portfolios that have both T-bills and risky securities. If another graph is drawn showing, say, ten portfolios constructed from different mixes of T-bills and the same risky portfolio, and the risky portfolio is a "good" one in the sense that it falls on the efficient frontier, it would look like Figure 8–12.

This portfolio has a number of interesting characteristics. Some dots fall to the left of the efficient frontier, indicating that these portfolios have less risk and a lower expected return than a 100% risky-security portfolio, a result of the presence of T-bills in these portfolios. The dots fall on a straight line as risk and return increase, because mathematically varying the mix of riskless and risky assets varies the weights

Figure 8–10

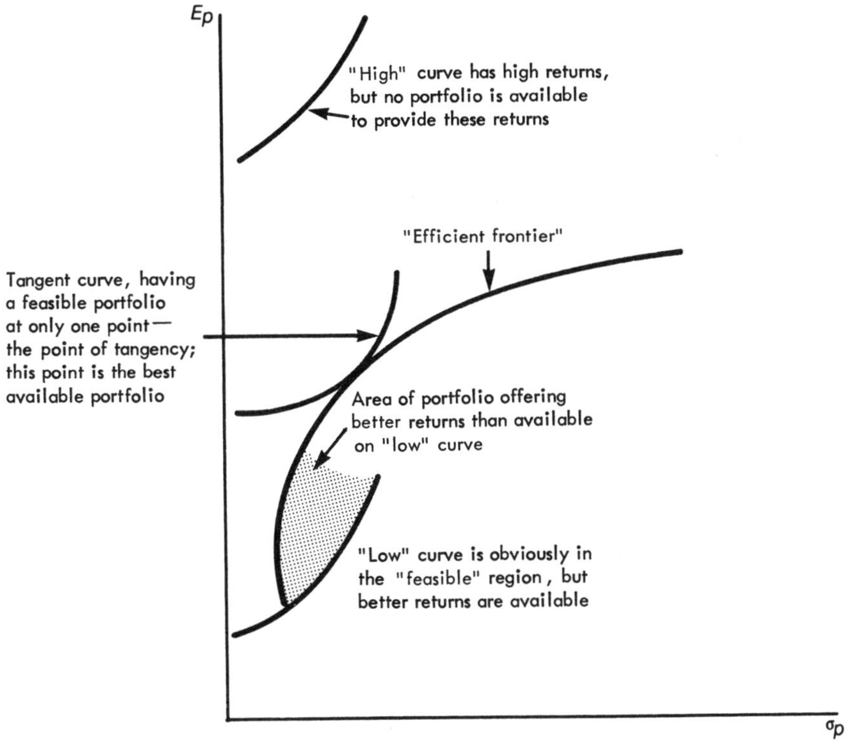

Figure 8–11

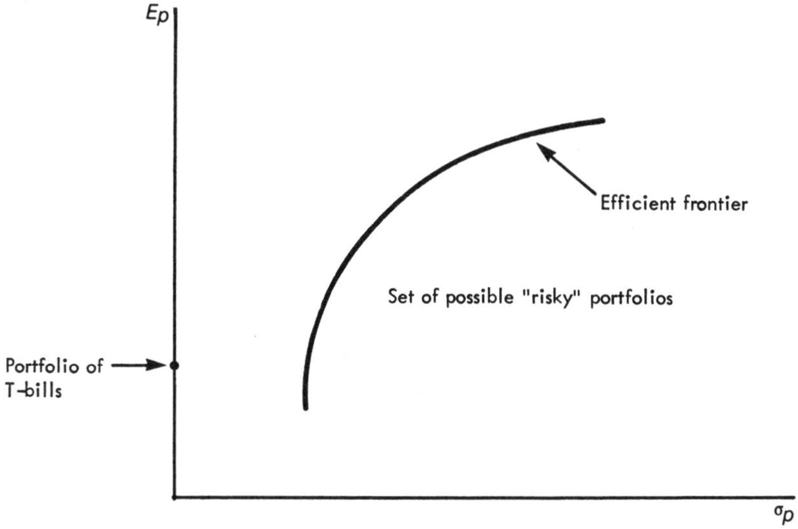

Figure 8-12

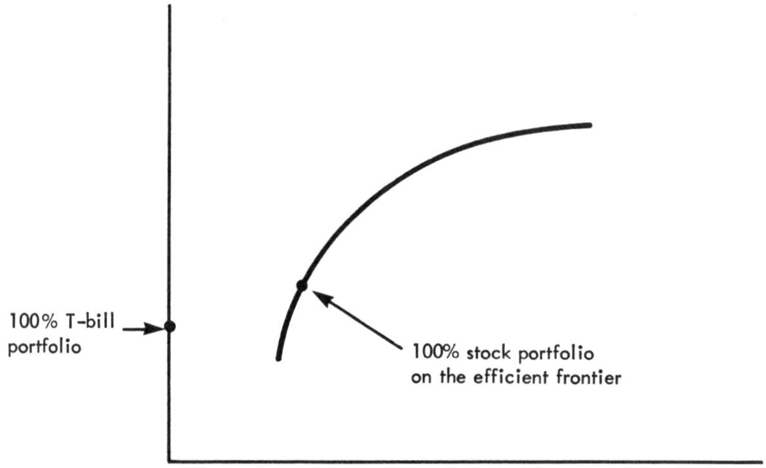

in a weighted total, which is a linear combination. The line rises as risk increases because investors would not purchase riskier assets unless they anticipated a higher return to compensate for the higher risk. The dots extend to the right of the efficient frontier (riskier than the 100% risky security portfolio) because the investor could (by assumption) borrow at the T-bill rate and buy more risky assets. Such a "leveraged' portfolio would be riskier than a "100% risky" investment: it would be, say, "120% risky." Also, the graph shows only ten possible portfolios. Actually, an infinite number of such portfolios are possible. As we plot more and more of them, we find that they become so dense that they form a complete straight line on the graph, and any point on this straight line is a portfolio that an investor could purchase by choosing one particular mix of T-bills and the risky-asset portfolio.

This analysis leads to a very interesting question: "Why did we choose that one particular risky portfolio?" One answer, of course, is that it was on the efficient frontier, but an infinite number of portfolios are on the efficient frontier and we arbitrarily chose only one. We could graph a straight line for any efficient portfolio. If we could locate a straight line that is "best," the problem will be greatly simplified. Figure 8-13 shows some possibilities.

Line *D* is the easiest to discuss because it is impossible. Because the straight line represents the set of portfolios that an investor could buy by varying the mix of T-bills and a risky portfolio, a feasible risky portfolio must be located somewhere on the line. Such is not the case for line *D;* line *D* simply portrays beautiful returns at each level of risk—returns so beautiful that no portfolio can be found that will achieve them. Line *A* is the line discussed in the preceding paragraph.

Figure 8–13

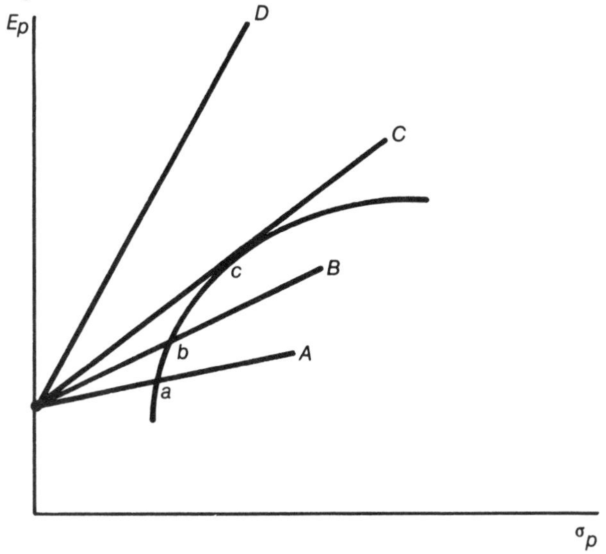

Comparing it to line *B*, we find that a portfolio built using the *b* portfolio on the efficient frontier has a higher return at each level of risk than an *a* portfolio (unless both are invested 100% in T-bills). Although both portfolios fall on the efficient frontier, the use of portfolio *b* to construct various portfolios that lie on line *B* clearly is better than using portfolio *a*. As can be seen from the graph, any line having a higher slope will have a higher return at each level of risk than a line with a lower slope. Consequently, the investor would prefer the highest feasible line, and this line will be the line tangent to the efficient frontier (line *C* in the graph). Any line with a higher slope would not be feasible—it would be like line *D*. Any line with a lower slope would be feasible, but would offer a lower return, like lines *A* and *B*.

This result can be shown in terms of the indifference-curve analysis by simply drawing the curves onto the last graph, as in Figure 8–14. The relationship of line *D* to the indifference curves is a moot point, inasmuch as the investor cannot achieve the results of line *D*. The fact that *D* is tangent to a high indifference curve simply shows that impossibly high returns would generate a high level of satisfaction. As we move to successively lower indifference curves, we find that they must touch line *C* before reaching the efficient frontier. Higher levels of satisfaction are available from line *C* than from the efficient frontier. All investors would logically prefer line *C* to any other investment, choosing their particular point on line *C* on the basis of the amount of risk that they will accept. From the standpoint of indifference curves,

Figure 8-14

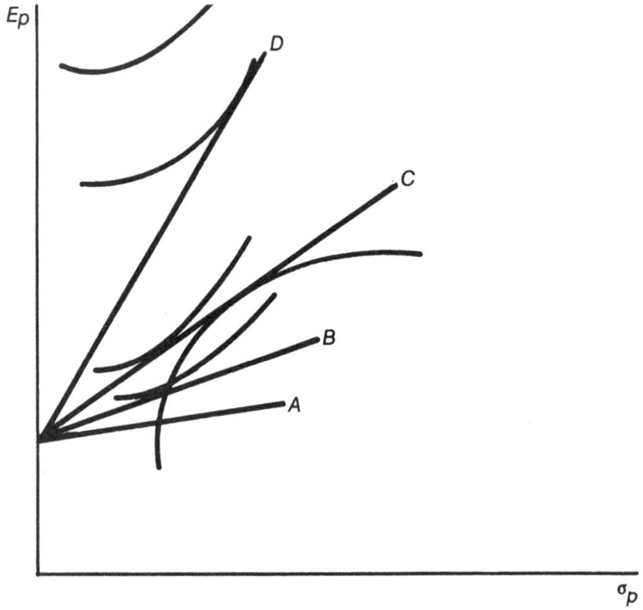

the portfolio chosen will be the point at which the investor's highest indifference curve touches line *C*. The preference of investors for line *C* has caused it to be called the "capital market line", or CML.

The fact that the theory leads us to conclude that investors will prefer the capital market line moves us easily into the next stage of the argument. The capital market line is constructed from T-bills and only one portfolio of risky assets. Because all investors prefer the CML, all invest in only one portfolio of risky assets (plus more or fewer T-bills). Because all investors hold the same securities and all securities are held by someone, the portfolio must be the aggregate of all available risky securities, the "market portfolio." The capital asset pricing model (CAPM) leads to the conclusion that all investors should own their proportionate share of all risky securities available, plus some T-bills to adjust the portfolio to the desired level of risk.

This model, however, began by assuming that all investors agree about the future returns and risks of all risky investments. Under this assumption, all investors end up holding the same set of risky securities. And if everyone holds the same risk assets, that set must be the "market portfolio." What happens when investors are allowed to have different expectations about future returns and risks? Basically, the capital asset pricing model then becomes valid for each individual investor, but not for the market as a whole. Each investor will have his own expectations, his own efficient frontier, and his own "capital market line." To behave logically, he would prefer his personal CML to his personal efficient frontier, so that he will vary risk by using his "best portfolio" in all cases and vary the percentage invested in T-bills. However, his "best portfolio" is not the same as some other investor's "best portfolio." The risky assets that each investor owns will be different, and his "best portfolio" would not necessarily be the "market portfolio."

In addition to the assumption of agreement, the CAPM has been criticized for assuming that the investor can borrow at the risk-free rate. The model develops a few technical difficulties if this assumption is removed. Other criticisms stem from the single uniform investment horizon considered. Because different investors have different time horizons, they conceivably may purchase different portfolios. Also, the idea of a risk-free rate of interest loses some validity in light of the single holding period or time horizon used in the model. If, for example, a five-year horizon is used, the risk-free interest rate probably would not be T-bills because a strategy of rolling T-bills over gives an unpredictable element in the five-year return. Five-year government bonds held to maturity would eliminate all risk other than a slight political risk if return is measured in nominal terms, but if return is measured in terms of real purchasing power the unpredictability of future inflation rates presents the investor with some risk.

Nevertheless, the CAPM presents the investor with a very useful way of looking at the investment problem. The model also has a great deal to say about the nature of risk for an individual security. The mathematical machinery of the CAPM establishes that (under conditions of agreement) the expected return of a security in excess of the risk-free rate will be proportional to the covariance of the security to the market, which, in turn, implies that the excess return on a security will be proportional to the excess return on the market. The beta coefficient, which measures the volatility of a stock to the market, can thus be used as a measure of a security's risk. The overall volatility of any portfolio can simply be computed as the weighted total of the beta coefficients of the stocks in the portfolio, using the diversification percentages as the weights. This approach divides risk into systematic risk and unique, or specific, risk. Systematic risk is the risk of a security common to all securities because they operate in a similar socio-economic environment. Unique risk is peculiar to the particular security. Unique risk can be diversified away because a large portfolio will have about as many unexpected favorable unique company developments as unexpected unfavorable unique company developments, and these will therefore cancel each other out. Systematic risk, however, cannot be diversified away, and this "commonality" of risk is considered in evaluating securities by using either covariance or the beta coefficient.

The main finding of the capital asset pricing model is that, even under conditions of disagreement, the investor should adjust his risk level by adjusting the percentage that he invests in very low-risk assets such as T-bills instead of adjusting his stock portfolio. Even this finding must be qualified, however. Allowing the investor to have certain risks in his life in addition to investment risks causes the machinery of the CAPM to indicate that different portfolios of risky assets are appropriate for different people. If it is valid to assume that expectations of investors are more or less in agreement, the main finding of the CAPM is that the investor is well advised to "buy the market." The rationale behind an index fund is to provide the investor with an opportunity to approximate the "buy the market" strategy.

ADDITIONAL READINGS IN PORTFOLIO THEORY

Analysts interested in additional information in the area of modern portfolio theory have available a vast literature from which to choose. As a starting point, the portfolio sections of three books should serve well, and additional readings can be selected from the books' bibliographies.

Sharpe, William F. *Investments.* Englewood Cliffs, N.J.: Prentice-Hall, Inc., 1978.

Lorie, James H., and Hamilton, Mary T. *The Stock Market: Theories and Evidence.* Homewood, Ill.: Richard D. Irwin, Inc., 1973.

Sharpe, William F. *Portfolio Theory and Capital Markets.* New York, N.Y.: McGraw-Hill Book Company, 1970.

Chapter 9

The computer and programming

Many of the techniques described earlier in this book involve the use of a computer. Although an analyst is not expected to be either a programmer or a computer scientist, an understanding of some of the fundamentals of how a computer works and how it can be used will enable him to use a computer more intelligently. A computer is a complex and flexible machine that is a combination of hardware and programming software. Programs are instructions to the computer telling it what to do and in what order. Special languages such as FORTRAN and COBOL have been designed to simplify programming by translating the instructions into the computer's machine language. These programs can be designed to perform very complex and repetitious steps with simple instructions. An illustration is given by an elementary program written in FORTRAN.

NATURE OF THE COMPUTER

The computer is the most powerful tool that has ever been made available to the financial analyst. Without it, only a few of the quantitative techniques described in this book could ever be applied in a practical fashion to complicated problems. Computer science is an extremely broad and highly technical area. This chapter, however, is not designed to be an exhaustive treatment of the nature or use of the computer. It is only an attempt to familiarize the financial analyst with the very basic principles by which a digital computer functions.

The computer is a machine, but it is not like any other type of machine used in business today. A businessman may buy a typewriter if he needs a machine to transfer words neatly from oral to written form. Or he may buy an adding machine to calculate certain values, graphic devices to provide displays, or a machine sorter to organize punchcard decks. The computer, however, is a "black box" par excellence; it is a machine that when properly programmed can behave as if it were a typewriter, adding machine, sorter, and the like. The computer, in other words, can be any combination of a number of machines, depending upon the particular program that tells it what to do. In a way, it is possible to say that the computer plus any given program equals a "black box" and that the computer can be as many "black boxes" as there are programs to guide it. Properly instructed, the computer can serve not only as a typewriter, sorter, adding machine, and the like, but also as an entire accounting system, an information system automatically reporting key facts to management, a multiple regression model, a linear programming model, and more. Each program converts the computer into a different type of "black box," and as a result "creates" a new machine. Naturally, the intrinsic value of the computer stems from the combination of the physical computer "hardware" and the instructions that constitute the programming "software"—from the combination of the computer's "labor force" and the programmer's "management."

The functions performed by any computer operating under the instructions of any given program can be divided into the three logical sections of Figure 9-1.

Figure 9-1

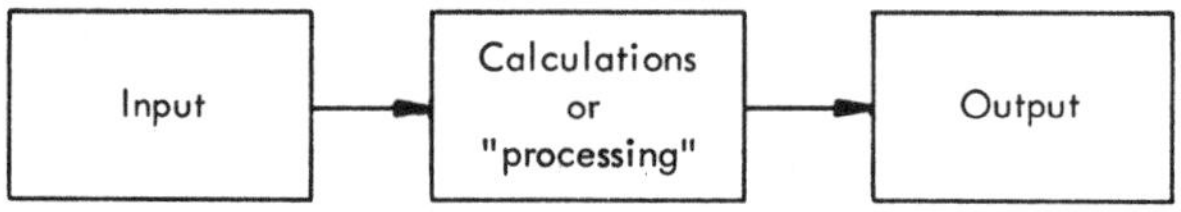

This division of functions can be seen to correspond to the natural requirements of any practical "black box":

1. Something must be put into the box for anything to happen at all.
2. The box must do something to the input or it has no practical value at all.
3. The results of the activity of the box on the input must be reported, or the calculations will be performed but the results will never be known by the researcher.

THE "CALCULATE" OR "PROCESS" FUNCTION

When computers are mentioned in everyday discussions, what is usually meant is the calculation or "thinking" aspect of a computer system. This function is the heart of any computer installation and is performed by the central processing unit (CPU). The simplest way to picture the CPU is to regard it as a "grid" of storage locations. Each storage location is capable of holding a number or letter and all of these locations taken together provide the computer with a "memory." Obviously, this memory is restricted to the number of storage locations present in any given CPU. The important point in working with the computer is to bear in mind that the computer is not capable of processing any information not in memory at the time the calculation is desired, i.e., the computer cannot calculate using numbers that it cannot find in one of its storage locations.

Figure 9–2 shows a hypothetical computer that has only 20 storage locations.

Figure 9–2

	Second digit of storage location									
First digit of storage location	0	1	2	3	4	5	6	7	8	9
0						2				
1								3		

The illustration shows that only two numbers have been stored in the computer memory (technically called core storage). Location number 5 contains the number (2), and the number (3) is stored in location number 17. If an instruction in the computer program were to add the contents of location number 5 to the contents of location 17 and store the result in location 12, core storage would have the appearance of Figure 9–3 after the instruction was performed.

Figure 9–3

	0	1	2	3	4	5	6	7	8	9
0						2				
1			5					3		

All computer instructions are in principle quite similar to the addition instruction just shown. They refer to the contents of storage locations and manipulate those contents in various ways, eventually storing the results of the manipulation in some other storage location. As a result of the nature of this process, all calculations are completely dependent upon the contents of core storage at the time that the calculation is made.

PROGRAMS

Just as a man with only a memory and no ability to use judgment in relating his memory or experience to practical problems is regarded as having limited value, so the value of the computer would be restricted without a program by which it can process the data in memory. *All* programs are step-by-step lists of instructions that the computer is to perform sequentially. The strength of the computer is that it follows these instructions in the minutest detail, without once deviating from the prescribed rules of operation. The weakness of the computer is its total inability to exercise human judgment on even the most minor matters. Therefore, the programmer is forced to describe his problem in the most precise detail without the slightest error or ambiguity.

Once a program has been written and is available to the computer in machine language, the program can be input to the computer at any time. This program can then be used to process whatever data the computer has in core storage. For example, if the program is designed to cause the computer to perform a simple regression analysis, the computer can use this model in connection with one set of data, output the results, and then read in another set of data, proceed by applying the regression model to this set, output the results, and so forth. When all simple regressions have been processed, the computer can then read a linear programming program into core storage, then read in the data for the first LP problem, perform the analysis, output the results, read in the data for the next LP problem, and so on. Putting this into a more concise form, any given program can be designed in such a way that it is capable of handling multiple sets of data, and any computer can execute any number of programs sequentially. Figure 9–4 shows what the core storage of a hypothetical computer might look like just before the program is to be executed.

Figure 9–4

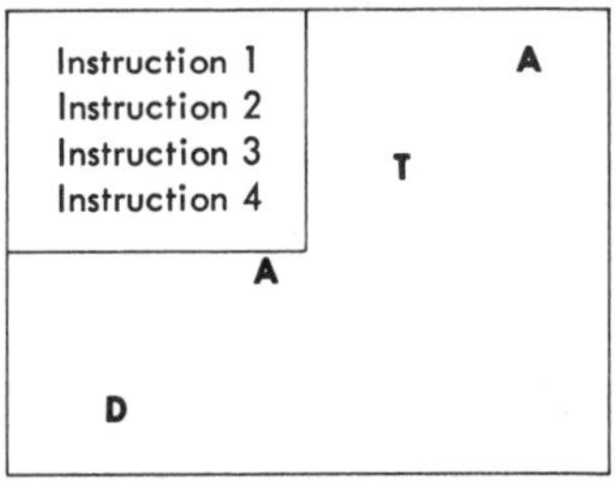

Because any program always will be executed sequentially by a computer, the machine will automatically access instruction 1 in the section of core that contains the program, perform whatever operation this instruction indicates, then access instruction 2, perform this operation, and so on. This process will be continued unless an instruction is encountered specifically commanding a different order of processing or informing the machine that no additional instructions are present within the program. The above diagram is obviously a simplification for several reasons. First, typical programs having practical application range from 300 to 10,000 or more instructions. Second, the amount of core storage actually occupied by the program depends solely upon the nature of that program. One program may occupy 80% of core while its data occupy only 10%, leaving 10% of core unused. Another program may occupy 10% of core, while its data require 85%. Core storage, in other words, consists of available storage locations; the computer is completely indifferent to the particular application's choice of storing instructions or data. The only restriction, of course, is the fact that the total of program instructions and data for processing must not exceed the limits of the memory of core.

A DEEPER APPRAISAL OF THE COMPUTER

Working with a computer is much more detailed than is commonly realized. The machine must receive an instruction for every single step of the analysis to be performed, and the data must be stored in the computer in a known location or the program would be unable to inform the machine of the specific numbers to be processed. In addition, every single instruction and piece of data must be input to the computer in such a way that it will be present in core storage at the specific time that the application requires it for processing. Finally, the results of the process must be output in some meaningful form. Unfortunately, from the professional programmer's standpoint there is a great deal more to the computer than this. In a digital computer, all contents of core storage must be in binary form. This means that every unit of information made available to the computer must be some arrangement of "1" or "0." This causes no problem if the actual number 0 or 1 is to be processed, but the number 2 must be "rephrased" in such a way that it will consist of an arrangement of 1's or 0's.

The easiest way to explain this binary number system is to review the ordinary decimal system that all investment analysts use daily. The decimal system gets its name from *decem*, the Latin word for the number 10, which is the base of the system. In other words, symbols called digits are used to represent zero and all positive whole numbers up to but not including the number 10. These symbols are easily recognized, for they are the numbers 0, 1, 2, 3, 4, 5, 6, 7, 8, and 9. The number 10, however, is not expressed by a single symbol; it is represented by a combination of the digits 1 and 0. When the digits 1 and 0 are seen together, people automatically recognize them as the number ten. But this automatic recognition is more a matter of tradition than mathematics. Mathematically, the concept involved could be called "placement value." The fact that the digit 1 is placed to the left of the digit 0 gives the digit 1 an added meaning. In the decimal system, the meaning is defined as "one set of ten." The 0 is the rightmost digit of the number and its meaning is "zero sets of one." In the decimal number 100, the 1 stands for "one set of ten times ten, or one set of one hundred." The leftmost 0, of course, stands for zero sets of ten, and the rightmost 0 stands for zero sets of one.

As can be seen from these examples, any number in the decimal, or base ten, system is actually the sum of the digits involved in the number weighted according to successive powers of the base of the system. Figure 9–5 may make this point clearer.

Figure 9–5

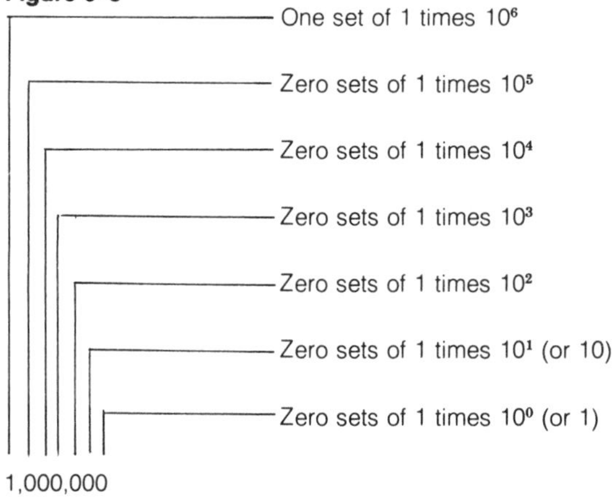

The decimal number 1,000,000 therefore implies:

$(1 \cdot 10^6) + (0 \cdot 10^5) + (0 \cdot 10^4) + (0 \cdot 10^3) + (0 \cdot 10^2) + (0 \cdot 10^1) + (0 \cdot 10^0) = 1{,}000{,}000.$

In the binary number system, the base of the system is the number 2, and in this case only the numbers 0 and 1 are used as fundamental digits. In order to express larger numbers, the binary system uses the same technique as the more familiar decimal system, assigning a "placement value" to the digits whenever numbers larger than one need to be represented. However, because the base of the binary system is 2, the placement value is weighted by powers of 2 instead of 10, as was the case in the decimal system. For example, in the binary system, the number 2 is represented as 10, meaning one set of 2 and zero sets of 1. The number 3 is represented by the value 11, meaning one set of 2 and one set of 1. The number 4 is represented by the value 100, meaning one set of 2 times 2 and zero sets of 2 and zero sets of 1. Table 9–1 shows the relationship between the structure of the decimal and the binary number systems. Using the information concerning number systems that has been developed, it is relatively easy to see how any decimal number can have a binary equivalent. Table 9–2 gives

Table 9–1

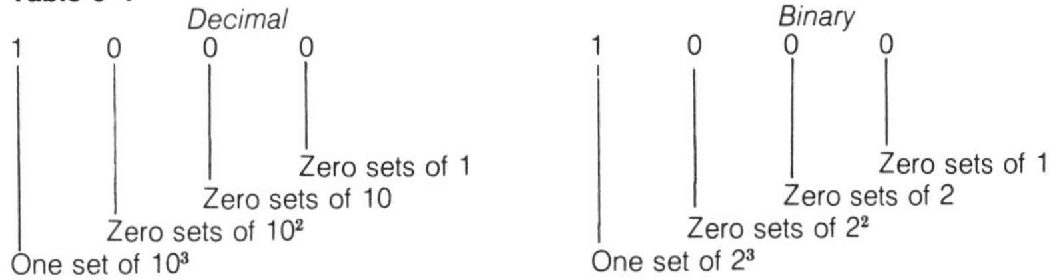

certain selected base ten numbers and the corresponding binary representation.

Table 9–2

Decimal number	*Equivalent binary number*
1	1
2	10
3	11
4	100
5	101
6	110
7	111
8	1000
9	1001
10	1010
25	11001
100	1100100

ASSEMBLERS

When a program is executed on a computer, all of the instructions and all of the data present in core storage are in binary form. In addition, all of the "storage locations" by which the program references the data have "addresses" that are in binary form. In other words, the programmer working solely in machine language would input to the computer only a combination of 1's and 0's for any application. This problem would be so enormous that it would virtually be impossible to use the computer in practical applications if computer scientists had not invented an escape from this mass of detail. The means of escape was, paradoxically, the computer itself. A computer program was written that was capable of receiving as input the programmer's instructions in a humanly intelligible form and provided as output the machine-language binary program. This program, (called an "assembler") permitted programmers to input reasonably intelligible statements to the computer and then converted these statements into the actual program that the computer could at some other time use to process data in an actual application. All modern computers of any reasonable size are now equipped with assembly programs.

The advantages of writing in assembly language instead of machine language are threefold. First, the programmer can refer to a storage location by some label that he can choose at will. If, for example, the programmer wishes to refer to a specific number as "X," he can do so in the assembly language and the assembler will automatically assign a storage location for "X" in the program. Second, if the programmer has reason to go to a specific instruction in the program from some other program location, he can easily label any assembly language statement and later write an instruction that goes to that label. The assembler will see to it that the instruction that "branches" to the labeled instruction will go to the correct core location. Third, the various types of instructions that can be processed by the computer can be referenced by alphabetic names, which the assembler then will convert automatically into their binary equivalent. Figure 9–6 shows how the computer uses the assembly program, assembly language statements, and input data to produce output.

Figure 9–6

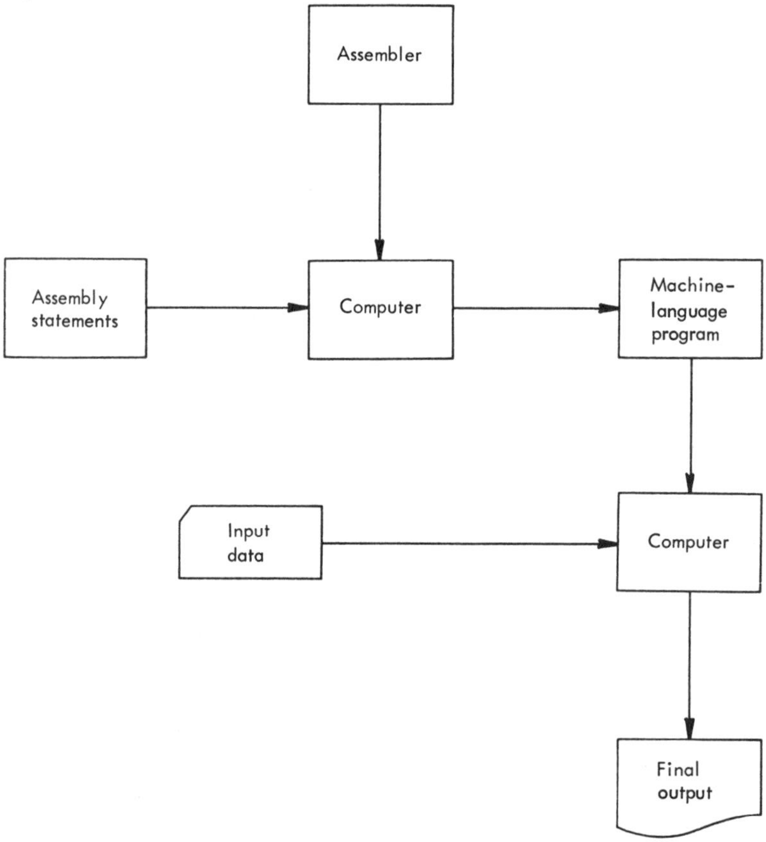

COMPILERS

The binary representation of data and the use of assembly language are areas over which the analyst need have little concern. They are included in this chapter only to show the structural means by which the computer solves problems for the analyst. Actually, the advent of compilers makes even assembly language statements too detailed to be considered in depth by anyone other than professional programmers. A compiler is a program by which the computer can write its own machine language program. In other words, computer science has for quite some time already achieved the fabled "self-programming computer." Actually, a compiler is a program that receives as input a number of English-like instructions and then converts these instructions into an assembly language program. The assembly language program is then converted automatically into a machine-language (binary) program. The machine is programming itself in the sense that it is creating a program it will later use in an actual application, but it is not by any means operating on its own. The machine-language or "object program" performs exactly the same set of operations specified by the programmer as input to the compiler. The computer simply handles the majority of the detail work necessary to "clean up" the program so that it will be capable of execution by the computer. By using a compiler, the programmer can write instructions in a high-level language that the computer can be made to understand, freeing the people who work with the computer from having to deal with the machine's actual characteristics.

Probably the best known compiler language is FORTRAN. When an investment analyst writes a FORTRAN program, it is manually keypunched and presented to the computer. The computer first reads the FORTRAN compiler so that it will be able to understand the FORTRAN instructions written by the analyst. Next, it reads the FORTRAN instructions the analyst has just written and had keypunched. These instructions are frequently referred to as the "source deck." The compiler converts the source deck into a set of assembly language instructions and turns control over to the assembly program. The assembler then uses the assembly language statements just created by the FORTRAN compiler as input and converts these into the machine-language program to be used to process actual data. The machine-language program can then be used to process actual data. The machine-language statements are usually punched on cards by the computer and are referred to as the "object deck." Summarizing the entire process, the computer is not capable of understanding FORTRAN statements. It has available, however, a FORTRAN compiler that *can* understand FORTRAN statements and can translate them into statements to be used by the assembler to create the machine-language statements directly intelligible to the computer itself. The process can be diagrammed as in Figure 9–7.

Figure 9–7

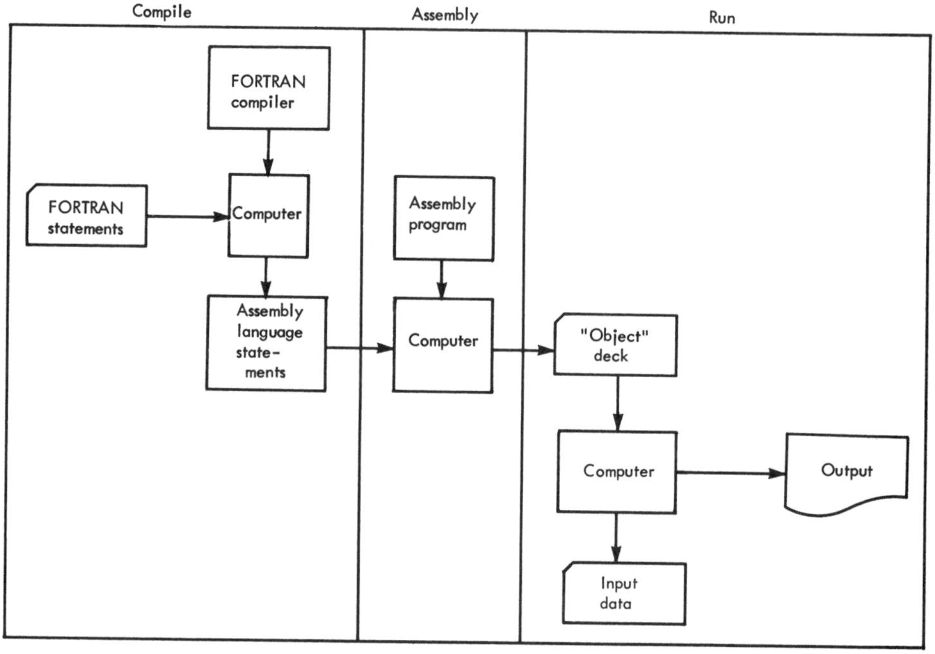

By using FORTRAN or any other compiler, anyone programming a computer can give specific commands in a language resembling English, or at least mathematical English. Each of these commands is independent of the specific computer language and usually will be translated into a number of machine-language computer instructions. The entire process of going from the FORTRAN coding sheet (written statements) to the computer output can be handled automatically by the operations division of any moderately large organization, unless the program has an error and must be "debugged." Extensive testing and debugging, however, are inevitable for programs of any magnitude.

A number of compilers or "languages" are available for programming and operate in a manner similar to the FORTRAN example shown above. All of these languages have essentially the same approach as FORTRAN, consisting of a set of statements indirectly usable by the computer. The best known high-level languages are FORTRAN, COBOL, ALGOL, PL/1, and BASIC.

FORTRAN stands for FORmula TRANslation and was designed as a mathematical language that could be used to process rather complicated mathematical problems and then report the results. As a consequence of the motives behind the design, FORTRAN is very useful in computational programs or programs having extremely complicated logic. However, it is more difficult to use efficiently in problems requiring complicated input-output, editing, or the handling of letters or symbols instead of numbers (called "alphanumeric" data).

COBOL, on the other hand, stands for COmmon Business-Oriented Language and as a result of the motives behind its design is a very powerful tool when the programmer is concerned with the arrangement of the data, editing results to create a businesslike report, speed in input and output of massive amounts of data, and controlling the validity of both the data and the processing. COBOL is, however, much less useful whenever extensive calculations are to be performed or complex logical operations are to be executed on a relatively small amount of data.

ALGOL is a language especially designed for the creation of computational models (called algorithms). As a result, ALGOL perhaps is even more powerful than FORTRAN in the strictly computational aspects of the computer. Unfortunately, it appears to be fairly limited in the nonmathematical portion of computer usage such as input-output.

PL/1 is a new language specifically designed to synthesize the mathematical capabilities of FORTRAN with the input-output and editing capabilities of COBOL. As a result, it is very useful for either scientific problems that for some reason require the handling of large amounts of data or for business problems that, because of the growing usage of quantitative techniques, now frequently require rather complicated mathematical manipulations.

BASIC is a simplified language very similar to FORTRAN but slightly easier to learn and slightly less flexible.

In addition to these general purpose languages, a number of special purpose programs are available that have certain language characteristics. Several of these are based on decision tables, a concept that unfortunately cannot be explored further because of considerations of space. Other special purpose languages are simulation-oriented, such as GPSS or Simscript, and still others are industry-oriented. From the general languages and the special-purpose languages, programmers can create a number of very general programs, each capable of handling a large number of diverse assignments. These software-packages, or systems, provide the computer user with a kind of middle ground lying between the creation of a large number of small special programs at a high total cost on the one hand and the extreme generality of the languages on the other.

FLOWCHARTING AND PROGRAM CHARACTERISTICS

The nature of a computer program already has been discussed in moderate detail. For example, it is already known that the program must be in binary machine-language form before it can be processed by a computer, that it must be present in core storage during processing, that it is a step-by-step sequence of instructions used by the computer to operate upon data available in core storage, and that every single, specific action taken by the computer must be clearly and completely defined in the program instructions. It also has been shown that a programmer can use a compiler or assembler in order to allow the computer to relieve him of a large proportion of the detail required to produce the actual instructions required in any particular application. This section is designed to show how a programmer can lay out the step-by-step definition of the program in order to be able to write instructions with a minimum possibility of logical error. This section also gives some insight into the types of instructions the computer is capable of executing. Unfortunately, this section also is an oversimplification, and it is important to remember that the functions included in the following flowcharts are not computer instructions *per se* but rather are logical processes that must first be converted into a number of specific computer instructions before they become intelligible even to a high-level compiler.

A flowchart is a diagram of the sequence by which the various processes to be executed in a program are to be performed. Flowcharts serve the dual purpose of defining the problem to facilitate programming and documenting the program so that a humanly intelligible record of the program's nature will be available if needed at some time in the future. In order to draw even the simplest flowchart, the following symbols need to be defined:

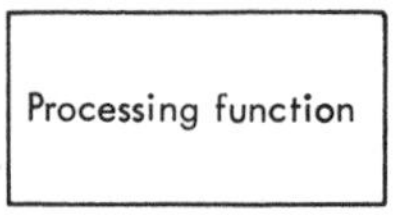

A rectangle is used to represent any operation performed strictly within the CPU and does not involve program control.

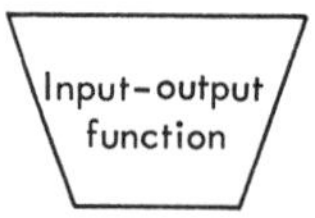

A trapezoid is used to represent any operation performed by the CPU that involves input or output.

Using these elementary symbols and showing the flow of processing by arrows, an extremely simple flowchart can be produced, as in Figure 9-8.

Figure 9–8

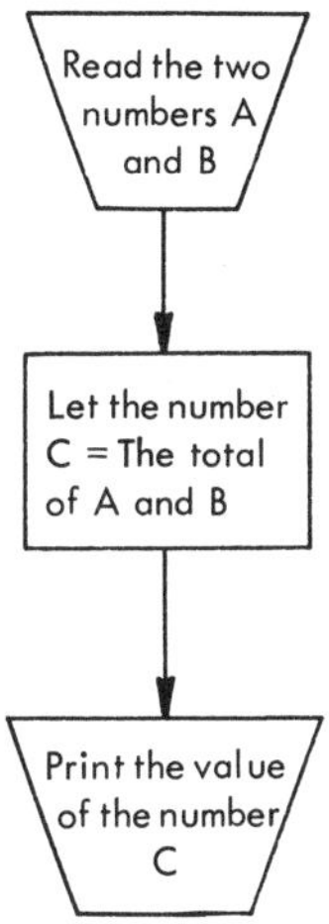

It is now possible to introduce an additional flowchart symbol that has great value in almost all computer applications:

When this symbol is encountered, the computer actually makes a "decision." It can interrogate some computer value and on the basis of the result continue processing *either* in the normal step-by-step procedure *or* branch to some other instruction not in the normal instruction sequence. The concept of branching is illustrated in the flowchart (Figure 9–9) of an extremely simple program that calculates and prints the absolute value of the sum of two numbers.

The value of the computer is greatly enhanced by the possibility of branching to alternative "lines" of processing based upon the nature of the data. But the value of the decision capability of the computer goes beyond that of simple branching and includes the concept of a loop. The flowchart shown in Figure 9–10 illustrates a program that uses a loop to permit the computer to perform a set of instructions over and over again on different data.

By using loops in various ways, the programmer can cause the computer to perform certain sets of instructions many times on slightly different data or, if he wishes, may slightly alter the instructions to be executed inside the loop and so perform an almost identical set of calculations on either the same data or different data. Obviously, processing plus branching and loops when merged into various combina-

Figure 9-9

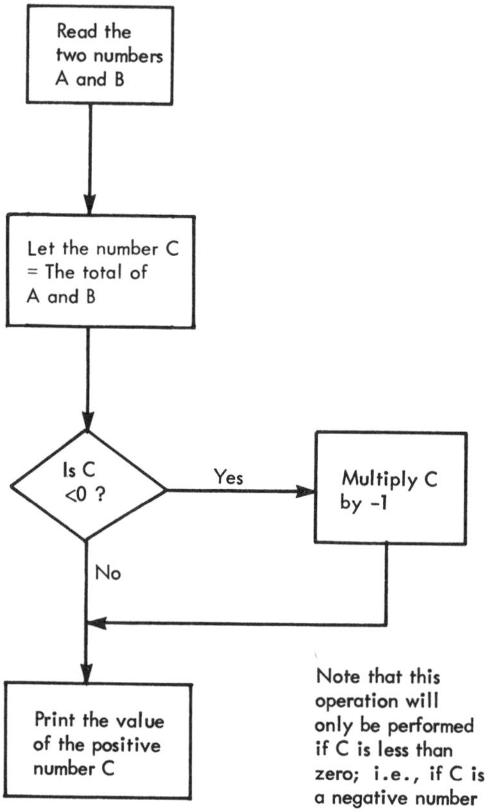

tions will permit the computer to handle almost any quantitative problem that can be strictly defined by a fixed procedure of any kind, almost without regard to complexity.

PROGRAMMING IN THE FORTRAN LANGUAGE

Basic elements

In order to provide a rough understanding of the nature of high-level compiler instructions, a brief sketch of one language and its characteristics may be used as an example. FORTRAN is chosen here because it is available on almost all computers and is quantitative in orientation. Two words of caution are necessary before this description. The first is obvious—this is not a text on programming, so that the following description is incomplete and will not in any way qualify a reader as a programmer. The second is that the wide variation in the

Figure 9–10

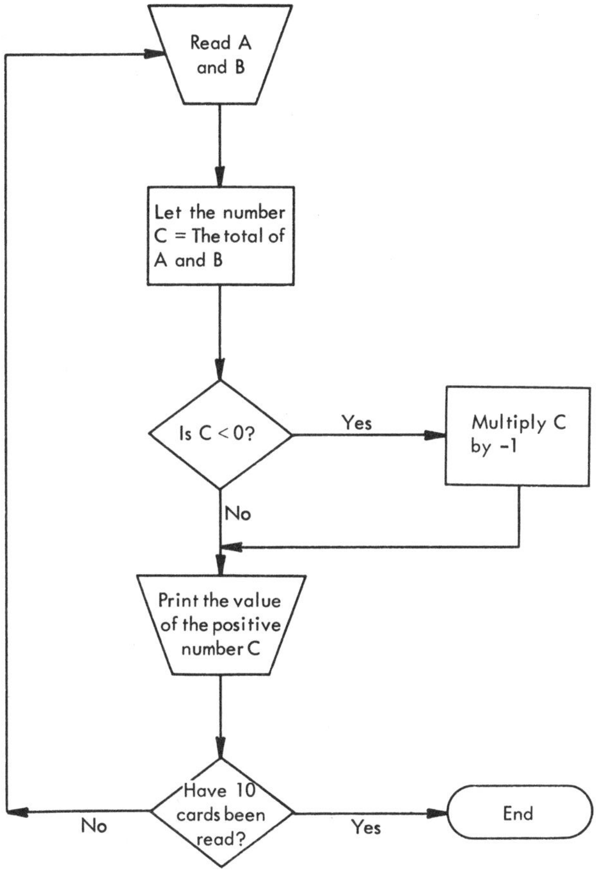

nature of languages makes the use of FORTRAN as a general example of all compilers a mild distortion of the nature and capability of high-level program statements. This comment is especially true if "FORTRAN" and "programming" are mistakenly assumed by a reader to be equivalent terms. All compilers do, however, have some functions in common and, although the forms of the statements and the arrangement of the program's functions may differ, all languages share with FORTRAN the following four categories of instructions:

1. Input-Output
2. Calculation
3. Control
4. General Purpose.

Any analyst with a little knowledge of FORTRAN and some support from computer specialists is capable of designing and writing his own simple programs. About all that has been said about FORTRAN up to this point is that it is a compiler that permits the analyst to write a set of statements indirectly understandable by the computer and that can be combined in a way that allows a large number of different processes to be defined for computer execution. Unfortunately, the only way possible to move more deeply into the use of this language is simply to jump into the middle of the programming problem and then attempt to dig back out. Accordingly, a complete computer program written in the FORTRAN language is now presented:

```
  READ 1, I, J
  K = I + J
  PRINT 2, K
1 FORMAT (I 4, I 4)
2 FORMAT (I 5)
  END
```

As has already been explained, the computer always processes any program in a step-by-step procedure. In FORTRAN, this characteristic of the nature of the computer's execution of the generated machine-language program is handled by the following convention. The computer will execute the FORTRAN instructions in order from top to bottom unless an instruction specifically demands that this order of processing be altered (that the computer "branches"). If the above program is used as an example, the statement "READ 1, I, J" will be executed first, followed by the statement "K = I + J." This "sequential" system by which the computer's actions "flow" through a program is shown diagrammatically in the flowcharts explained in the preceding section. In a sense, both the order of statements in a FORTRAN program and the order of operations in a flowchart are a model of the computer's behavior during the execution of a given program. Both provide a visual representation of the sequence of events, but flowcharts appear to provide a clearer insight into the nature of a procedure and are therefore frequently used to point out graphically the logical structure implied in the FORTRAN program's instructions. The accompanying diagram (Figure 9–11) shows the relationship between the flowchart and the FORTRAN statements in the example program. On the left is what may be called a "functional" flowchart, which describes the type of processes involved in our example program. The flowchart on the right indicates the corresponding FORTRAN instruction that permits the computer to execute the required process:

Formats

Continuing our discussion of this very simple program, we see two FORMAT statements immediately following the PRINT statement in

Figure 9–11

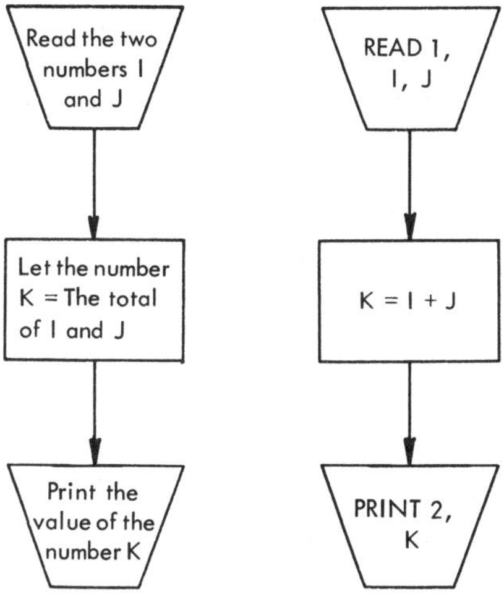

the program listing. Each of the FORMAT statements is preceded by a statement number, or label, that permits the program to refer to the particular statement. By using this statement number, the READ instruction at the top of the program can easily refer to FORMAT statement one, and the PRINT instruction can refer to FORMAT two. The use of statement numbers, in other words, enables any FORTRAN program to establish a kind of interstatement communications, without which high-level languages such as FORTRAN would be impossible. In this particular case, statement numbers permit input-ouput statements to refer to the FORMAT statements that describe to the computer the nature of the data being read-in or printed-out.

This formatting procedure is necessary because the computer is not able to understand a number given to it until that number has been fully defined, and this definition is the function of the FORMAT statement. The computer must be told how many digits are in the number, whether the number has a decimal point, and how many digits are to the right of the decimal point. It must even be told that the number is a number and not a letter.

Needless to say, a large variety of FORMAT instructions is possible in the FORTRAN language, but it is sufficient here simply to indicate that in the sample program the FORMAT statement number one defines two numbers of four digits each (I4, I4) and both of these numbers are integers (they have no decimal point). FORMAT 2 defines one five-digit integer (I5). Notice that, because the READ statement refers to FORMAT 1, the computer will read the two numbers *described* in that FORMAT statement and *named* in the READ statement (I and J). The PRINT statement refers to FORMAT 2, which defines one five-digit integer. The PRINT statement lists one number to be printed (the number K). *All numbers in a FORTRAN program are named in the input-output statement and described more fully in an associated format statement.* In addition, it is worth noting that *any* number input to the computer or output from the computer must be "formatted," unless the particular FORTRAN compiler permits unformatted statements when using tape or disc.

Calculations

The computer treats integers in a way completely different from the treatment given numbers that have a decimal point (called "real" numbers). The name the programmer assigns to any number that is an integer must begin with any of the letters I, J, K, L, M, N; the name assigned to any real number must begin with any of the other letters. In addition, the two types of numbers cannot be "mixed" in the same mathematical statement (although some compilers will allow mixed-mode calculations).

Arithmetic statements constitute an extremely large segment of FORTRAN and present no serious problem to anyone first encountering the language. FORTRAN simply sets the variable on the left-hand side of the equation equal to the expression on the right-hand side. For example, the statement

$$C = A + B$$

will cause the computer to set the value of C equal to the sum of the values of A and B. Only three important points need to be kept in mind when writing a FORTRAN arithmetic statement:

1. Integer numbers and real numbers cannot both be written in the same statement in many compilers.
2. The notation used in FORTRAN is slightly different from notation common in mathematics. The symbol * is used for multiplication; *A**B* is the same as $(A)(B)$, or $A \times B$, in mathematical notation. Also, ** is used to denote an exponent; *A***2 is the notation for A^2; *A***3 is A^3; and so on.
3. A FORTRAN equation is really an instruction to make the left-hand number equal to the value of the right-hand expression, and it is not a strict mathematical equation. For example, the statement $B = B + 1$ is perfectly legitimate because it instructs the computer to make the new value of *B* equal to "the value currently in *B* plus the value of the number 'one.'" It demands that "*B*" be made one larger than it was. A few examples of simple FORTRAN arithmetic statements are given below as examples:

FORTRAN notation	MATHEMATICAL notation
A= B+ C	$A = B + C$
A= B**2+ C**2	$A = B^2 + C^2$
X= B*(A+ C)	$X = B(A + C)$
A= A+ 1	---------------

The last expression is legitimate because it is not a mathematical equation. It is an instruction to make the number called *A* one greater than it was. If the old *A* equaled 8, the new *A* would equal 9.

In more complicated arithmetic statements, many different numbers may be combined by a large number of operations, which immediately raises the question of the order in which various operations are to be performed. In mathematics, for example, $2 + (4 \div 2)$ does not equal $(2 + 4) \div 2$. It is important when calculating to know whether to add or divide first because different answers would be obtained. In FORTRAN it is important to write the instruction in such a way that the computer will perform the calculations in the correct order for the same reason. Fortunately, this problem is handled in FORTRAN in almost exactly the same way as in ordinary mathematics. For example, parentheses are used to indicate the order of operation in exactly the same way as normal mathematical statements. In the absence of parentheses, the following priorities, or order of operations, are observed:

1. Exponentiation
2. Multiplication and division
3. Addition and subtraction.

Therefore the following FORTRAN statements produce the following corresponding mathematical results:

FORTRAN statement	Mathematical result
A= B**2*C	$A = (B^2)(C)$
A= B+ C*D**2	$A = B + (C)(D^2)$
A= B/C+ D	$A = \frac{B}{C} + D$
A = B**2/C + D*4.0	$A = \frac{B^2}{C} + 4D$
A= B**2*2.0+ C	$A = 2B^2 + C$

If operations have the same priority, they are performed from left to right:

FORTRAN statement	Mathematical result
A= B*C/D	$A = \frac{BC}{D}$
A= B+ C− D	$A = (B + C) - D$
A= B+ C− D/E*F	$A = B + C - \frac{D}{E}(F)$

FORTRAN statement	*Mathematical result*
A= B**2+ C**3 − D*4.0/E	$A = B^2 + C^3 - \frac{4D}{E}$
A= B*C/D+ 4.0 − E	$A = \frac{BC}{D} + 4 - E$

The problem of correctly stating the order of operations is not severe and a little care in the phrasing of the computer statements should eliminate the possibility of error. Parentheses may be used freely in order to define very clearly the precise sequence of operation. The FORTRAN language places no restrictions on parentheses and as many may be used as are desired, even if they are superfluous. In fact, the fluent use of parentheses in formulas is generally regarded as one of the characteristics of the precise programmer.

Program control

FORTRAN provides a number of control statements by which the programmer can alter the normal sequential top-to-bottom sequence by which his statements are executed. Only three of these control statements will be considered in this section:

1. The GO TO statement
2. The IF statement
3. The DO statement.

The GO TO statement tells the computer to "branch" to a statement located somewhere else in the program. Obviously, this branch is unconditional, i.e., the computer is given absolutely no option in the matter and will inevitably branch to the designated statement.

The IF statement is more useful because it is conditional. It tells the computer to go to a statement located somewhere else in the program if, and *only* if, some specific condition is present. The computer must "decide" whether or not the branch is to be taken, i.e., whether or not the condition is present. Figure 9–12 shows the syntax involved in the FORTRAN IF statement and explains the meaning of the various parts of the statement.

Figure 9–12

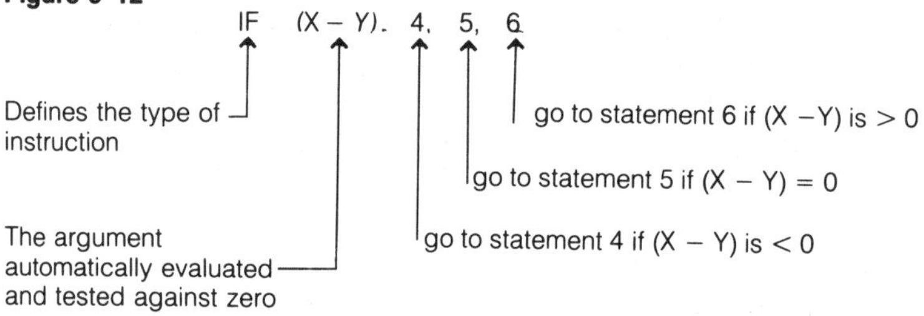

Figure 9–13 shows a flowchart that was used as an example in the section on flowcharts, but on the left is an identical flowchart that shows the specific FORTRAN statements enabling the computer to execute the specified functions.

Figure 9–13

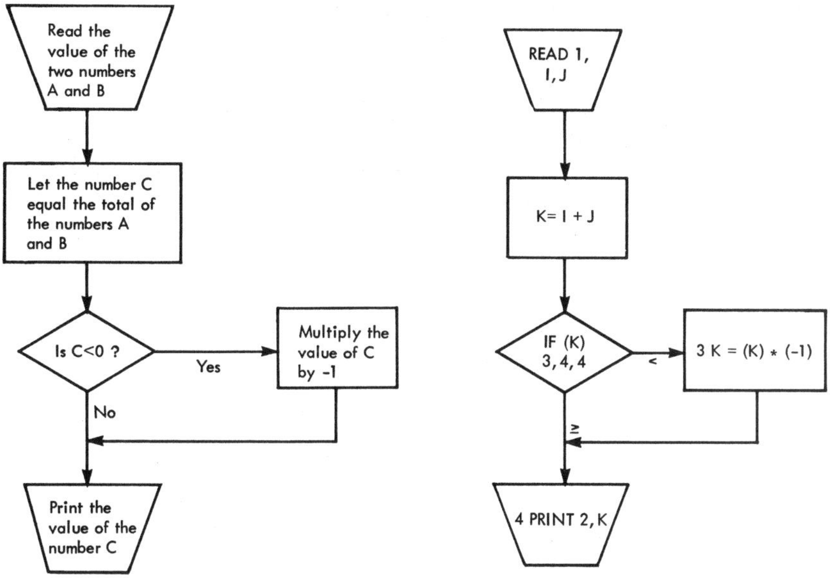

From the above example, it can be seen that the flowchart is a diagram of the following FORTRAN computer program:

```
  READ 1, I, J
  K = I + J
  IF (K) 3, 4, 4
3 K = (K)*(−1)
4 PRINT 2, K
1 FORMAT (I 4, I 4)
2 FORMAT (I 5)
  END
```

This program will add two numbers, just as before. It therefore performs exactly the same function as the first sample program. But because of the conditional branch (the ability of the computer to "decide"), it will multiply all negative values of K by -1 in order to make them positive. In effect, the program produces the absolute value of the sum of any two numbers.

The DO statement greatly adds to the power of FORTRAN programs by automatically creating a loop wherever the programmer finds one necessary. The DO statement merely specifies the aspects or parameters that define a loop, and the compiler will see to it that the proper set of instructions is repeated the correct number of times. The defining parameters of any loop whether specified by a DO statement or not are as follows:

1. The beginning of the loop must be defined.
2. The end of the loop must be stated.
3. The counter used in the loop must be defined.
4. The number of times that the loop is to be performed must be stated.

The DO statement accomplishes the task of defining these parameters and actually allows even more flexibility, as will become apparent. The syntax of the DO statement is explained by Figure 9–14.

Figure 9–14

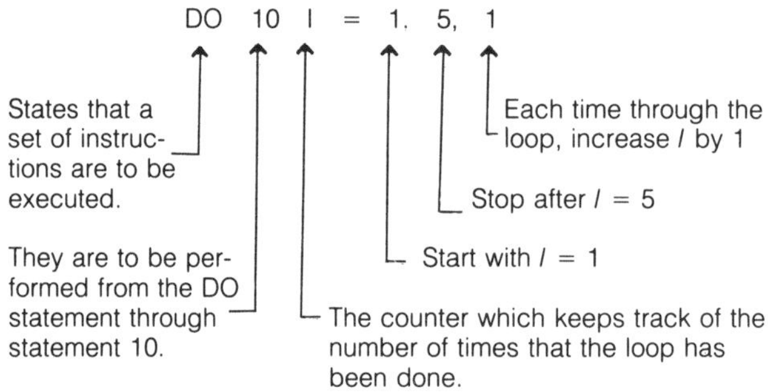

The following examples show several DO statements on the left with a verbal description of the same instruction on the right:

DO 10 I = 1, 5, 1 .... Do everything through statement 10 five times, increasing I by one each time the loop is performed.

DO 10 I = 1, 5 .... Same as above. The compiler assumes that the counter is to be increased by one each time the loop is to be performed if no entry is made.

DO 10 J = 1, 5 .... Same as above, except that J will be increased instead of I.

DO 10 J = 1, 10 .... Same as above, except that the loop will be performed ten times instead of five.

DO 20 J = 1, 10 .... Same as above, except that all statements through statement 20 will be performed for each loop.

Because the DO statement was specifically designed to assist the programmer in creating loops, the example of a loop shown in Figure 9–10 can be programmed more easily using a DO statement than by using the IF statement. The DO statement program corresponding to this flowchart is listed below on the left, and the IF statement program that is capable (though less easily) of performing the same function is stated on the right:

```
  DO 4 M = 1, 10, 1
  READ 1, I, J
  K = I + J
  IF (K) 3, 4, 4
3 K = (K)*(-1)
4 PRINT 2, K
1 FORMAT (I 4, I 4)
2 FORMAT (I 5)
  END
```

```
  M = 0
5 READ 1, I, J
  K = I + J
  IF (K) 3, 4, 4
3 K = (K)*(-1)
4 PRINT 2, K
1 FORMAT (I 4, I 4)
2 FORMAT (I 5)
  M = M + 1
  IF (M - 10) 5, 6, 6
6 CONTINUE
  END
```

The real power of the DO loop, however, is not utilized unless used in connection with subscripted variables. Examining subscripted variables, it is possible to draw on the fairly extensive description of the use of subscripts already given in previous chapters. For example, the most common measure of central tendency is given by the formula $\Sigma X_i/N$ where $i = 1, 2, 3, \ldots N$. Because each of the numbers to be included in the average is defined in computer language as being *X(I)* and *I* varies from 1 to *N*, it is possible to write a program to compute the arithmetic mean *by simply letting the counter of the DO loop be the subscript value* and then performing the DO loop ten times. The following section of a program (Table 9–3) should be able to handle the entire problem. The DO loop is boxed. Note that the FORMAT and END statements are not present because this example is only a program segment, not a complete program.

The first time through the loop, *I* will be equal to 1, which means that the expression *X(I)* will mean $X(1)$. The computer will read a card that contains the value of $X(1)$, and then will add this value into the total. Next, the program will loop back and make *I* equal to 2, which in turn makes *X(I)* equal to $X(2)$. A card is then read that contains the number $X(2)$, this number is added to the total, and so on. After this process has been performed *N* times, the program "falls through" the loop and processes the instructions outside of the loop—in this case dividing the total by *N* and printing the answer.

Table 9-3

TOTAL = 0.0	Sets the value of $\Sigma X_i = 0.0$
DO 1 I = 1, N	Indicates that the addition is to be performed N times.
READ 2, X(I)	Reads a value for X_i each time through the loop.
1 TOTAL = TOTAL + X(I)	Adds X_i to the total, ΣX_i
DIV = N	By the time this statement is reached, the loop is complete and ΣX_i is therefore the sum of all of the X_i that have been read.
AVE = TOTAL/DIV	Divides ΣX_i by N
PRINT 3, AVE	Prints the average

The power of the DO loop and subscript combination can be increased even further by the use of doubly subscripted arrays. These arrays are entire tables of numbers that can be represented as, for example, a_{ij}. In this notation, i is the row number of the particular element in the table, and j is the column number. The FORTRAN notation A (I,J) is therefore equivalent to the mathematical notation a_{ij}. It is possible to have one DO loop cause computations to be performed for each row of the table in turn, and within this loop have another DO loop that causes the computations to be performed for each column in turn. Table 9-4 is an example.

Table 9-4

```
DO 1 I = 1, 10
DO 1 J = 1, 5
1 A(I, J) = 0.0
```

This statement will cause the following statements to be performed first for the first row of the table, then for the second, and so forth through the tenth.

These two statements will cause each column of the row under consideration to be set equal to zero. These statements are performed for every row, hence all elements a_{ij} are set equal to zero.

The use of nested DO loops is, of course, not restricted to problems involving subscripted arrays, although this is their most important application.

Program structure

One additional major concept in the technical aspects of programming needs to be developed. Subroutines are vital to any reasonably complex programming problem, especially in mathematical applications. A subroutine is a set of computer statements that perform a specific function and can be treated as a logical whole. A program can refer to the subroutine whenever the function that the subroutine performs is needed. Any reasonably large program will typically process in the normal sequential fashion but will periodically transfer control to a subroutine when a specific task needs to be performed, then return control to the main line coding until another subroutine is called, and so forth. One of the simplest examples of a subroutine might be a set of instructions that, when given the numeric value of x, returns to the program the value of log x.

From the simplest subroutine to the most complex, the common characteristic of these tools is that they are black boxes. In the simple example just given, the input to the box is x, the output is log x. The input to a complex subroutine might be a large array of data and the output might be the results of a complete multiple correlation analysis. The principle in both cases is the same, and subroutines can easily be seen to be smaller black boxes used by the computer program that is itself a black box from the standpoint of the user. It is even possible for a complex subroutine to utilize or "call" a number of other, more basic subroutines in order to accomplish its function more easily. In fact, in more sophisticated mathematical languages it is even possible for a subroutine to call itself in order to facilitate processing.

The programmer has available a large number of already prepared, or "canned," subroutines and certainly has the option of writing his own subroutines to perform whatever set of functions might be needed. In writing large programs, he will attempt to locate particular functions or operations that are a logical unity and can be reduced to a subroutine. Ideally, the program can be reduced to the sequential processing of routine after routine, leaving no work at all for the main line program. In practical work, however, this procedure is seldom possible, and after all routines have been written a main line program remains to control the order in which the routines are performed. The advantage of this approach is that it "fragments" the problem into a set of clearly defined functions connected by a basic skeleton of logic. The fundamental, underlying logic therefore becomes much clearer and errors are less frequent. If errors occur, they can usually be seen immediately to have been caused by a certain subroutine. A 30-statement subroutine can then be corrected instead of a 2,000-statement main program. The time-saving can be substantial.

Several basic facts about programming can be gleaned from the discussion of subroutines. First, the problems of program organization make large programs disproportionately more difficult than small ones. A 2,000-statement program is not just ten times more difficult than one with 200 statements, it is an altogether different world. Second, the problem of the programmer is not really one of being certain that every comma is in the right place, as is commonly supposed. Although it is true that attention to detail is important, the characteristic that most distinguishes a good programmer from a mediocre one is the ability to structure the logic of extremely large problems as a whole. Instead of hacking away at the problem one piece at a time, he will view the total problem, break it into its fundamental units, delineate the relationships between these units, code these main line relationships, and then insert the pieces (the subroutines) into their properly defined place within the structured whole.

Although the analyst can write smaller programs using a high-level compiler, he probably will have to rely upon the professional programmer to provide the larger ones. The problems involved in this relationship are basically problems of discovering which results would be valuable and finding ways in which those results can be obtained. This is the subject of the next chapter.

Chapter 10

Computer usage

With an understanding of how a computer works, some further consideration must be given to how to use this instrument most effectively: A good computer program must be applicable to a real problem and stated in sufficiently general terms so that it can be applied to many similar problems. It is most useful when the problem is repetitive in nature. Because the computer can process data much faster than input can be given the computer or output can be provided, a tradeoff must be reached to balance the time and money spent on proper programming against the speed and cost reduction provided by superior programming. A computer *system* deals not with one problem but the organization of computer output to meet the users' total needs. Establishment of such a system requires defining the structure and organization of the user, defining his needs, and defining the input before the integrated programming can begin. After the system is installed, programs must be modified and updated and computer runs controlled. Only by approaching the computer as an information system rather than a solver of a particular problem can maximum utilization of modern computer technology be achieved.

INTRODUCTION

One of the most common mistakes among people inexperienced with computers is the assumption that the use of the computer is identical with the problem of programming the calculations or internal processing involved in any particular problem. Actually, this is by far the simplest aspect of computer work. The availability of high-level compilers has made both the calculations and logic requirements of any project so simple that more bottlenecks occur in keeping the mathematics correct than in translating the mathematics into a machine workable form. The really difficult portions of any particular computer project can be placed into three categories:

1. Applications and communications.
2. Run time and input-output.
3. Computer systems in the context of business systems.

APPLICATIONS AND COMMUNICATIONS

Highly professional programming has become such a difficult subject that it is almost impossible for programmers to understand fully all aspects of the science. In the little time that is available for self-education, the programmer must deepen his understanding of the characteristics of peripheral devices, the nature of existing compilers, and the more unusual characteristics of the particular machine he uses. In addition, he must keep aware of the new programming techniques constantly being developed, new languages available, and new programs that may have been made available for public use. He must keep up to date on all business standards and documentation requirements of the company for which he works, the system used by the team running the machine to control the flow of programs, and the management structure used in the programming division to maintain communications and coordination among the programming staff. To make matters worse, the technology in the industry is changing so rapidly that anything that he learns will be obsolete in five years because new machines, new languages and techniques, and new management devices will have replaced completely the ones he spent so much time studying.

The research analyst is in approximately the same situation, for he is responsible for estimates of financial results in several industries, which would be taxing even if needed for only one company for which internal financial records were accessible. In addition, the techniques by which he makes his estimates are undergoing a revolutionary change as the quantitative approach becomes more dominant in the investment industry. The requirements for these two different professions of computer science and investments indirectly produce the most significant problem in the application of computer science to the investment field. One man knows the problems that need to be solved and another knows the solution techniques that may be applied to problems in general, but no single person is capable of being acquainted with both the problem and the solution. Because of this, communication difficulties surround every computer project undertaken.

The investment analyst can state in his technical jargon what needs to be done, but the computer programmer is not sufficiently acquainted with the investment industry to be able to understand the highly developed terminology used for investment work and so is forced to ask detailed questions. Unfortunately, these questions appear to an investment analyst to be either highly trivial (such as how many digits go to the right of the decimal point), or completely incomprehensible because they are couched in the *computer analyst's* jargon ("My round-off error can't be helped in any compiler-written program because I can't go beyond 64-bit double-precision in the model 50"). Adding to the confusion is the unfortunate fact that quantitative techniques have already developed to the point where no single person can be an expert in all statistical and mathematical models, and so a three- or four-direction communication confusion results. In this kind of environment, it is quite possible to have three or four highly skilled individuals involved in a computerization effort and still accomplish nothing because of the lack of direction stemming from an absence of coordination. In many cases, adding more people to the project simply increases this problem and actually *lowers* efficiency.

A knowledge of a few of the basic principles known to be requirements of a good computer program may assist the financial analyst in making the initial move to break this communication deadlock. The two keys to any good computer project are applicability and generality. Any computer program must apply to a real problem in investments or it cannot have any value regardless of its cost. But the program must solve reasonably general problems or it will not be used sufficiently to justify its cost. Figure 10–1 is an example of one of the most elementary programs possible on a computer.

Figure 10–1

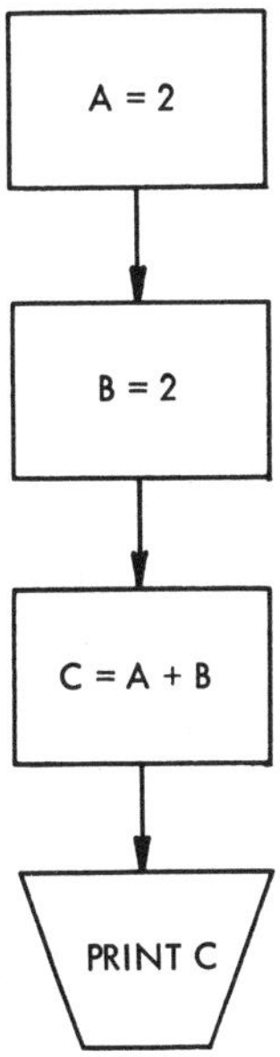

This program would have value only if the sum of two and two were desired. The problem is not sufficiently general because this problem obviously does not occur too frequently and even when it does occur it can be solved without resort to a computer run. Figure 10–2 is substantially superior to the one just analyzed.

Figure 10–2

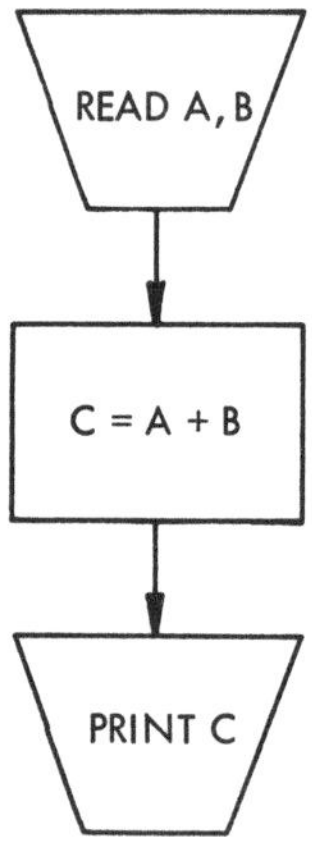

This program will work whenever the sum of any two numbers is desired regardless of what particular numbers are involved. Such a program is a substantial improvement because the problem is encountered much more frequently, but a program could be even more valuable if the statement

```
C = (A**2)*(B**4)/(A +B)**3,
```

which is a computer-language version of

$$C = A^2B^4/(A + B)^3,$$

were substituted for $C = A + B$. A frequently used complex calculation, in other words, is just as easy for the computer as a frequently used simple one. This produces one of the very basic peculiarities of computer work: *the value of the computer rises as the complexity of the problem increases.* The computer has a very marked tendency to make difficult problems easy. On the other hand, because it requires such specific instructions, it also has a tendency to make simple jobs quite difficult.

By using general variables in the program, a given set of calculations can be performed on different data. For example, a simple regression can be run on two variables and the program will still apply to another set of two variables related to a completely different investment problem. Another important ingredient in any computer program is repetition. For example, if the sum of two numbers were needed, it would be very easy to use a hand calculator and avoid a computer run. But if this sum were needed on, say, 5,000 different sets of two numbers, the computer becomes substantially more valuable, as shown in Figure 10–3.

Figure 10–3

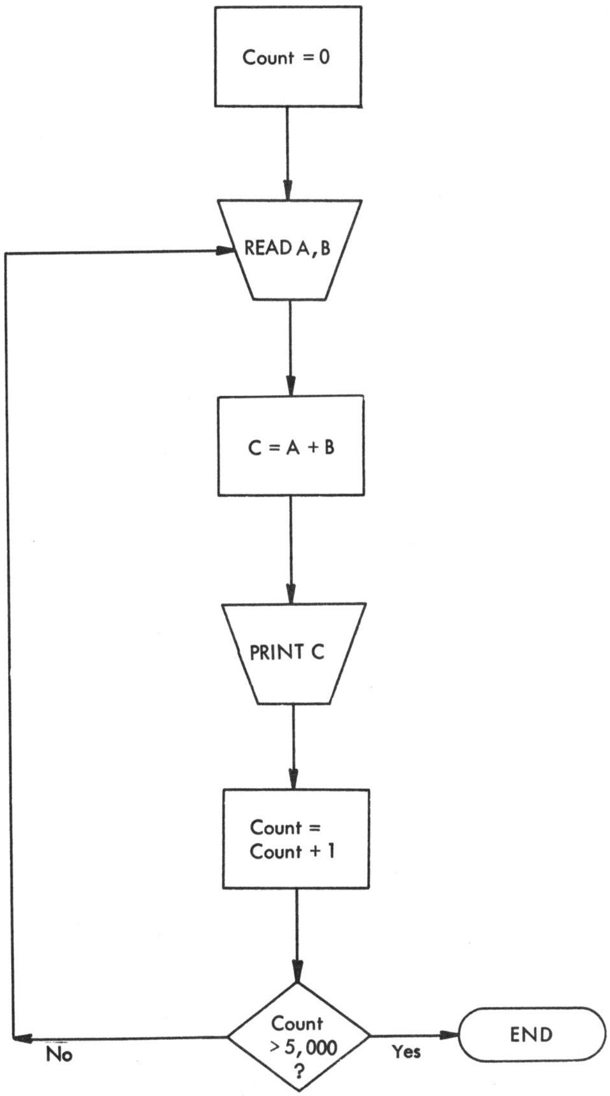

Summarizing, for a program to be valuable, it is usually necessary that it be quite general, applying to large numbers of slightly different types of problems. In addition, the problem to be solved must be encountered repetitively, so that the cost of the program can be allocated to a large number of different sets of data, all of which have the same nature.

One of the most common misuses of the computer is the development of a one-time job of moderate complexity. While it is true that an engineer may write a program, run it once, and then throw it away, this approach is seldom valuable in a business environment. The engineer has complicated mathematics built into a simple program with little input-output. As a result, the engineer may save three man-months by using an 80-statement program. The financial man who requests a one-time job typically has need for light mathematics, a moderately difficult program, and rather large input-output. As a result, the analyst may save one man-day with a 200-statement program. The large cost of a *general* program can be spread over many different computer runs and possibly over a number of fairly diverse applications. But the moderate cost of a program used *once* is all applied to the one computer run that results. Once again, the computer has a knack for making the simple difficult and the difficult simple; it can also make the expensive almost free and the moderate cost the highest.

One very interesting point is that this discussion of the reasons why a program has a high value points very strongly toward the use of mathematical models. Mathematical models have all of the desirable characteristics of a computer application. They are very general, applying to numerous sets of data and a large number of application areas. They do not go out of date and so require little modification. They can be of use in virtually every industry, allowing the cost to be spread among a number of different applications. In fact, most mathematical models are available as "canned" packages from computer manufacturers and so have very little cost to the user other than the education of the analysts in the characteristics of the program. As will be shown in later sections of this chapter, fortunately these models have low input-output requirements and they can be more precisely defined than would ever be possible in a nonmathematical area.

RUN TIME AND INPUT-OUTPUT

The chapter on computer programming divided the computer into three basic functions of input, processing, and output. After this distinction was made, the subjects of input and output were promptly eliminated from consideration in the development of the nature of the computer that followed. This distortion, unfortunately, is both necessary and misleading. It is necessary because the processing function of the computer must be fairly well understood before input-output can be discussed. It is misleading because the majority of the purely technical problems in the computer industry stem from input-output difficulties. In other words, if the only problems encountered by programmers were machine-oriented problems, the majority of the programmer's time would be spent treating the input that feeds the computer and constructing the commands that create the output from the computer. (In fact, however, the first section of this chapter shows that the largest problems of the programming function are not technical at all but rather deal with the very human problem of coordination).

Input-output problems result from three major facts:

1. The computer is substantially slower in inputting raw data and outputting results than it is in actually processing values already present in core.
2. A number of input-output (IO) devices are available, and it is necessary to know their characteristics and to choose the correct device for each particular application.
3. Input by its very nature means input to the computer *from* human beings. Output means output going *to* human beings. (This statement is only partially true, for the computer is quite capable of generating output and then at a later time using these data as input without any human intervention.) Nevertheless, all data used by computers *initially* come from people and the final output of any computer project must eventually be given to human beings or the project will not be relevant to human problems.

The fact that the computer is significantly faster when performing internal processing than when reading data or writing results produces a major programming problem. In fact, this difficulty is the reason why this section is called "run time and input-output." The computer in a very simple application might be required to read two numbers, add them together, and print the result. Unfortunately, it takes so much time to read the two numbers that the computer must sit idly waiting for the numbers to be placed in core storage. Depending upon the particular input-output device being used, the computer may wait as many as 1,000 seconds for every second that it has data available for processing.

A number of sophisticated ways are used to get around this problem. The most obvious is simply to develop faster IO devices. Unfortunately, computer technology seems to be able to develop faster CPU's (central processing units) more easily than faster IO units, and as a result any gain in input-output speed is quickly offset by newer CPU's that once again widen the disparity. In order to break away from this race in hardware development, programmers have under their own control a number of possibilities:

1. The IO device used in any application must be the fastest practical.
2. While the machine is waiting for data to come in from one IO unit,

the program can be designed in such a way that it goes to another IO unit and starts to use input from this alternate source. By properly staggering the input and output commands among a number of units, it may be possible for a programmer to reduce run time substantially.

3. Instead of reading input into only one area in core storage, the programmer may alternately read data into two different areas. The computer can then process area A while information is being read into area B. Hopefully, by the time area A has been finished, area B will be ready for processing. While area B is then being processed, data is read into area A. This process of switching back and forth between input areas is called "input buffering." In effect, the technique allows the computer to perform IO operations and processing at the same time.
4. A number of programs may be placed in core at one time, permitting the computer to process whichever program may have data available at any given time. In actual practice, this "multiprogramming environment" is frequently used, and each program has buffered IO as well.

The variety of input-output devices cannot be described in any book not essentially devoted to the subject. Nevertheless, a speaking acquaintance with the most frequently used types of IO units is important in order to understand the problems the programmer may encounter and the effect that these problems have on the development costs and run time that is charged to the investment department.

A body of data fed into a computer is technically referred to as a "data set" or a "file." Examples of files might be the assets held in the various portfolios analyzed by the investment division, the analyst's estimates concerning next year's results for all stocks covered by the research department, the historical record of 500 economic time-series, or the financial history of a number of companies frequently analyzed. Any data set can be regarded from a human standpoint as being a stack or pile of information through which he can browse in any manner that he chooses. Unfortunately, however, the computer must access any data set by means of a fixed procedure. If, for example, the analyst's estimates on the companies currently on the recommended list are punched onto cards to be fed into the computer, the computer must access the first card first, then the second, and so on. The cards must be in the proper order (the order specified by the program) if valid results are to be obtained. Most IO devices are designed for the processing of sequential files, but some devices have the ability to permit random access. With random access, the computer is able to select the correct data from the entire data set in any order whatsoever. The computer therefore has the ability to use a "pick and choose" method for accessing information.

The most important IO devices for processing sequential files are card readers, card punches, and magnetic tape. The card reader permits the machine to access at rates as high as 1,000 cards per minute information that has been punched onto cards. The advantage of the card reader is that an analyst can punch virtually any information onto cards and so convert it into a computer readable form. The disadvantage is that the extremely slow speed of the reader causes the computer to spend a very high percentage of its time idly waiting for input to be made available.

Card punches are output devices by which the computer can convert the results of its calculations into punched cards, which then may be stored and later used as input. The card punch, however, is even slower than the reader, with the most rapid units operating at about 500 cards per minute. The advantage of the card punch is that it permits the computer to create machine readable output, relieving the analyst from the task of examining printed output and then manually punching the information for use in a later study. The disadvantage, of course, is that the punch is slower than the reader.

Magnetic tape units can be used both for input and output and have the advantage of being substantially more efficient than cards. The fastest tape units are approximately 150 times as fast as the best card readers. The advantage of the use of magnetic tape is its high speed and availability of both input and output. The disadvantage is that the programming of a tape-oriented system is slightly more difficult than when cards are used. A secondary but not inconsiderable value of magnetic tape is the compactness of the data set.

Less important sequential IO devices include the computer console (the control typewriter actually connected to the computer), optical reading devices capable of sensing visual characters, punched paper tape, and online terminals that provide a typewriter connected to the computer at a location physically remote from the machine.

The most important random access input-output devices are disc and drum. The use of disc units is slightly slower than tape if the application deals only with a sequential file. However, the random access feature makes it substantially more efficient if the data cannot easily be given to the computer in a simple, well-ordered way. The advantage of disc is therefore its random access capabilities and the ability to store very large data files. The disadvantages are essentially the same as for magnetic tape. The use of a high-speed drum as an input-output device is very efficient, allowing data to be provided to the computer at a very high speed and in a random access environment. Unfortunately, a large amount of data cannot be permanently stored on a high speed drum in a cost-efficient way, so that files must be placed on this unit from other IO devices for any particular application and for only a short period of time.

As a result of the technical characteristics of these input-output devices, the programmer working on an investment project will prefer sequential files to random access files because of the greater speed. In addition, he will use tape or disc instead of cards at every possible point. He will be willing to read data from cards once, but he will have a strong tendency to try to store it as a permanent file on some other medium, most likely disc. If a high-speed drum is available, he will probably want to load the data file on the drum before processing. When the programmer's concern to minimize run time by optimum use of IO hardware is coupled with his design of the actual program using buffering techniques and multiple IO devices, a program having essentially simple logic can easily become very complicated. Because of this fact, the reduction of run time almost inevitably produces an increase in project development cost. If the program's instructions are to be efficient and lower the computer charges, additional time must be spent on the program's development, with a corresponding increase in the development cost. Trading off development and efficiency costs by using the "best" level of input-output sophistication is one of the most important decisions in the control of costs on a computer project. On one side is the investment analyst's inherent desire for the flexibility that simplicity in program design produces (and the associated high computer charges). On the other hand is the programmer's almost pathological drive toward the maximum in technological sophistication (with correspondingly high development costs). Unfortunately, the balancing of these opposed positions becomes substantially more complicated when consideration is given to the massive problem of computer systems.

COMPUTER SYSTEMS AND BUSINESS SYSTEMS

Once the analyst has completed the rather time-consuming job of learning elementary programming, he or she can use the computer for assistance in solving a number of specific problems. Unfortunately, this approach of using the computer "one program at a time" is only the most elementary of applications. In order to understand how computers are used in business today, it is necessary to undertake the substantially more difficult subject of systems theory and the design and use of the computer system. In this approach, the computer is no longer seen as simply a tool to which various members of the investment department occasionally present various isolated problems. Instead, it is seen as the device by which the department's total information requirements can be continuously satisfied in a unified, systematic manner.

In the systems approach, the total investment function is considered a single operating unit having a definite set of informational needs. The computer programs must, of course, satisfy those needs, which is not possible if attempted on a program-by-program basis. The needs must be evaluated as a complete, integrated system of requirements, and their resolution must come from a complete, integrated system of computer instructions. Therefore, in any really satisfactory computer application to investments, each statement in any given program must be related to all other such statements but also all programs must be interrelated.

This approach of viewing the department as a single unit having information needs and the computer applications as a single unit satisfying those needs is the first aspect of systems theory. The first step, then, is to regard the problems and the solutions in their entirety, in a manner very similar to the way the department head and the computer-applications head regard their operations when undertaking long-range planning. Unfortunately, the second step is more difficult. In actual practice, the two functions are deeply interwoven. The analysts have information needs, such as company data or statistical results. They have information output that must be summarized by the computer and then given to the portfolio managers. The managers also receive information concerning their accounts. Their decisions are information output, and so forth. Systems theory in its broadest application refers not to either the investment or the computer function; it refers rather to the analysis of the systematic and interrelated operating unit resulting from integrating the two functions in day-to-day operations. The balance of this chapter discusses various aspects of the design of specifically *computer* systems that at least in part satisfy the requirements of *business* systems.

Any computer system is completely dependent upon its data base. This is axiomatic, for although ten related programs may use a single data set (or calculations resulting from this set), no program can ever be designed that pulls numbers out of thin air in order to begin calculations. All of the solutions that any computer system can provide are constrained by the initial human input, which is then processed and maintained automatically. The second major constraint on the system stems from the output requirements. Because the computer is used to provide information, the nature of the reports needed heavily determines the nature of the system. Because of these two limiting factors, work in computer systems naturally emphasizes a number of input-output principles.

Data should be input to the system only once, and the computer should handle all further manipulations needed. All data needed for any reports must, of course, be input at some time or other, but it is important to avoid the precalculation of data before it is given to the computer. After all, the computer was designed for calculations and it is inefficient to perform them by hand. Output should be tailored to the needs of the user. It should meet his requirements directly, and no further calculations based upon the output should be necessary. In order to avoid inundating the user with output, all reports should be relevant. Going a step beyond this, it is possible to use exception output, i.e., output printed only if it is unusual for some reason.

If the analyst has at least a rudimentary understanding of the problems involved in building and operating a computer system, he can utilize the computer more effectively in his work, but more important is the fact that he will see more clearly the nature of his position in the context of the overall effort of the investment research team. The system is built by first analyzing the function and structure of the investment department. Next, the particular information needed by each member of the department is strictly defined. The reports are then designed, and their frequency is determined (weekly, monthly, etc.). Once all of the output has been specified, the input required to produce the desired results is deduced from the calculations. The most efficient form in which these data can be prepared for the computer is then determined. After all of this has been completed, the actual programs needed to produce the desired results are specified and then designed. The specifications for each program can then be used for the programming (called "coding") of the system. The programs are coded in a logical order that permits portions of the total system to be "phased in" before the total project is complete. Once the system is complete and tested, each program will be closely related to every other program.

These design considerations must be understood when the investment department undertakes any computer effort. As can easily be seen, the nature of the system makes modification extremely difficult, for a number of programs will be affected. If the definition of the needed information is not complete, additional input may be needed, and this requires a redesign running through the entire length of the system. Errors in specifying calculations are usually less serious because they are often unique to one program, but it may be difficult to detect that an error in definition has occurred if the difference in the results is small. The most important point that can be drawn from the nature of system design is the fact that individual programs cannot be written on a one-at-a-time basis and then combined into an integrated system. A successful computer effort requires a complete definition before the project is undertaken.

Once a system is operational, it must be maintained in an operating environment. This is really two problems. First, the programs must continuously be modified and updated. Second, the computer runs that provide the investment output must be controlled. This control requires the scheduling of machine runs, the orderly distribution of output, and the accurate preparation of input. The input provides the majority of problems. It must be correctly entered on forms in accordance with a strict schedule based on the timing of the machine runs. It is then keypunched, checked for errors, and given to the computer. The majority of difficulties in either the accuracy or the timing of output can almost always be traced to a problem at some point in the input preparation process.

A discussion of computer systems would hardly be complete without some comment concerning time-sharing computer applications (called real-time systems). Any computer having real-time capabilities can be programmed in such a way that it will provide simultaneous service to a number of users working with different programs. For example, one computer owned by an independent computer service company might at any one time be processing the programs of 30 users located in different cities but connected to the CPU by telephone lines and teletype terminals. The CPU would spend a short time on a portion of user A's job, then move to user B's job, and so on. Whenever user A's job requires input or output, the CPU automatically transfers to B's job until A's program is once again ready for processing. Because input-output is so much slower than processing, this feature permits the CPU to process someone else's job instead of simply waiting for data. As a result, the CPU is used much more efficiently, and each user is charged only for the amount of CPU time that was actually spent on his program.

Organizationally, this approach to computer usage results in sharing of the cost of a single computer among many users. This produces two aspects of real-time that are radically different from the investment department's standpoint. First, a company having an investment department may introduce an internal real-time system in which the investment function will participate. Second, the investment department may contract with a time-sharing service bureau to become a user of a computer that is outside the company.

The first alternative, an in-house real-time system, is extremely sophisticated and also extremely complicated. Terminals can be located in the investment department to provide immediate access to all accounting data, statistical output, standard reports, and the like. In addition, any job not efficient in a time-sharing environment can still be processed by the more traditional batch methods if necessary. This type of system provides both the flexibility of real-time terminals and the efficiency of batch processing. Its drawbacks are that it requires a top-management commitment to the implementation of the system, a high degree of coordination between the investment function and the computer function, an extremely high level of software (i.e., systems and programming) expertise, a high cost for design and implementation, and a high cost for computer processing (primarily because of the larger number of applications computerized).

The second alternative, using an outside computer, produces almost the reverse situation. Because the computer company makes available to all users a large number of operational programs, the need for computer sophistication is kept to a minimum. If fact, it is possible to run such an arrangement without even having a programmer, let alone a systems analyst. Because the investment department is billed only for the time actually used, the computer charges can be kept low. The operating environment is simplified because all data are entered directly on the terminal. No liaison with the in-house computer staff is required.

This time-sharing approach also has drawbacks, however. First, although dollar costs can be kept quite low, the charges will tend to be higher than batch processing on an application-by-application basis. This tendency can become quite pronounced on large jobs. Second, because the programs supplied by the hardware company must be quite general, they cannot be well integrated into the investment system. If, alternatively, the money is spent to build an integrated system for the time-sharing application, computer usage costs can be much higher than in batch processing. The approach is very limited in input-output. Data entered by hand on the teletype and output are printed at about 120 *words* per minute. Because of the simplified operations, the answers are given in a reduced *lapse*-time, but the fact that the analyst is tied to the slow input-output increases the project's *man*-time, raising costs. A general accounting system cannot be utilized on a time-sharing computer. In calculating costs, the charge for time on the terminal is frequently 10 to 20 times the charge for the CPU time in terms of dollars paid per month. This terminal cost must be coupled with the cost per hour of the analyst tied up at the terminal.

Man-machine conversation can, as the above paragraph shows, be a very expensive approach. This expense, of course, must be weighed carefully against the numerous benefits stemming from the time-sharing environment. One practical approach is to use both computer modes, with each project's individual characteristics determining the computer to be used or whether the computer should be used at all. In general, the time-sharing terminal can be used to gain access to canned programs that can handle small jobs quickly, while the batch mode can be used for the overall system and the large statistical projects. Another, more sophisticated, solution is the use of *remote batch* systems, which have all of the beneficial features of batch processing and in addition allow the use of a remote terminal located in the investment division. This combination permits lower costs and the processing of more complex programs without encountering a high lapse time. If, however, the investment division is quite small, the only option available may be time-sharing, in which case the only choice is whether this approach can be taken on at least a few projects more efficiently than hand methods. This will usually be the case; even if usage is low, only the time used is charged to the investment department.

ADDITIONAL READINGS IN COMPUTER USAGE

Naylor, Thomas H.; Balintfy, Joseph L.; Burdick, Donald S.; and Chu, Kong. *Computer Simulation Technique*. New York: John Wiley & Sons, Inc., 1966.

This book will substantially expand anyone's concept concerning the capabilities of the computer and the problems it can solve (340 pages). The book covers simulation technique, where the computer is programmed to behave as if it were a gas station, or an inventory system, or an economy. The presentation is almost completely verbal, and no knowledge of the computer is assumed. The nature of simulation experiments, examples of possible simulation applications, and several special-purpose simulation languages are discussed at some length. The two chapters on random numbers and probability distributions can be skipped without damaging the presentation if technical aspects of the approach are not needed.

Rosen, Saul (Ed). *Programming Systems and Languages*. New York: McGraw-Hill Book Company, 1967.

This book of readings discusses the characteristics of software on a more advanced level than is encountered in the books written to popularize one or another of the various languages available. Fortran, Algol, Cobol, and PL/1 are covered in the first 159 pages. The next 202 pages discuss the methods by which compilers operate. List processing and string processing are two advanced techniques in problem solving, and 153 pages are devoted to a description of five languages specializing in these approaches. The remaining 214 pages discuss operating systems, which are the software support systems that provide the computer with the general control environment necessary for particular applications programs to run.

Weinberg, Gerald M. *PL/1 Programming Primer*. New York: McGraw-Hill Book Company, 1966.

This book is an excellent introduction to the PL/1 language (260 pages). The statements and concepts are introduced in a logical order of increasing complexity and the grammatical aspects of the instructions are subordinated to their actual problem-solving characteristics through the use of applications in the main body of the text.

APPENDIX A: LOGARITHMS

N	0	1	2	3	4	5	6	7	8	9
10	0000	0043	0086	0128	0170	0212	0253	0294	0334	0374
11	0414	0453	0492	0531	0569	0607	0645	0682	0719	0755
12	0792	0828	0864	0899	0934	0969	1004	1038	1072	1106
13	1139	1173	1206	1239	1271	1303	1335	1367	1399	1430
14	1461	1492	1523	1553	1584	1614	1644	1673	1703	1732
15	1761	1790	1818	1847	1875	1903	1931	1959	1987	2014
16	2041	2068	2095	2122	2148	2175	2201	2227	2253	2279
17	2304	2330	2355	2380	2405	2430	2455	2480	2504	2529
18	2553	2577	2601	2625	2648	2672	2695	2718	2742	2765
19	2788	2810	2833	2856	2878	2900	2923	2945	2967	2989
20	3010	3032	3054	3075	3096	3118	3139	3160	3181	3201
21	3222	3243	3263	3284	3304	3324	3345	3365	3385	3404
22	3424	3444	3464	3483	3502	3522	3541	3560	3579	3598
23	3617	3636	3655	3674	3692	3711	3729	3747	3766	3784
24	3802	3820	3838	3856	3874	3892	3909	3927	3945	3962
25	3979	3997	4014	4031	4048	4065	4082	4099	4116	4133
26	4150	4166	4183	4200	4216	4232	4249	4265	4281	4298
27	4314	4330	4346	4362	4378	4393	4409	4425	4440	4456
28	4472	4487	4502	4518	4533	4548	4564	4579	4594	4609
29	4624	4639	4654	4669	4683	4698	1713	4728	4742	4757
30	4771	4786	4800	4814	4829	4843	4857	4871	4886	4900
31	4914	4928	4942	4955	4969	4983	4997	5011	5024	5038
32	5051	5065	5079	5092	5105	5119	5132	5145	5159	5172
33	5185	5198	5211	5224	5237	5250	5263	5276	5289	5302
34	5315	5328	5340	5353	5366	5378	5391	5403	5416	5428
35	5441	5453	5465	5478	5490	5502	5514	5527	5539	5551
36	5563	5575	5587	5599	5611	5623	5635	5647	5658	5670
37	5682	5694	5705	5717	5729	5740	5752	5763	5775	5786
38	5798	5809	5821	5832	5843	5855	5866	5877	5888	5899
39	5911	5922	5933	5944	5955	5966	5977	5988	5999	6010
40	6021	6031	6042	6053	6064	6075	6085	6096	6107	6117
41	6128	6138	6149	6160	6170	6180	6191	6201	6212	6222
42	6232	6243	6253	6263	6274	6284	6294	6304	6314	6325
43	6336	6345	6355	6365	6375	6385	6395	6405	6415	6425
44	6435	6444	6454	6464	6474	6484	6493	6503	6513	6522
45	6532	6542	6551	6561	6571	6580	6590	6599	6609	6618
46	6628	6637	6646	6656	6665	6675	6684	6693	6702	6712
47	6721	6730	6739	6749	6758	6767	6776	6785	6794	6803
48	6812	6821	6830	6839	6848	6857	6866	6875	6884	6893
49	6902	6911	6920	6928	6937	6946	6955	6964	6972	6981
50	6990	6998	7007	7016	7024	7033	7042	7050	7059	7067
51	7076	7084	7093	7101	7110	7118	7126	7135	7143	7152
52	7160	7168	7177	7185	7193	7202	7210	7218	7226	7235
53	7243	7251	7259	7267	7275	7284	7292	7300	7308	7316
54	7324	7332	7340	7348	7356	7364	7372	7380	7388	7396

APPENDIX A *(continued)*

N	0	1	2	3	4	5	6	7	8	9
55	7404	7412	7419	7427	7435	7443	7451	7459	7466	7474
56	7482	7490	7497	7505	7513	7520	7528	7536	6543	7551
57	7559	7566	7574	7582	7589	7597	7604	7612	7619	7627
58	7634	7642	7649	7657	7664	7672	7679	7686	7694	7701
59	7709	7716	7723	7731	7738	7745	7752	7760	7767	7774
60	7782	7789	7796	7803	7810	7818	7825	7832	7839	7846
61	7853	7860	7868	7875	7882	7889	7896	7903	7910	7917
62	7924	7931	7938	7945	7952	7959	7966	7973	7980	7987
63	7993	8000	8007	8014	8021	8028	8035	8041	8048	8055
64	8062	8069	8075	8082	8089	8096	8102	8109	8116	8122
65	8129	8136	8142	8149	8156	8162	8169	8176	8182	8189
66	8195	8202	8209	8215	8222	8228	8235	8241	8248	8254
67	8261	8267	8274	8280	8287	8293	8299	8306	8312	8319
68	8325	8331	8338	8344	8351	8357	8363	8370	8376	8382
69	8388	8395	8401	8407	8414	8420	8426	8432	8439	8445
70	8451	8457	8463	8470	8476	8482	8488	8494	8500	8506
71	8513	8519	8525	8531	8537	8543	8549	8555	8561	8567
72	8573	8579	8585	8591	8597	8603	8609	8615	8621	8627
73	8633	8639	8645	8651	8657	8663	8669	8675	8681	8688
74	8692	8698	8704	8710	8716	8722	8727	8733	8739	8745
75	8751	8756	8762	8768	8774	8779	8785	8791	8797	8802
76	8808	8814	8820	8825	8831	8837	8842	8848	8854	8859
77	8865	8871	8876	8882	8887	8893	8899	8904	8910	8915
78	8921	8927	8932	8938	8943	8949	8954	8960	8965	8971
79	8976	8982	8987	8993	8998	9004	9009	9015	9020	9025
80	9031	9036	9042	9047	9053	9058	9063	9069	9074	9079
81	9085	9090	9096	9101	9106	9112	09117	9122	9128	9133
82	9138	9143	9149	9154	9159	9165	9170	9175	9180	9186
83	9191	9196	9201	9206	9212	9217	9222	9227	9232	9238
84	9243	9248	9253	9258	9263	9269	9274	9279	9284	9289
85	9294	9299	9304	9309	9315	9320	9325	9330	9335	9340
86	9345	9350	9355	9360	9365	9370	9375	9380	9385	9390
87	9395	9400	9405	9410	9415	9420	9425	9430	9435	9440
88	9445	9450	9455	9460	9465	9469	9474	9479	9484	9489
89	9494	9499	9504	9509	9513	9518	9523	9528	9533	9538
90	9542	9547	9552	9557	9562	9566	9571	9576	9581	9586
91	9590	9595	9600	9605	9609	9614	9619	9625	9628	9633
92	9638	9643	9647	9652	9657	9661	9666	9671	9675	9680
93	9685	9689	9694	9699	9703	9708	9713	9717	9722	9727
94	9731	9736	9741	9745	9750	9754	9759	9763	9768	9773
95	9777	9782	9786	9791	9795	9800	9805	9809	9814	9818
96	9823	9827	9832	9836	9841	9845	9850	9854	9859	9863
97	9868	9872	9877	9881	9886	9890	9894	9899	9903	9908
98	9912	9917	9921	9926	9930	9934	9939	9943	9948	9952
99	9956	9961	9965	9969	9974	9978	9983	9987	9991	9996

APPENDIX B: PRESENT VALUE AND COMPARED GROWTH TABLES

Table B-1: Future Value of $1

$$F_n = P(1 + r)^n$$

Periods	2%	2 1/2%	3%	4%	5%	6%	8%	10%
1	1.0200	1.0250	1.0300	1.0400	1.0500	1.0600	1.0800	1.1000
2	1.0404	1.0506	1.0609	1.0816	1.1025	1.1236	1.1664	1.2100
3	1.0612	1.0769	1.0927	1.1249	1.1576	1.1910	1.2597	1.3310
4	1.0824	1.1038	1.1255	1.1699	1.2155	1.2625	1.3605	1.4641
5	1.1041	1.1314	1.1593	1.2167	1.2763	1.3382	1.4693	1.6105
6	1.1262	1.1597	1.1941	1.2653	1.3401	1.4185	1.5869	1.7716
7	1.1487	1.1887	1.2299	1.3159	1.4071	1.5036	1.7138	1.9488
8	1.1717	1.2184	1.2668	1.3686	1.4775	1.5938	1.8509	2.1436
9	1.1951	1.2489	1.3048	1.4233	1.5513	1.6895	1.9990	2.3589
10	1.2190	1.2801	1.3439	1.4802	1.6289	1.7908	2.1589	2.5938
11	1.2434	1.3121	1.3842	1.5395	1.7103	1.8983	2.3316	2.8532
12	1.2682	1.3449	1.4258	1.6010	1.7959	2.0122	2.5182	3.1385
13	1.2936	1.3785	1.4685	1.6651	1.8856	2.1329	2.7196	3.4524
14	1.3195	1.4130	1.5126	1.7317	1.9799	2.2609	2.9372	3.7976
15	1.3459	1.4483	1.5580	1.8009	2.0709	2.3966	3.1722	4.1774
16	1.3728	1.4845	1.6047	1.8730	2.1829	2.5404	3.4259	4.5951
17	1.4002	1.5216	1.6528	1.9479	2.2920	2.6928	3.7000	5.0545
18	1.4282	1.5597	1.7024	2.0258	2.4066	2.8543	3.9960	5.5600
19	1.4568	1.5987	1.7535	2.1068	2.5270	3.0256	4.3157	6.1160
20	1.4859	1.6386	1.8061	2.1911	2.6533	3.2071	4.6610	6.7276
22	1.5460	1.7216	1.9161	2.3699	2.9253	3.6035	5.4365	8.1404
24	1.6084	1.8087	2.0328	2.5633	3.2251	4.0489	6.3412	9.8498
26	1.6734	1.9003	2.1566	2.7725	3.5557	4.5494	7.3964	11.9183
28	1.7410	1.9965	2.2879	2.9987	3.9201	5.117	8.6271	14.4211
30	1.8114	2.0976	2.4273	3.2434	4.3219	5.7435	10.0627	17.4495
32	1.8845	2.2038	2.5751	3.5081	4.7649	6.4534	11.7371	21.1140
34	1.9607	2.3153	2.7319	3.7943	5.2533	7.2510	13.6901	25.5479
36	2.0399	2.4325	2.8983	4.1039	5.7918	8.1473	15.9682	30.9130
38	2.1223	2.5557	3.0748	4.4388	6.3855	9.1543	18.6253	37.4047
40	2.2080	2.6851	3.2620	4.8010	7.0400	10.2857	21.7245	45.2597
42	2.2972	2.8210	3.4607	5.1928	7.7616	11.5570	25.3395	54.7643
44	2.3901	2.9638	3.6715	5.6165	8.5572	12.9855	29.5560	66.2648
46	2.4866	3.1139	3.8950	6.0748	9.4343	14.5905	34.4741	80.1804
48	2.5871	3.2715	4.1323	6.5705	10.4013	16.3939	40.2106	97.0182
50	2.6916	3.4371	4.3839	7.1067	11.4674	18.4202	46.9016	117.3920
60	3.2810	4.3998	5.8916	10.5196	18.6792	32.9877	101.2571	304.4846

Source: Myron J. Gordon and Gordon Shillinglaw, *Accounting: A Management Approach*, 4th ed. (Homewood, Ill.: Richard D. Irwin, 1969), p. 784. ©1969 by Richard D. Irwin, Inc.

Table B-2. Present Value of $1

$$P_n = F(1+r)^{-n}$$

Years Hence	1%	2%	4%	6%	8%	10%	12%	14%	15%	16%	18%	20%	22%	24%	25%	26%	28%	30%	35%	40%	45%	50%
1	0.990	0.980	0.962	0.943	0.926	0.909	0.893	0.877	0.870	0.862	0.847	0.833	0.820	0.806	0.800	0.794	0.781	0.769	0.741	0.714	0.690	0.667
2	0.980	0.961	0.925	0.890	0.857	0.826	0.797	0.769	0.756	0.743	0.718	0.694	0.672	0.650	0.640	0.630	0.610	0.592	0.549	0.510	0.476	0.444
3	0.971	0.942	0.889	0.840	0.794	0.751	0.712	0.675	0.658	0.641	0.609	0.579	0.551	0.524	0.512	0.500	0.477	0.455	0.406	0.364	0.328	0.296
4	0.961	0.924	0.855	0.792	0.735	0.683	0.636	0.592	0.572	0.552	0.516	0.482	0.451	0.423	0.410	0.397	0.373	0.350	0.301	0.260	0.226	0.198
5	0.951	0.906	0.822	0.747	0.681	0.621	0.567	0.519	0.497	0.476	0.437	0.402	0.370	0.341	0.328	0.315	0.291	0.269	0.223	0.186	0.156	0.132
6	0.942	0.888	0.790	0.705	0.630	0.564	0.507	0.456	0.432	0.410	0.370	0.335	0.303	0.275	0.262	0.250	0.227	0.207	0.165	0.133	0.108	0.088
7	0.933	0.871	0.760	0.665	0.583	0.513	0.452	0.400	0.376	0.354	0.314	0.279	0.249	0.222	0.210	0.198	0.178	0.159	0.122	0.095	0.074	0.059
8	0.923	0.853	0.731	0.627	0.540	0.467	0.404	0.351	0.327	0.305	0.266	0.233	0.204	0.179	0.168	0.157	0.139	0.123	0.091	0.068	0.051	0.039
9	0.914	0.837	0.703	0.592	0.500	0.424	0.361	0.308	0.284	0.263	0.225	0.194	0.167	0.144	0.134	0.125	0.108	0.094	0.067	0.048	0.035	0.026
10	0.905	0.820	0.676	0.558	0.463	0.386	0.322	0.270	0.247	0.227	0.191	0.162	0.137	0.116	0.107	0.099	0.085	0.073	0.050	0.035	0.024	0.017
11	0.896	0.804	0.650	0.527	0.429	0.350	0.287	0.237	0.215	0.195	0.162	0.135	0.112	0.094	0.086	0.079	0.066	0.056	0.037	0.025	0.017	0.012
12	0.887	0.788	0.625	0.497	0.397	0.319	0.257	0.208	0.187	0.168	0.137	0.112	0.092	0.076	0.069	0.062	0.052	0.043	0.027	0.018	0.012	0.008
13	0.879	0.773	0.601	0.469	0.368	0.290	0.229	0.182	0.163	0.145	0.116	0.093	0.075	0.061	0.055	0.050	0.040	0.033	0.020	0.013	0.008	0.005
14	0.870	0.758	0.577	0.442	0.340	0.263	0.205	0.160	0.141	0.125	0.099	0.078	0.062	0.049	0.044	0.039	0.032	0.025	0.015	0.009	0.006	0.003
15	0.861	0.743	0.555	0.417	0.315	0.239	0.183	0.140	0.123	0.108	0.084	0.065	0.051	0.040	0.035	0.031	0.025	0.020	0.011	0.006	0.004	0.002
16	0.853	0.728	0.534	0.394	0.292	0.218	0.163	0.123	0.107	0.093	0.071	0.054	0.042	0.032	0.028	0.025	0.019	0.015	0.008	0.005	0.003	0.002
17	0.844	0.714	0.513	0.371	0.270	0.198	0.146	0.108	0.093	0.080	0.060	0.045	0.034	0.026	0.023	0.020	0.015	0.012	0.006	0.003	0.002	0.001
18	0.836	0.700	0.494	0.350	0.250	0.180	0.130	0.095	0.081	0.069	0.051	0.038	0.028	0.021	0.018	0.016	0.012	0.009	0.005	0.002	0.001	0.001
19	0.828	0.686	0.475	0.331	0.232	0.164	0.166	0.083	0.070	0.060	0.043	0.031	0.023	0.017	0.014	0.012	0.009	0.007	0.003	0.002	0.001	
20	0.820	0.673	0.456	0.312	0.215	0.149	0.104	0.073	0.061	0.051	0.037	0.026	0.019	0.014	0.012	0.010	0.007	0.005	0.002	0.001	0.001	
21	0.811	0.660	0.439	0.294	0.199	0.135	0.093	0.064	0.053	0.044	0.031	0.022	0.015	0.011	0.009	0.008	0.006	0.004	0.002	0.001		
22	0.803	0.647	0.422	0.278	0.184	0.123	0.083	0.056	0.046	0.038	0.026	0.018	0.013	0.009	0.007	0.006	0.004	0.003	0.001	0.001		
23	0.795	0.634	0.406	0.262	0.170	0.112	0.074	0.049	0.040	0.033	0.022	0.015	0.010	0.007	0.006	0.005	0.003	0.002	0.001			
24	0.788	0.622	0.390	0.247	0.158	0.102	0.066	0.043	0.035	0.028	0.019	0.013	0.008	0.006	0.005	0.004	0.003	0.002	0.001			
25	0.780	0.610	0.375	0.233	0.146	0.092	0.059	0.038	0.030	0.024	0.016	0.010	0.007	0.005	0.004	0.003	0.002	0.001	0.001			
26	0.772	0.598	0.361	0.220	0.135	0.084	0.053	0.033	0.026	0.021	0.014	0.009	0.006	0.004	0.003	0.002	0.002	0.001				
27	0.764	0.586	0.347	0.207	0.125	0.076	0.047	0.029	0.023	0.018	0.011	0.007	0.005	0.003	0.002	0.002	0.001	0.001				
28	0.757	0.574	0.333	0.196	0.116	0.069	0.042	0.026	0.020	0.016	0.010	0.006	0.004	0.002	0.002	0.002	0.001	0.001				
29	0.749	0.563	0.321	0.185	0.107	0.063	0.037	0.022	0.017	0.014	0.008	0.005	0.003	0.002	0.002	0.001	0.001	0.001				
30	0.742	0.552	0.308	0.174	0.099	0.057	0.033	0.020	0.015	0.012	0.007	0.004	0.003	0.002	0.001	0.001	0.001					
40	0.672	0.453	0.208	0.097	0.046	0.022	0.011	0.005	0.004	0.003	0.001	0.001										
50	0.608	0.372	0.141	0.054	0.021	0.009	0.003	0.001	0.001	0.001												

Source: Robert N. Anthony, *Management Accounting: Text and Cases* 4th ed. (Homewood, Ill.: Richard D. Irwin, 1970), p. 777. ©1970 by Richard D. Irwin, Inc.

Table B-3: Future Value of Annuity of $1 in Arrears

$$F = A\left[\frac{(1+r)^n - 1}{r}\right]$$

Periods	2%	2 1/2%	3%	4%	5%	6%	8%	10%
1	1.0000	1.0000	1.0000	1.0000	1.0000	1.0000	1.0000	1.0000
2	2.0200	2.0250	2.0300	2.0400	2.0500	2.0600	2.0800	2.1000
3	3.0604	3.0756	3.0909	3.1216	3.1525	3.1836	3.2464	3.3100
4	4.1216	4.1525	4.1836	4.2465	4.3101	4.3746	4.5061	4.6410
5	5.2040	5.2563	5.3091	5.4163	5.5256	5.6371	5.8666	6.1051
6	6.3081	6.3877	6.4684	6.6330	6.8019	6.9753	7.3359	7.7156
7	7.4343	7.5474	7.6625	7.8983	8.1420	8.3938	8.9228	9.4872
8	8.5830	8.7361	8.8923	9.2142	9.5491	9.8975	10.6366	11.4360
9	9.7546	9.9545	10.1591	10.5828	11.0266	11.4913	12.4876	13.5796
10	10.9497	11.2034	11.4639	12.0061	12.5779	13.1808	14.4866	15.9376
11	12.1687	12.4835	12.8078	13.4864	14.2068	14.9716	16.6455	18.5314
12	13.4121	13.7956	14.1920	15.0258	15.9171	16.8699	18.9771	21.3846
13	14.6803	15.1404	15.6178	16.6268	17.7130	18.8821	21.4953	24.5231
14	15.9739	16.5190	17.0863	18.2919	19.5986	21.0151	24.2149	27.9755
15	17.2934	17.9319	18.5989	20.0236	21.5786	23.2760	27.1521	31.7731
16	18.6393	19.3802	20.1569	21.8245	23.6575	25.6725	30.3243	35.9503
17	20.0121	20.8647	21.7616	23.6975	25.8404	28.2129	33.7502	40.5456
18	21.4123	22.3863	23.4144	25.6454	28.1324	30.9057	37.4502	45.6001
19	22.8406	23.9460	25.1169	27.6712	30.5390	33.7600	41.4463	51.1601
20	24.2974	25.5447	26.8704	29.7781	33.0660	36.7856	45.7620	57.2761
22	27.2990	28.8629	30.5368	34.2480	38.5052	43.3923	55.4568	71.4041
24	30.4219	32.3490	34.4265	39.0826	44.5020	50.8156	66.7648	88.4989
26	33.6709	36.0117	38.5530	44.3117	51.1135	59.1564	79.9544	109.1835
28	37.0512	39.8598	42.9309	49.9676	58.4026	68.5281	95.3388	134.2119
30	40.5681	43.9027	47.5754	56.0849	66.4388	79.0582	113.2832	164.4962
32	44.2270	48.1503	52.5028	62.7015	75.2988	90.8898	134.2135	201.1402
34	48.0338	52.6129	57.7302	69.8579	85.0670	104.1838	158.6267	245.4796
36	51.9944	57.3014	63.2759	77.5983	95.8363	119.1209	187.1021	299.1302
38	56.1149	62.2273	69.1594	85.9703	107.7095	135.9042	220.3159	364.0475
40	60.4020	67.4026	75.4013	95.0255	120.7998	154.7620	259.0565	442.5974
42	64.8622	72.8398	82.0232	104.8196	135.2318	175.9505	304.2435	537.6428
44	69.5027	78.5523	89.0484	115.4129	151.1430	199.7580	356.9496	652.6478
46	74.3306	84.5540	96.5015	126.8706	168.6852	226.5081	418.4261	791.8039
48	79.3535	90.8596	104.4084	139.2632	188.0254	256.5645	490.1322	960.1827
50	84.5794	97.4843	112.7969	152.6671	209.3480	290.3359	573.7702	1163.9209
60	114.0515	135.9916	163.0534	237.9907	353.5837	533.1282	1253.2133	3034.8470

Source: Myron J. Gordon and Gordon Shillinglaw, *Accounting: A Management Approach* 4th ed. (Homewood, Ill.: Richard D. Irwin, 1969), p. 785. ©1969 by Richard D. Irwin, Inc.

Note: To convert this table to values of an annuity in advance, take one more period and subtract 1,000.

Table B-4. Present Value of Annuity of $1 in Arrears

$$P_A = A\left[\frac{1-(1+r)^{-n}}{r}\right]$$

Periods (n)	1%	1 1/2%	2%	2 1/2%	3%	3 1/2%	4%	4 1/2%	5%	6%	7%
1	0.9901	0.9852	0.9804	0.9756	0.9709	0.9662	0.9615	0.9569	0.9524	0.9434	0.9346
2	1.9704	1.9559	1.9416	1.9274	1.9135	1.8997	1.8861	1.8727	1.8594	1.8334	1.8080
3	2.9410	2.9122	2.8839	2.8560	2.8286	2.8016	2.7751	2.7490	2.7232	2.6730	2.6243
4	3.9020	3.8544	3.8077	3.7620	3.7171	3.6731	3.6299	3.5875	3.5460	3.4651	3.3872
5	4.8534	4.7826	4.7135	4.6458	4.5797	4.5151	4.4518	4.3900	4.3295	4.2124	4.1002
6	5.7955	5.6972	5.6014	5.5081	5.4172	5.3286	5.2421	5.1579	5.0757	4.9173	4.7665
7	6.7282	6.5982	6.4720	6.3494	6.2303	6.1145	6.0021	5.8927	5.7864	5.5824	5.3893
8	7.6517	7.4859	7.3255	7.1701	7.0197	6.8740	6.7327	6.5959	6.4632	6.2098	5.9713
9	8.5660	8.3605	8.1622	7.9709	7.7861	7.6077	7.4353	7.2688	7.1078	6.8017	6.5152
10	9.4713	9.2222	8.9826	8.7521	8.5302	8.3166	8.1109	7.9127	7.7217	7.3601	7.0236
11	10.3676	10.0711	9.7868	9.5142	9.2526	9.0016	8.7605	8.5289	8.3064	7.8869	7.4987
12	11.2551	10.9075	10.5753	10.2578	9.9540	9.6633	9.3851	9.1186	8.8633	8.3838	7.9427
13	12.1337	11.7315	11.3484	10.9832	10.6350	10.3027	9.9856	9.6829	9.3936	8.8527	8.3577
14	13.0037	12.5434	12.1062	11.6909	11.2961	10.9205	10.5631	10.2228	9.8986	9.2950	8.7455
15	13.8651	13.3432	12.8493	12.3814	11.9379	11.5174	11.1184	10.7395	10.3797	9.7122	9.1079
16	14.7179	14.1313	13.5777	13.0550	12.5611	12.0941	11.6523	11.2340	10.8378	10.1059	9.4466
17	15.5623	14.9076	14.2919	13.7122	13.1661	12.6513	12.1657	11.7072	11.2741	10.4773	9.7632
18	16.3983	15.6726	14.9920	14.3534	13.7535	13.1897	12.6593	12.1600	11.6896	10.8276	10.0591
19	17.2260	16.4262	15.6785	14.9789	14.3238	13.7098	13.1339	12.5933	12.0853	11.1581	10.3356
20	18.0456	17.1686	16.3514	15.5892	14.8775	14.2124	13.5903	13.0079	12.4622	11.4699	10.5940
21	18.8570	17.9001	17.0112	16.1845	15.4150	14.6980	14.0292	13.4047	12.8212	11.7640	10.8355
22	19.6604	18.6208	17.6580	16.7654	15.9369	15.1671	14.4511	13.7844	13.1630	12.0416	11.0612
23	20.4558	19.3309	18.2922	17.3321	16.4436	15.6204	14.8568	14.1478	13.4886	12.3034	11.2722
24	21.2434	20.0304	18.9139	17.8850	16.9355	16.0584	15.2470	14.4955	13.7986	12.5504	11.4693
25	22.0232	20.7196	19.5235	18.4244	17.4131	16.4815	15.6221	14.8282	14.0939	12.7834	11.6536
26	22.7952	21.3986	20.1210	18.9506	17.8768	16.8904	15.9828	15.1466	14.3752	13.0032	11.8258
27	23.5596	22.0676	20.7069	19.4640	18.3270	17.2854	16.3296	15.4513	14.6430	13.2105	11.9867
28	24.3164	22.7267	21.2813	19.9649	18.7641	17.6670	16.6631	15.7429	14.8981	13.4062	12.1371
29	25.0658	23.3761	21.8444	20.4535	19.1885	18.0358	16.9837	16.0219	15.1411	13.5907	12.2777
30	25.8077	24.0158	22.3965	20.9303	19.6004	18.3920	17.2920	16.2889	15.3725	13.7648	12.4090
40	32.8347	29.9158	27.3555	25.1028	23.1148	21.3551	19.7928	18.4016	17.1591	15.0463	13.3317
50	39.1961	34.9997	31.4236	28.3623	25.7298	23.4556	21.4822	19.7620	18.2559	15.7619	13.8007

Source: Myron J. Gordon and Gordon Shillinglaw, *Accounting: A Management Approach* 4th ed. (Homewood, Ill.: Richard D. Irwin, 1969), pp. 788-89. © by Richard D. Irwin, Inc.

Note: To convert this table to values of an annuity in advance, take one less period and add 1,000.

8%	10%	12%	14%	15%	16%	18%	20%	22%	24%	25%	26%	28%	30%	40%	50%
0.9259	0.9091	0.893	0.877	0.870	0.862	0.847	0.833	0.820	0.806	0.800	0.794	0.781	0.769	0.714	0.667
1.7833	1.7355	1.690	1.647	1.626	1.605	1.566	1.528	1.492	1.457	1.440	1.424	1.392	1.361	1.224	1.111
2.5771	2.4869	2.402	2.322	2.283	2.246	2.174	2.106	2.042	1.981	1.952	1.923	1.868	1.816	1.589	1.407
3.3121	3.1699	3.037	2.914	2.855	2.798	2.690	2.589	2.494	2.404	2.362	2.320	2.241	2.166	1.849	1.605
3.9927	3.7908	3.605	3.433	3.352	3.274	3.127	2.991	2.864	2.745	2.689	2.635	2.532	2.436	2.035	1.737
4.6229	4.3553	4.111	3.889	3.784	3.685	3.498	3.326	3.167	3.020	2.951	2.885	2.759	2.643	2.168	1.824
5.2064	4.8684	4.564	4.288	4.160	4.039	3.812	3.605	3.416	3.242	3.161	3.083	2.937	2.802	2.263	1.883
5.7466	5.3349	4.968	4.639	4.487	4.344	4.078	3.837	3.619	3.421	3.329	3.241	3.076	2.925	2.331	1.922
6.2469	5.7590	5.328	4.946	4.772	4.607	4.303	4.031	3.786	3.566	3.463	3.366	3.184	3.019	2.379	1.948
6.7101	6.1446	5.650	5.216	5.019	4.833	4.494	4.192	3.923	3.682	3.571	3.465	3.269	3.092	2.414	1.965
7.1390	6.4951	5.988	5.453	5.234	5.029	4.656	4.327	4.035	3.776	3.656	3.544	3.335	3.147	2.438	1.977
7.5361	6.8137	6.194	5.660	5.421	5.197	4.793	4.439	4.127	3.851	3.725	3.606	3.387	3.190	2.456	1.985
7.9038	7.1034	6.424	5.842	5.583	5.342	4.910	4.533	4.203	3.912	3.780	3.656	3.427	3.223	2.468	1.990
8.2442	7.3667	6.628	6.002	5.724	5.468	5.008	4.611	4.265	3.962	3.824	3.695	3.459	6.249	2.477	1.993
8.5595	7.6061	6.811	6.142	5.847	5.575	5.092	4.675	4.315	4.001	3.859	3.726	3.483	3.268	2.484	1.995
8.8514	7.8237	6.974	6.265	5.954	5.669	5.162	4.730	4.357	4.033	3.887	3.751	3.503	3.283	2.489	1.997
9.1216	8.0216	7.120	6.373	6.047	5.749	5.222	4.775	4.391	4.059	3.910	3.771	3.518	3.295	2.492	1.998
9.3719	8.2014	7.250	6.467	6.128	5.818	5.273	4.812	4.419	4.080	3.928	3.786	3.529	3.304	2.494	1.999
9.6036	8.3649	7.366	6.550	6.198	5.877	5.316	4.844	4.442	4.097	3.942	3.799	3.539	3.311	2.496	1.999
9.8181	8.5136	7.469	6.623	6.259	5.929	5.353	4.870	4.460	4.110	3.954	3.808	3.546	3.316	2.497	1.999
10.0168	8.6487	7.562	6.687	6.312	5.973	5.384	4.891	4.476	4.121	3.963	3.816	3.551	3.320	2.498	2.000
10.2007	8.7715	7.645	6.743	6.359	6.011	5.410	4.909	4.488	4.130	3.970	3.822	3.556	3.323	2.498	2.000
10.3711	8.8832	7.718	6.792	6.399	6.044	5.432	4.925	4.499	4.137	3.976	3.827	3.559	3.325	2.499	2.000
10.5288	8.9847	7.784	6.835	6.434	6.073	5.451	4.937	4.507	4.143	3.981	3.831	3.562	3.327	2.499	2.000
10.6748	9.0770	7.843	6.873	6.464	6.097	5.467	4.948	4.514	4.147	3.985	3.834	3.564	3.329	2.499	2.000
10.8100	9.1609	7.896	6.906	6.491	6.118	5.480	4.956	4.520	4.151	3.988	3.837	3.566	3.330	2.500	2.000
10.9352	9.2372	7.943	6.935	6.514	6.136	5.492	4.964	4.524	4.154	3.990	3.839	3.567	3.331	2.500	2.000
11.0511	9.3066	7.984	6.961	6.534	6.152	5.502	4.970	4.528	4.157	3.992	3.840	3.568	3.331	2.500	2.000
11.1584	9.3696	8.022	6.983	6.551	6.166	5.510	4.975	4.531	4.159	3.994	3.841	3.569	3.332	2.500	2.000
11.2578	9.4269	8.055	7.003	6.566	6.177	5.517	4.979	4.534	4.160	3.995	3.842	3.569	3.332	2.500	2.000
11.9246	9.7791	8.244	7.105	6.642	6.234	5.548	4.997	4.544	4.166	3.999	3.846	3.571	3.333	2.500	2.000
12.2335	9.9148	8.304	7.133	6.661	6.246	5.554	4.999	4.545	4.167	4.000	3.846	3.571	3.333	2.500	2.000

APPENDIX C: PERCENTAGE POINTS OF THE T DISTRIBUTION*

Probabilities refer to the sum of the two-tail areas. For a single tail divide the probability by 2.

	Probability (*P*).												
n	.9	.8	.7	.6	.5	.4	.3	.2	.1	.05	.02	.01	.001
1	.158	.325	.510	.727	1.000	1.376	1.963	3.078	6.314	12.706	31.821	63.657	636.619
2	.142	.289	.445	.617	.816	1.061	1.386	1.886	2.920	4.303	6.965	9.925	31.598
3	.137	.277	.424	.584	.765	.978	1.250	1.638	2.353	3.182	4.541	5.841	12.941
4	.134	.271	.414	.569	.741	.941	1.190	1.533	2.132	2.776	3.747	4.604	8.610
5	.132	.267	.408	.559	.727	.920	1.156	1.476	2.015	2.571	3.365	4.032	6.859
6	.131	.265	.404	.553	.718	.906	1.134	1.440	1.943	2.447	3.143	3.707	5.959
7	.130	.263	.402	.549	.711	.896	1.119	1.415	1.895	2.365	2.998	3.499	5.405
8	.130	.262	.399	.546	.706	.889	1.108	1.397	1.860	2.306	2.896	3.355	5.041
9	.129	.261	.398	.543	.703	.883	1.100	1.383	1.833	2.262	2.821	3.250	4.781
10	.129	.260	.397	.542	.700	.879	1.093	1.372	1.812	2.228	2.764	3.169	4.587
11	.129	.260	.396	.540	.697	.876	1.088	1.363	1.796	2.201	2.718	3.106	4.437
12	.128	.259	.395	.539	.695	.873	1.083	1.356	1.782	2.179	2.681	3.055	4.318
13	.128	.259	.394	.538	.694	.870	1.079	1.350	1.771	2.160	2.650	3.012	4.221
14	.128	.258	.393	.537	.692	.868	1.076	1.345	1.761	2.145	2.624	2.977	4.140
15	.128	.258	.393	.536	.691	.866	1.074	1.341	1.753	2.131	2.602	2.947	4.073
16	.128	.258	.392	.535	.690	.865	1.071	1.337	1.746	2.120	2.583	2.921	4.015
17	.128	.257	.392	.534	.689	.863	1.069	1.333	1.740	2.110	2.567	2.898	3.965
18	.127	.257	.392	.534	.688	.862	1.067	1.330	1.734	2.101	2.552	2.878	3.922
19	.127	.257	.391	.533	.688	.861	1.066	1.328	1.729	2.093	2.539	2.861	3.883
20	.127	.257	.391	.533	.687	.860	1.064	1.325	1.725	2.086	2.528	2.845	3.850
21	.127	.257	.391	.532	.686	.859	1.063	1.323	1.721	2.080	2.518	2.831	3.819
22	.127	.256	.390	.532	.686	.858	1.061	1.321	1.717	2.074	2.508	2.819	3.792
23	.127	.256	.390	.532	.685	.858	1.060	1.319	1.714	2.069	2.500	2.807	3.767
24	.127	.256	.390	.531	.685	.857	1.059	1.318	1.711	2.064	2.492	2.797	3.745
25	.127	.256	.390	.531	.684	.856	1.058	1.316	1.708	2.060	2.485	2.787	3.725
26	.127	.256	.390	.531	.684	.856	1.058	1.315	1.706	2.056	2.479	2.779	3.707
27	.127	.256	.389	.531	.684	.855	1.057	1.314	1.703	2.052	2.473	2.771	3.690
28	.127	.256	.389	.530	.683	.855	1.056	1.313	1.701	2.048	2.467	2.763	3.674
29	.127	.256	.389	.530	.683	.854	1.055	1.311	1.699	2.045	2.462	2.756	3.659
30	.127	.256	.389	.530	.683	.854	1.055	1.310	1.697	2.042	2.457	2.750	3.646
40	.126	.255	.388	.529	.681	.851	1.050	1.303	1.684	2.021	2.423	2.704	3.551
60	.126	.254	.387	.527	.679	.848	1.046	1.296	1.671	2.000	2.390	2.660	3.460
120	.126	.254	.386	.526	.677	.845	1.041	1.289	1.658	1.980	2.358	2.617	3.373
∞	.126	.253	.385	.524	.674	.842	1.036	1.282	1.645	1.960	2.326	2.576	3.291

*Appendix C is reprinted from Table III of R. A. Fisher and F. Yates, *Statistical Tables for Biological, Agricultural and Medical Research* published by Oliver & Boyd, Ltd., Edinburgh, by permission of the authors and publishers.

APPENDIX D: PERCENTAGE POINTS OF THE F DISTRIBUTION

Each entry is the percent point of F which is exceeded by the proportion of values of F listed at the head of its column for degrees of freedom n_1 listed in the major caption and n_2 listed in the stub.

	$n_1 = 1$			$n_1 = 2$			$n_1 = 3$			$n_1 = 4$			$n_1 = 5$		
n_2	.05	**.01**	.001	.05	**.01**	.001	.05	**.01**	.001	.05	**.01**	.001	.05	**.01**	.001
1	161.45	4,052.2	405,284	199.50	4,999.5	500,000	215.71	5,403.3	540,379	224.58	5,624.6	562,500	230.16	5,763.7	576,405
2	18.513	98.503	998.5	19.000	99.000	999.0	19.164	99.166	999.2	19.247	99.249	999.2	19.296	99.299	999.3
3	10.128	34.116	167.5	9.552	30.817	148.5	9.277	29.457	141.1	9.117	28.710	137.1	9.014	23.237	134.6
4	7.709	21.198	74.14	6.944	18.000	61.25	6.591	16.694	56.18	6.388	15.977	53.44	6.256	15.522	51.71
5	6.608	16.258	47.04	5.786	13.274	36.61	5.410	12.060	33.20	5.192	11.392	31.09	5.050	10.967	29.75
6	5.987	13.745	35.51	5.143	10.925	27.00	4.757	9.779	23.70	4.534	9.148	21.90	4.387	8.746	20.81
7	5.591	12.246	29.22	4.737	9.547	21.69	4.347	8.451	18.77	4.120	7.847	17.19	3.972	7.460	16.21
8	5.318	11.259	25.42	4.459	8.649	18.49	4.066	7.591	15.83	3.838	7.006	14.39	3.688	6.632	13.49
9	5.117	10.561	22.86	4.256	8.022	16.39	3.863	6.992	13.90	3.633	6.422	12.56	3.482	6.057	11.71
10	4.965	10.044	21.04	4.103	7.559	14.91	3.708	6.552	12.55	3.478	5.994	11.28	3.326	5.636	10.48
11	4.844	9.646	19.69	3.982	7.206	13.81	3.587	6.217	11.56	3.357	5.668	10.35	3.204	5.316	9.58
12	4.747	9.330	18.64	3.885	6.927	12.97	3.490	5.953	10.80	3.259	5.412	9.63	3.106	5.064	8.89
13	4.667	9.074	17.81	3.806	6.701	12.31	3.410	5.739	10.21	3.179	5.205	9.07	3.025	4.862	8.35
14	4.600	8.862	17.14	3.739	6.515	11.78	3.344	5.564	9.73	3.112	5.035	8.62	2.958	4.695	7.92
15	4.543	8.683	16.59	3.682	6.359	11.34	3.287	5.417	9.34	3.056	4.893	8.25	2.901	4.556	7.57
16	4.494	8.531	16.12	3.634	6.226	10.97	3.239	5.292	9.00	3.007	4.773	7.94	2.852	4.437	7.27
17	4.451	8.400	15.72	3.592	6.112	10.66	3.197	5.185	8.73	2.965	4.669	7.68	2.810	4.336	7.02
18	4.414	8.285	15.38	3.555	6.013	10.39	3.160	5.092	8.49	2.928	4.579	7.46	2.773	4.248	6.81
19	4.381	8.185	15.08	3.522	5.926	10.16	3.127	5.010	8.28	2.895	4.500	7.26	2.740	4.171	6.61
20	4.351	8.096	14.82	3.493	5.849	9.95	3.098	4.938	8.10	2.866	4.431	7.10	2.711	4.103	6.46
21	4.325	8.017	14.59	3.467	5.780	9.77	3.072	4.874	7.94	2.840	4.369	6.95	2.685	4.042	6.32
22	4.301	7.945	14.38	3.443	5.719	9.61	3.049	4.817	7.80	2.817	4.313	6.81	2.661	3.988	6.19
23	4.279	7.881	14.19	3.422	5.664	9.47	3.028	4.765	7.67	2.795	4.264	6.69	2.640	3.939	6.08
24	4.260	7.823	14.03	3.403	5.614	9.34	3.009	4.718	7.55	2.776	4.218	6.59	2.621	3.895	5.98
25	4.242	7.770	13.88	3.385	5.568	9.22	2.991	4.676	7.45	2.759	4.177	6.49	2.603	3.855	5.88
26	4.225	7.721	13.74	3.369	5.526	9.12	2.975	4.637	7.36	2.743	4.140	6.41	2.587	3.818	5.80
27	4.210	7.677	13.61	3.354	5.488	9.02	2.960	4.601	7.27	2.728	4.106	6.35	2.572	3.785	5.73
28	4.196	7.636	13.50	3.340	5.453	8.93	2.947	4.568	7.19	2.714	4.074	6.25	2.558	3.754	5.66
29	4.183	7.598	13.39	3.328	5.421	8.85	2.934	4.538	7.12	2.701	4.045	6.19	2.545	3.725	5.59
30	4.171	7.563	13.29	3.316	5.390	8.77	2.922	4.510	7.05	2.690	4.018	6.12	2.534	3.699	5.53
40	4.085	7.314	12.61	3.232	5.178	8.25	2.839	4.313	6.60	2.606	3.828	5.70	2.450	3.514	5.13
60	4.001	7.077	11.97	3.150	4.977	7.76	2.758	4.126	6.17	2.525	3.649	5.31	2.368	3.339	4.76
120	3.920	6.851	11.38	3.072	4.786	7.31	2.680	3.949	5.79	2.447	3.480	4.95	2.290	3.174	4.42
∞	3.841	6.635	10.83	2.996	4.605	.91	2.605	3.782	5.42	2.372	3.319	4.62	2.214	3.017	4.10

APPENDIX D (continued)

	$n_1 = 6$			$n_1 = 8$			$n_1 = 12$			$n_1 = 24$			$n_1 = \infty$		
n_2	.05	**.01**	.001	.05	**.01**	.001	.05	**.01**	.001	.05	**.01**	.001	.05	**.01**	.001
1	233.99	5,859.0	585,937	238.88	5,981.6	598,144	243.91	6,106.3	610,667	249.05	6,234.6	623,497	254.32	6,366.0	636,619
2	19.330	99.332	999.3	19.371	99.374	999.4	19.413	99.416	999.4	19.454	99.458	999.5	19.496	99.501	999.5
3	8.941	27.911	132.8	8.845	27.489	130.6	8.745	27.052	128.3	8.638	26.598	125.9	8.527	26.125	123.5
4	6.163	15.207	50.53	6.041	14.799	49.00	5.912	14.274	47.41	5.774	13.929	45.77	5.628	13.463	44.05
5	4.950	10.672	28.84	4.818	10.289	27.64	4.678	9.888	26.42	4.527	9.467	25.14	4.365	9.020	23.78
6	4.284	8.466	20.03	4.147	8.102	19.03	4.000	7.718	17.99	3.841	7.313	16.89	3.669	6.880	15.75
7	3.866	7.191	15.52	3.726	6.840	14.63	3.575	6.469	13.71	3.410	6.074	12.73	3.230	5.650	11.69
8	3.581	6.371	12.86	3.438	6.029	12.04	3.284	5.667	11.19	3.115	5.279	10.30	2.928	4.859	9.34
9	3.374	5.802	11.13	3.230	5.467	10.37	3.073	5.111	9.57	2.900	4.729	8.72	2.707	4.311	7.81
10	3.217	5.286	9.92	3.072	5.057	9.20	2.913	4.706	8.45	2.737	4.327	7.64	2.538	3.909	6.76
11	3.095	5.069	9.05	2.948	4.745	8.35	2.788	4.397	7.63	2.609	4.021	6.85	2.405	3.602	6.00
12	2.996	4.821	8.38	2.849	4.499	7.71	2.687	4.155	7.00	2.505	3.780	6.25	2.296	3.361	5.42
13	2.915	4.620	7.86	2.767	4.202	7.21	2.604	3.960	6.52	2.420	3.587	5.78	2.206	3.165	4.97
14	2.848	4.456	7.43	2.699	4.140	6.80	2.534	3.800	6.13	2.349	3.427	5.41	2.131	3.004	4.60
15	2.790	4.218	7.09	2.641	4.004	6.47	2.475	3.666	5.81	2.288	3.294	5.10	2.066	2.868	4.31
16	2.741	4.202	6.81	2.591	3.890	6.19	2.425	3.553	5.55	2.235	3.181	4.85	2.010	2.753	4.06
17	2.699	4.102	6.56	2.548	3.791	5.96	2.381	3.455	5.32	2.190	3.083	4.63	1.960	2.653	3.85
18	2.661	4.015	6.35	2.510	3.705	5.76	2.342	3.371	5.13	2.150	2.999	4.45	1.917	2.566	3.67
19	2.628	3.929	6.18	2.477	6.631	5.59	2.308	3.296	4.97	2.114	2.925	4.29	1.878	2.489	3.52
20	2.599	3.871	6.02	2.447	3.564	5.44	2.278	3.231	4.82	2.083	2.859	4.15	1.843	2.421	3.38
21	2.573	3.812	5.88	2.421	3.506	5.31	2.250	3.173	4.70	2.054	2.801	4.03	1.812	2.360	3.26
22	2.549	3.758	5.76	2.397	3.453	5.19	2.226	3.121	4.58	2.028	2.749	3.92	1.783	2.305	3.15
23	2.528	3.710	5.65	2.375	3.406	5.09	2.204	3.074	4.48	2.005	2.702	3.82	1.757	2.256	3.05
24	2.508	3.667	5.55	2.355	3.263	4.99	2.183	3.032	4.39	1.984	2.659	3.74	1.733	2.211	2.97
25	2.490	3.627	5.46	2.337	3.324	4.91	2.165	2.993	4.31	1.964	2.620	3.66	1.711	2.169	2.89
26	2.474	3.591	5.38	2.321	3.288	4.83	2.148	2.958	4.24	1.946	2.585	3.59	1.691	2.132	2.82
27	2.459	3.558	5.31	2.305	3.256	4.76	2.132	2.926	4.17	1.930	2.552	3.52	1.672	2.096	2.75
28	2.445	3.528	5.24	2.291	3.226	4.69	2.118	2.896	4.11	1.915	2.522	3.46	1.654	2.064	2.70
29	2.432	3.499	5.18	2.278	3.198	4.64	2.104	2.869	4.05	1.901	2.495	3.41	1.638	2.034	2.64
30	2.421	3.474	5.12	2.266	3.173	4.58	2.092	2.843	4.00	1.887	2.469	3.36	1.622	2.006	2.59
40	2.336	3.291	4.73	2.180	2.993	4.21	2.004	2.665	3.64	1.793	2.288	3.01	1.509	1.305	2.23
60	2.254	3.119	4.37	2.097	2.823	3.87	1.917	2.496	3.31	1.700	2.115	2.69	1.389	1.601	1.90
120	2.175	2.954	4.04	2.016	2.663	3.55	1.834	2.336	3.08	1.608	1.950	2.40	1.254	1.380	1.56
∞	2.099	2.802	3.74	1.938	2.511	3.27	1.752	2.185	2.74	1.517	1.791	2.13	1.000	1.000	1.00

Source: Frederick E. Croxton and Dudley J. Cowden, *Practical Business Statistics*, 2nd ed. (New York: Prentice-Hall, Inc., 1948), pp. 514 and 515. Reprinted by permission of the publisher.

Values of *F* at the .05 and .01 points were taken, by permission, from Maxine Merrington and Catherine M. Thompson, "New Tables of Statistical Variables," Biometrika, Vol. XXXIII, Part I, pp. 80, 81, 84, and 85. Values of *F* at the .001 point were taken from Table V of R. A. Fisher and F. Yates, *Statistical Tables for Biological, Agricultural and Medical Research*, Oliver and Boyd, Ltd., Edinburgh, 1938, by permission of the author and publishers. The first reference gives *F* values to five digits at the .50, .25, .10, .05, .025, .01, and .005 points and for values of n_1 in addition to those shown in the above table. The second reference gives *F* values to three or more digits at the .20, .05, .01, and .001 points.

APPENDIX E: PERCENTAGE POINTS OF THE χ^2 DISTRIBUTION*

Each entry is a percent point of χ^2. It is exceeded by the proportion (P) of values of χ^2 listed in the column heading for the number of degrees of freedom (n) given in the stub.

n.	P=.99.	.98.	.95.	.90.	.80.	.70.	.50.	.30.	.20.	.10.	.05.	.02.	.01.
1	.000157	.000628	.00393	.0158	.0642	.148	.455	1.074	1.642	2.706	3.841	5.412	6.635
2	.0201	.0404	.103	.211	.446	.713	1.386	2.408	3.219	4.605	5.991	7.824	9.210
3	.115	.185	.352	.584	1.005	1.424	2.366	3.665	4.642	6.251	7.815	9.837	11.345
4	.297	.429	.711	1.064	1.649	2.195	3.357	4.878	5.989	7.779	9.488	11.668	13.277
5	.554	.752	1.145	1.610	2.343	3.000	4.351	6.064	7.289	9.236	11.070	13.388	15.086
6	.872	1.134	1.635	2.204	3.070	3.828	5.348	7.231	8.558	10.645	12.592	15.033	16.812
7	1.239	1.564	2.167	2.833	3.822	4.671	6.346	8.383	9.803	12.017	14.067	16.622	18.475
8	1.646	2.032	2.733	3.490	4.594	5.527	7.344	9.524	11.030	13.362	15.507	18.168	20.090
9	2.088	2.532	3.325	4.168	5.380	6.393	8.343	10.656	12.242	14.684	16.919	19.679	21.666
10	2.558	3.059	3.940	4.865	6.179	7.267	9.342	11.781	13.442	15.987	18.307	21.161	23.209
11	3.053	3.609	4.575	5.578	6.989	8.148	10.341	12.899	14.631	17.275	19.675	22.618	24.725
12	3.571	4.178	5.226	6.304	7.807	9.034	11.340	14.011	15.812	18.549	21.026	24.054	26.217
13	4.107	4.765	5.892	7.042	8.634	9.926	12.340	15.119	16.985	19.812	22.362	25.472	27.688
14	4.660	5.368	6.571	7.790	9.467	10.821	13.339	16.222	18.151	21.064	23.685	26.873	29.141
15	5.229	5.985	7.261	8.547	10.307	11.721	14.339	17.322	19.311	22.307	24.996	28.259	30.578
16	5.812	6.614	7.962	9.312	11.152	12.624	15.338	18.418	20.465	23.542	26.296	29.633	32.000
17	6.408	7.255	8.672	10.085	12.002	13.531	16.338	19.511	21.615	24.769	27.587	30.995	33.409
18	7.015	7.906	9.390	10.865	12.857	14.440	17.338	20.601	22.760	25.989	28.869	32.346	34.805
19	7.633	8.567	10.117	11.651	13.716	15.352	18.338	21.689	23.900	27.204	30.144	33.687	36.191
20	8.260	9.237	10.851	12.443	14.578	16.266	19.337	22.775	25.038	28.412	31.410	35.020	37.566
21	8.897	9.915	11.591	13.240	15.445	17.182	20.337	23.858	26.171	29.615	32.671	36.343	38.932
22	9.542	10.600	12.338	14.041	16.314	18.101	21.337	24.939	27.301	30.813	33.924	37.659	40.289
23	10.196	11.293	13.091	14.848	17.187	19.021	22.337	26.018	28.429	32.007	35.172	38.968	41.638
24	10.856	11.992	13.848	15.659	18.062	19.943	23.337	27.096	29.553	33.196	36.415	40.270	42.980
25	11.524	12.697	14.611	16.473	18.940	20.867	24.337	28.172	30.675	34.382	37.652	41.566	44.314
26	12.198	13.409	15.379	17.292	19.820	21.792	25.336	29.246	31.795	35.563	38.885	42.856	45.642
27	12.879	14.125	16.151	18.114	20.703	22.719	26.336	30.319	32.912	36.741	40.113	44.140	46.963
28	13.565	14.847	16.928	18.939	21.588	23.647	27.336	31.391	34.027	37.916	41.337	45.419	48.278
29	14.256	15.574	17.798	19.768	22.475	24.577	28.336	32.461	35.139	39.087	42.557	46.693	49.588
30	14.953	16.306	18.493	20.599	23.364	25.508	29.336	33.530	36.250	40.256	43.773	47.962	50.892

For larger values of n_2 the expression $\sqrt{2\chi^2} - \sqrt{2n-1}$ may be used as a normal deviate with unit variance.

*Reprinted from Table III, pp. 112-13, of R. A. Fisher, *Statistical Methods for Research Workers,* 11th ed., published by Oliver and Boyd, Ltd., Edinburgh, by permission of author and publishers.

Index